D1247681

THE RHETORIC OF STRUGGLE

CRITICAL STUDIES IN
BLACK LIFE AND CULTURE
(VOL. 20)

GARLAND REFERENCE LIBRARY
OF SOCIAL SCIENCE
(VOL. 701)

CRITICAL STUDIES IN BLACK LIFE AND CULTURE
C. James Trotman, Advisory Editor

THE RHETORIC OF STRUGGLE
Public Address by
African American Women

edited by
Robbie Jean Walker

I.C.C. LIBRARY

GARLAND PUBLISHING, INC. • NEW YORK & LONDON
1992

Library of Congress Cataloging-in-Publication Data

The rhetoric of struggle : public address by African American women /
edited by Robbie Jean Walker.
      p. cm. — (Critical studies in Black life and culture ; v.
20) (Garland reference library of social science ; v. 701)
   Includes bibliographical references.
   ISBN 0–8240–7268–5
   1. Speeches, addresses, etc., American—Afro-American authors.
2. Speeches, addresses, etc., American—Women authors. 3. Afro-
Americans—Civil rights. 4. Afro-American orators. 5. Afro-
American women. I. Walker, Robbie Jean, 1939– . II. Series.
III. Series: Garland reference library of social science ; v. 701.
PS663.N4R47   1992
815.008'09287—dc20   91–40684
                                                                          CIP

Printed on acid-free, 250-year-life paper
Manufactured in the United States of America

Dedication

To the memory of my parents
Sarah Bertha Lacey Walker and Dallas Almus Walker
Two brothers—Hilmer and Hansel
My sisters and brothers who continue to sustain me
Odus, Kenneth, Ruby, Willow,
Doris, Dorothy, Dallas, Edwin, and their offspring
All of whose essence and aspirations are so inextricably
bound to mine that I dare not call this work mine alone.

Contents

Contents

Acknowledgments

This work is prepared with assistance from a research grant-in-aid from the office of Research and Development at Auburn University at Montgomery. I also owe thanks to Esme Rahn, Manuscript Associate at Moorland-Spingarn Research Center at Howard University; Rosalyn Joyce Larkin for lodging, encouragement, and research assistance during my frequent research trips to Washington, D.C.; Robert Kilpatrick for his extraordinary resourcefulness and his generous arrangement of contacts; Dorisetta Michelle Walker and Jimmie Lee Felder for patiently reading and rereading portions of the manuscript; Scott F. Beaver and Ann Depas-Orange, my graduate students, for course projects that provided valuable insights and perspectives; Professor Edward P. J. Corbett for his letter that encouraged me to undertake the work; Sylvia Smiley for her technical assistance and general cooperation; Walter E. Stewart, Professor of Politics at Mount Holyoke College, for continuing with our collaborative manuscript while I completed this project, and Anne L. Moore for her loyalty, guidance, and expertise in the preparation of this manuscript.

Preface

Continuing efforts to research and record the contributions of African American women represent one of the remarkable attitudinal transformations of our time. Unfortunately, the resulting presentations are often fragmentary and fail to dramatize appropriately the accrued influence of these contributions. Such has been the fate of public address by African American women. *The Rhetoric Of Struggle* attempts to confer continuity and focus to a genre that so dramatically clarifies the dynamics of our cultural legacy. This work, then, is at once corrective and exploratory. It seeks first to counteract the effect of the fragmentation that implicitly distorts the vigor and passion with which African American women have defined and defended national values. It seeks as well to identify and explicate those rhetorical features that characterize and distinguish the oratory of African American women and justify its inclusion in a canon traditionally synonymous with cultural influence.

Indeed, among the several cultural indicators used to assess the evolving status and preoccupations of a group, perhaps none is more revelatory than its public address. The tremendous insight into cultural context afforded by the visual arts, imaginative or creative literature, and music is significant. Yet the authority and codification inherent in public address render it a singularly illuminating index of the prevailing concerns of a group or an era. This status derives in part from the historical ordering of spoken and written discourse in developing civilizations and cultures, the spoken language usually preceding the written one. One can infer the status of oratory in our times by noting the descriptors used to characterize *Vital Speeches Of The Day*, one of the primary national vehicles for the presentation of contemporary speeches. The descriptors used most recently read: "the best thoughts of the best minds in current national questions" and "the important addresses of the leading molders of public opinion."

Speeches selected for inclusion here span more than a century and demonstrate the remarkable diversity and breadth of oratory by women. Although the speeches do indeed reflect historical connections, the presentation is not linearly historical. Specific references will often date the speeches, but the thematic focus is not necessarily evolutionary or identifiable by era. This situation is reflective of the realities. African Americans, having suffered numerous reversals and failing to progress in a linear fashion as have other ethnic groups in this country, are frequently forced by circumstances to return to the same themes again and again. But the addresses do bespeak a vitality that attests to the active participation of African American women in national affairs and their intellectual reflections on the significant philosophical and moral matters that have engaged the energies of other segments of the population.

Several "firsts" grace the selections and provide a historical glimpse into significant achievements. There is the unofficial first feminist address by an African American woman—Sojourner Truth's 1851 speech before the Woman's Rights Convention in Akron, Ohio, a speech rendered memorable by the refrain "and ain't I a woman?" Fanny Jackson Coppin graduated from Oberlin College in 1865, and Alice Moore Dunbar's notes state that she was the first African American woman to graduate from college. Other sources differ, the discrepancy apparently deriving from distinctions between two-year and four-year certificates. Coppin's emphasis on industrial opportunity may not receive enthusiastic philosophical endorsement today, but her plea was indeed an eloquent one: "It seems necessary that we should make known to the good men and women who are so solicitous about our souls, and our minds, that we haven't quite got rid of our bodies yet, and until we do, we must feed and clothe them; and this attitude of keeping us out of work forces us back upon charity."

Two other "firsts" from the latter half of the twentieth century complement the selections. There is Barbara Jordan's Keynote Address before the Democratic National Convention in 1976, representing the first time this prestigious position had been accorded a woman of African descent, and Shirley Chisholm's first speech before the House of Representatives in 1969 represents another historical milestone, the election to Congress of the first African American woman. These examples are illustrative of the accomplishments of women and dramatize the possibilities of advancement in spite of adversities, adversities spawned by discrimination deriving from both race and gender. Other speakers presented in this volume were also forerunners in their respective professions. Yet the legacy of a group does not inhere solely in the exotic and the unusual but accrues as increasing numbers lend their varying talents to the continuing concerns of humanity and make their contributions in less spectacular arenas. This work attempts to highlight women in the latter category as well, in an effort to demonstrate the necessarily inclusive character of the cultural legacy. This legacy encompasses an amalgam of themes and emphases as African American women have confronted the multitude of social and political concerns affecting their status and the status of the race in general. So multifaceted have been the expectations and role of African American women in this society, so ambiguous and fraught with reversals has been their progress, that a strictly chronological presentation of the oratory would appear repetitive. The struggle has by no means been a linearly progressive one. For in each era of their existence women of African descent have confronted essentially the same kinds of problems and invoked the same or similar survival strategies. The errors, the reversals, or other derivatives of thwarted ambitions and deferred dreams yield a cyclical or recursive pattern. Thus, a thematic, or goal-centered, model seems more accurately reflective of the African American woman's struggle.

Freedom from physical slavery and psychological enslavement has been a recurrent theme in human history; certainly this theme has been a standard one for African Americans. The first division of this work, "Breaking the Shackles: The Struggle for Freedom," contains addresses that speak to the issue of basic human freedom and efforts to grasp more firmly the continuously retreating gains made by the race. History and experience dramatize the imperative of vigilance since freedom and political gains have proved ephemeral. Such has particularly been the reality for African Americans. One need only recall the Black Codes that essentially reconstructed the restrictive attributes of formal slavery, systematically eroding social and political gains made by African Americans during Reconstruction or the decisions of the United States Supreme Court described so aptly by noted historian Carter G. Woodson. He characterizes as "reactionary" a series of decisions "by which the Civil Rights Act of 1875 was finally nullified" (Woodson 1924, 177). Some of the speeches in the first division, then, are appeals for idealized rights while others are passionate appeals for the restoration of rights and privileges enjoyed briefly and subsequently snatched away. Since this pattern was a recurring one, speeches in this section are not confined to a particular historical period.

The second section, "Contending For Equality: The Struggle for Women's Rights And Progress," contains speeches that address the peculiar constraints of gender in this society. Neither the addresses selected for this work nor the facts of history confirm a pathological divisive force separating African American females and males. Yet this dimension of the struggle at times evokes responses to restraints imposed by men of color, the restraints often reflective of those imposed by the larger society. Orations in this section speak as well to the sometimes chaotic and frequently puzzling symbiotic relationship between women of color and white women. In an intense suffrage battle in the 1890s African American women discovered that it wasn't just racist politicians who put up obstacles to their enfranchisement. White women, including suffragists who should have been their natural allies, often became their most formidable adversaries (Giddings 1984, 66). For white suffrage leaders either acquiesced to, or took advantage of, the anti-Black sentiment in the period. So the struggle for suffrage on the part of African American Women was one twice fought, and speeches concerning suffrage for them will span more than a century.

The notion of transcendence is endemic to the human spirit, so this attribute in African American women is not, in itself, unique. What is unique is their perpetual belief in the possibility of transcendence when considered in relation to their protracted subordinated status and their exploitation at the hands of others. Speeches in the third division of this work, "Laying Claim To The Promise: The Struggle for Empowerment," dramatize the struggle for more than basic rights. Although the speeches do indeed continue to cherish basic freedoms, they do much more. They address pursuing expanding aspirations, seeking the abundant life, and surviving whole.

Some of the more technical features will be treated separately and presented at the conclusion of the general analysis. This division on the surface may seem arbitrary, but the prevailing consideration in this decision is that these technical sections can be bypassed by those readers whose primary interest resides in the thematic cultural and historical focus. In many instances, the rhetorical features are themselves critical to the interpretation and in those cases no attempt is made to distinguish between form and content.

A glossary of terms is presented at the end of the work. The general terms of the rhetorical model are defined briefly here, with most of the definitions based on those given by Professor Edward P.J. Corbett in *Classical Rhetoric For The Modern Student*. Corbett's comprehensive presentation of the specifics of classical rhetoric is an invaluable source and commendable for both its inclusion and consistent translations from the classical canon.

Classical rhetoricians identified lines of argument or common topics based on what many theorists perceive to be innate organizing properties of the human mind. The intent of the enterprise was to invent or discover arguments. Corbett uses the terms "suggesters" . . . "prompters" . . . and "initiators" to describe the function of the common topics in relation to discourse (Corbett 1971, 108). The common topics, he explains, suggest "general strategies of development" and include definition, comparison, relationship, circumstance, and testimony.

Corbett makes the following distinction between common topics and special topics: "Common topics were depositories of general arguments that one could resort to when discussing virtually any subject. Special topics, on the other hand, were more particular lines of argument that one could resort to when discussing some particular subject" (Corbett 1971, 146). Special topics generally perform specific functions in each of three major categories of discourse recognized in the classical canon: deliberative, forensic, and epideictic. Deliberative oratory has as its aim persuading others to the point of view espoused by the speaker, forensic oratory seeks to defend or condemn, and epideictic oratory has inspiration as its primary objective. In attempts to achieve the desired ends of a given category of oratory, speakers employ specific special topics. The special topics of the expedient and inexpedient are associated with deliberative oratory; justice and injustice with forensic oratory; honor and dishonor with epideictic oratory. In either category, the special topics serve to underscore positive and negative consequences of particular courses of action.

Arrangement is the second component of the five-part organizational outline of the classical canon that includes invention, arrangement, memory, delivery, and style. Arrangement encompasses the ordering of the argument, the typical pattern including introduction, statement of fact, confirmation, refutation, and conclusion. The crucial consideration governing arrangement is the disposition or readiness of the audience which determines the essential features of all divisions of the discourse: the nature and length of the introduction, the amount of time devoted to the confirmation (proof) and refutation, the ordering of major points of evidence, and the nature of the conclusion.

Schemes and tropes belong to the figurative dimension of language and denote transference of word order or transference of meaning, respectively. Both schemes and tropes are categorized as figures of speech in Corbett's classification that subscribes to Quintilian's definition of *Figura*: "any deviation, either in thought or expression, from the ordinary and simple method of speaking, a change analogous to the different positions our bodies assume when we sit down, lie down, or look back. . . . Let the definition of a figure, therefore, be a form of speech artfully varied from common usage" (qtd. in Corbett 1971, 460). The familiar quotation, "I came, I saw, I conquered," is categorized as a scheme (asyndeton) since it involves a deviation in order, "the deliberate omission of conjunctions between a series of . . . clauses"(469). "Litotes [the] deliberate use of understatement, not to deceive someone but to enhance the impressiveness of what we say" is a trope, a transference of meaning. An example of a trope is Saint Paul's statement, " I am a citizen of no mean city" (Corbett 1971, 487). A list of schemes and tropes with definitions is included in the glossary.

Linguistic features of paragraphs and sentences include usages and techniques to which rhetoricians and linguists attribute rhetorical significance. Movement within paragraphs, sentence openers, types and lengths of sentences, and length of paragraphs are among the considerations in this component of the analysis. The application of the linguistic component of the analysis will vary from one work to another due to peculiar internal dynamics in the works themselves, the pivotal criterion being the extent to which the individual orators blended content with form.

The classical canon includes as well three modes of persuasion: *logos* (rational appeal), *ethos* (ethical appeal), and *pathos*, (emotional appeal). Consideration of these modes of persuasion are interspersed throughout the individual analyses to assess the extent to which speakers fulfilled traditional expectations.

The author of this work acknowledges an impressive body of previous scholarship that motivated this current effort and provided the substantive background informing this study. *American Orators of The Twentieth Century* by Bernard K. Duffy and Halford R. Ryan (1987) presents a particularly instructive overview of research sources in American public address. The appealing feature of this presentation is its illustration of the evolutionary pattern of scholarly works devoted to public address. The trends demonstrated in their overview will be noted here.

Perhaps the standard references for public address are the three volumes of *A History and Criticism of American Public Address* by William Norwood Brigance and Marie Hochmuth Nichols (1943,1955). These volumes offer scholarly analyses of important speeches but do not include texts of the speeches. Brigance notes the importance of oratory in the shaping of human affairs. He explains that "most of the mighty movements affecting the destiny of the American nation have gathered strength in obscure places from the talk of nameless men, and gained final momentum from leaders who could state in common words the needs and hopes of common people" (Brigance 1945, vii). Despite the absence of speech texts, Brigance's work retains its reputation as a standard source. The next wave of books devoted to the study of public address, however, attempted to fill the void left by Brigance and Nichols' work by providing speech texts as well as the circumstances surrounding the rhetorical act and biographical information about the speakers. Representative of this organizational pattern is *American Speeches* (1954) edited by Wayland Maxfield Parrish and Marie Hochmuth Nichols. That work also included a section on rhetorical criticism, "The Study of Speeches," that has been influential in the evolving aesthetic standards for the evaluation of public address.

Later editions became more inclusive, adding speeches by less important speakers. Duffy and Ryan cite as an example of this expansion *Contemporary Forum: American Speeches of Twentieth Century Issues* (1962) edited by Ernest J. Wrage and Barnet Baskerville. Kathleen Jamieson edited a collection of speeches organized according to genre, *Critical Anthology of Public Speeches* (1978). A collection of particular relevance to this study is Judith Anderson's *Outspoken Women: Speeches By American Women Reformers 1635-1935* (1985). Duffy and Ryan applaud Anderson's inclusion of "hard-to-find texts of speeches by women orators and . . . a fine historical overview of the role and successes of American on the political platform" (Duffy and Ryan 1978, 430).

A final innovation noted by the editors of *American Orators of The Twentieth Century* is John Graham's *Great American Speeches 1898-1963* (1970). The innovative contribution of this work was the combination of speech texts and previously published analyses of these texts in one volume. Other volumes addressed particular issues or historical periods. Examples of these specialized treatments include *Presidential Rhetoric (1961 to the Present)* edited by Theodore Windt in 1983 and *The Agitator In American Society* (1968) edited by Charles W. Lomas.

A revised edition of *History and Criticism of American Public Address* (1960) includes a chapter uniquely relevant to this current work. Doris G. Yoakam's contribution to that volume entitled "Women's Introduction to The American Platform" (Nichols 1955, 153-192) explicates the role of women orators in the early nineteenth century, referred to as "the age of experimentation." Certainly the contributions of A. Craig Baird, Lester Thonssen, Waldo Braden, and Owen Peterson should be acknowledged here. These names represent editors of *Representative American Speeches*, a series published each year since 1937. Paula Giddings' *When And Where I Enter* (1988) served as an invaluable factual and scholarly source, and Dorothy Sterling's *We Are Your Sisters* (1984) proved to be not only an outstanding scholarly reference, but also an inspirational source cogently confirming the accomplishments and the possibilities of African American women. This list is by no means exhaustive but stands at best as a partial acknowledgment of the continuing scholarly commitment to the preservation of significant public address.

Introduction

The tradition of respect for public address is rooted in the classical antecedents of Greek and Roman oratory. The classical period, deemed by some to extend from the fifth century B.C. to the first quarter of the nineteenth century, produced rhetoricians of such distinction that greatness at some points in history became practically synonymous with rhetoric and oratory. Even the names of Aristotle, Demosthenes, Quintilian, and Cicero—to mention a few outstanding representatives of the art—immediately evoke images of the authority and excellence that inhere in the rhetorical tradition. Some contemporaries of Quintilian criticized his methods, notably his unrelenting insistence on discipline and excellence in the training of rhetors. Quintilian evinced his high regard for the discipline in his response, intimating that man had indeed accomplished more difficult feats but none more important. Students of rhetoric frequently refer to his eloquent query: " . . . has not man succeeded in crossing the high seas, in learning the number and the courses of the stars, and almost measuring the universe itself—all of them accomplishments of less importance than oratory. . .?" Although the word *rhetoric* has accrued some pejorative connotations across time, the art of oratory has generally been accorded a place of respect in the significant transactions of history.

The oratory of African Americans retains significant features established in the classical system and modern mainstream oratory. But the unique struggle of African Americans has rendered necessary some adaptations peculiar to the survival imperatives of a disadvantaged people. So pervasive and unique has been the racial theme that classifications of discourse frequently become blurred in the public address of African Americans. Graduation speeches

1

and keynote addresses, for example, would in the classical rhetorical system be categorized as ceremonial or epideictic discourse and thereby exempt from some of the imperatives of logic assumed in forensic and deliberative discourse. But, as the editors of *The Negro Speaks* note, the African American orator "is inevitably involved with the problems that confront Negroes as a group. Consequently, when he [or she] mounts the platform to speak for a university convocation or commencement, to keynote a conference or convention, to inspire a mammoth civil rights rally or a march on Washington, his [or her] speech reflects a concern for both the general problems of our democracy and the specific problems of the race" (Williams and Williams 1970, X1-X11).

African American oratory not only carries its own unique imperatives, but it singularly clarifies the character and texture of the race struggle. Philip S. Foner, editor of *The Voice of Black America* (1972) attests to this enhancing aspect of oratory. Commenting on the comparative influence of oratory and written works by African Americans, Foner argues that "although oratory is only one form that black Americans have used throughout history to assert their worth and to validate their claim to human rights, it is a singularly important one. Perhaps even more than writers, black orators helped to demolish the myth of the natural inferiority of black people" (Foner 1972, 2). African American orators seemed able to confer credibility on their art in a way that the writers often could not, considering persistent challenges to the true authorship of many of the written works. Foner also justifies the polemical nature of most of the speeches, attributing this feature to the reality that "there never was a time when the black American was not outraged at the conditions imposed on him" (Foner 1972, 8).

In commemoration of the fiftieth anniversary of the Emancipation Proclamation, Alice Moore Dunbar edited *Masterpieces of Negro Eloquence* (1913). Dunbar considered it appropriate to acknowledge "the birth of the Negro into manhood," stating as her goal the collection of "some few of the speeches he made to help win his manhood, his place in the economy of the nation, his right to stand with his face to the sun" (Preface, n.p.). Dunbar's claim for the accomplishments wrought by the oratory may be somewhat exaggerated, but the force of this medium in setting before the American public the tragic plight of an oppressed people cannot be denied.

Several works in the African American tradition have contributed to the direction and focus of this current volume. Two bibliographical sources in particular suggested the possibilities and parameters of a work of this nature. And a number of speech collections, six of which will be described in this section, provided numerous hours of inspirational reading as well as the speeches that partially make up this work. Acknowledgment of general sources is located at the end of the Preface.

Black Rhetoric: A Guide to Afro-American Communication (1976) by Robert W. Glenn is a remarkably instructive bibliographical guide to speeches and essays by African Americans. The first section presents a general bibliography of useful sources; other sections contain a comprehensive listing of anthologies accompanied by descriptive information relative to the type of material emphasized in the anthologies, dates, and representative examples of specific types of items. A topical listing of books and essays, and a comprehensive bibliographical listing of more than 2,400 speeches and essays combine to qualify this source as one of the most valuable single references consulted for this current work. *The Oratory Of Negro Leaders 1900-*

1968 (1969) by Marcus H. Boulware was similarly helpful in clarifying the nature and direction of African American oratory. A particularly valuable chapter in Boulware's work is one entitled "Public Addresses of Negro Women" (Boulware 1969, 98-113). References in the chapter cited provided a productive avenue of exploration that influenced the selection of speeches for this collection.

Six speech collections have been selected for discussion in this section. The value of these collections in the conception and preparation of this current work is two-fold. These collections not only provided some of the speech texts in this study but also afforded scholarly, instructive models that suggested the complementary role a work such as the one attempted here could fulfill in continuing the scholarship in this discipline. Descriptions of these collections focus primarily on scope and organizing principles.

Masterpieces of Negro Eloquence, edited by Alice Moore Dunbar, was first published in 1914 and reprinted in 1970. *Masterpieces* contains fifty-one speeches—four by women. Brief introductory statements and footnotes provide limited biographical information, dates, and places where the speeches were delivered. Alice Moore Dunbar (Nelson) edited another collection, *The Dunbar Speaker and Entertainer* in 1920. This work is divided into sections (oratorical and commemorative), under the general heading "The Best Prose and Poetic Selections By and About the Negro Race." *The Dunbar Speaker* contains twenty-eight speeches (or poems) in the two sections—five by women.

Rhetoric of Racial Revolt (1964) edited by Roy L. Hill, contains forty-two speeches—four by women. The organizational arrangement is according to historical periods. Speeches presented in this collection range from Frederick Douglass's "Fourth of July Oration" in 1852 to Martin Luther King's "I Have A Dream" in 1963. Analyses of content, style, and organization grouped by historical periods complement the collection of speeches. *The Negro Speaks* (1970), edited by Jamye Coleman Williams and McDonald Williams, contains twenty-three speeches—five by women. The organizing principle of this work is purpose. Categories of purpose are: to articulate problems, to arouse the national conscience, to affirm rights and responsibilities, to assess the past and chart the future, to inspire, and to enunciate black awareness. Well-researched biographical sketches precede the speech texts.

Speech texts in *The Rhetoric of Black Americans* (1971), edited by James L. Golden and Richard D. Rieke, span more than two hundred years. The organizing principle of this volume is ideological orientation. Assimilation, separation, and revolution are the three ideological constructs represented. Fifty-seven speech texts are presented in this work—one by a woman. Philip S. Foner edited *The Voice of Black America* (1972), a collection containing selected speeches presented between 1797 and 1971. This anthology is divided into two parts and six sections: The Antebellum Period, The Civil War and Reconstruction, The Post-Reconstruction, World War I to World War II, Post-World War II, and Civil Rights to Black Power. Short introductory sections containing relevant historical information and aspects of the rhetorical situation precede the speech texts. The work contains one hundred and ninety-eight speeches—nine by women.

In addition to providing information about the substantive and organizational features of speech collections, the descriptions reveal another significant consideration: the limited representation of public address by African American women even in works rooted in our own tradition. Sociological and cultural factors such as the smaller actual number of women speakers or the failure of women to record their speeches for posterity may be invoked to explain the proportional disparity. Some truth may well inhere in both claims. Yet neither claim, nor a combination of the two, is sufficient to justify the disparity, considering speech texts that are available.

Mary McLeod Bethune, herself a consummate orator, illuminates to some extent the nature of this disparity in her exposition of the "accidental" nature of greatness. Equating the struggle of African American women with the struggle of the race, she argued that "the failure of one group to have shining representatives is more apt to be due to lack of opportunity in these fields from which they are barred by social pressure than lack of capacity" (Bethune Papers, Box 3, Folder 13). Certainly the oratory selected for this volume is its own eloquent attestation of capacity. The underrepresentation noted may well derive from value judgments incongruent with the cultural significance of the contributions. This current volume thus attempts a revised, or corrective, construct that duly acknowledges the substantial contribution of this genre to our cultural legacy and to note as well distinctive features: its very audacity and themes of transcendence, a seemingly unwarranted sense of transcendence when viewed in relation to objective criteria.

Several practical and philosophical considerations informed the rhetorical problems of inclusion and significance for this work. Some decisions were arbitrary, such as the one to include a dozen speeches for each of the three thematic divisions. And although the initial quality attracting a rhetorical critic to a given work is the intrinsic worth of the discourse, that consideration alone did not govern selection. One prevailing criterion was that selections accurately reflect the character and texture of the African American woman's struggle and her place in this society, that a given speech communicate something larger than itself by clarifying the continuity and/or discordance in the continuing concerns of the group that define its world vision as comprehensively as possible. Thus, significance as a criterion involved more than the popularity or fame of a speaker, or, in some cases, the public attention attending the rhetorical act. In some instances the selection of one speech by a given orator over another speech derived not necessarily from the comparative intrinsic worth of the pieces, but in some thematic complementarity of the selected piece that illuminates facets of the struggle deemed essential to a comprehensive portrait of the African American across time. This assembly of works, therefore, will omit some brilliantly crafted and memorable speeches, a regrettable omission that continuing scholarship in the discipline should certainly correct.

The artistic problem of selection or inclusion is a necessarily demanding enterprise. Selecting one speech by a given speaker over an equally compelling one ranks high among the several agonizing choices confronting this author. No less demanding is the problem of methodology, the awesome and humbling task of formulating criteria that do justice to the features demonstrating sufficient significance to justify the work. The latter consideration is discussed in the next section.

Rhetorical criticism is an evolving art, as it should be, reflecting the inclination of theorists and critics to acknowledge limitations of the traditional classical approach and explore the possibilities of alternative critical approaches. Two seminal works in this tradition note several restrictive features of the classical canon, designated variously as Aristotelian, Neo-Aristotelian, or traditional. Edwin Black's *Rhetorical Criticism: A Study in Method* (1965, 1978) is a work highly critical of Aristotelian criticism, noting that the enterprise of rhetorical criticism is considerably less logical than the classical canon acknowledges and that the traditional canon accounts for, less substantially than it should, the complete rhetorical transaction. Robert L. Scott and Bernard L. Brock pose similar challenges to the traditional system in *Methods of Rhetorical Criticism: A Twentieth Century Perspective* (1980) and propose several potentially promising alternative critical methods.

Edwin Black argues that "Neo-Aristotelianism is founded upon a restrictive view of human behavior" and notes that "there are discourses that function in ways not dreamed of in Aristotle's *Rhetoric*" (Black 1978, 131). Black's primary challenge seems to be directed toward the fixed, *a priori* standards of the classical canon that fail to reflect the fluidity of human experience. He projects a theoretical construct for evaluating oral discourse based on the "intensity of conviction . . . promoted in audiences" and suggests for consideration two provocative orientations to analysis based on the principle of audience conviction.

Bernard L. Brock and Robert L. Scott concur with the substance of Black's "arguments about the insufficiency of neo-Aristotelianism," while disagreeing with some of the specific features of his descriptions (Brock and Scott 1980, 23). They define and explore the analytical potential of four general rhetorical perspectives: traditional, experiential, "new rhetorics," and the meta-critical approach. The traditional perspective, according to their description, concentrates on the speaker and the speaker's response to the unique rhetorical problems posed by the rhetorical situation. Assumptions informing the traditional perspective derive from established, relatively stable principles espoused by Aristotle (Brock and Scott 35, 36). Eclecticism is the distinguishing characteristic of the experiential perspective that acknowledges the necessity of continually applying fresh methodology. This perspective emphasizes the restrictive influences of fixed patterns and proposes flexible analytical strategies that accurately reflect the fluidity of human experience.

Two approaches, the language-action approach and the dramatistic approach, comprise the "new rhetorics" perspective. The language-action approach is "based on the assumption that the rhetorical critic should begin analysis with the speaker's or writer's use of language" (Brock and Scott 271). Language is perceived as the embodiment of action, rather than a reflection of action. The dramatistic approach derives from the theory of Kenneth Burke, who "shifts the rhetoric from persuasion (the speaker's purpose) to identification (the result of all the components in the rhetorical act)." He [Burke] highlights the psychological constituent of rhetoric by concentrating on the analysis of motives" (Brock and Scott 273).

The genre approach focuses on "congregations of rhetorical discourses that share similar strategies, situations, and effects" (Brock and Scott 294). Critics subscribing to this perspective assemble bodies of rhetorical discourse reflecting similarities sufficient to represent types or classes. Brock and Scott place the genre approach under the general rubric of meta-critical perspective. Completing the meta-critical perspective is the "movements" approach that attempts "to discover. . . the rhetorical pattern inherent in the movement selected for investigation." This method is essentially historical in its substantive effects.

Roderick P. Hart summarizes several emphases in the imperatives for rhetorical criticism in *Modern Rhetorical Criticism* (1990). These include gathering information about the speeches, understanding the general topic, researching the specific topic, gathering information about the audience, researching the social background of the message, understanding the verbal environment, accessing popular commentary, and accessing scholarly commentary (Hart 463-

486). Robert Cathcart captures the essence of these perspectives using more straightforward organizational principles. In *Post Communication: Rhetorical Analysis and Evaluation* (1981), Cathcart enumerates four possible foci in speech analysis based on the rhetorical variable stressed in a given analysis, noting that the critic's intentions determine the approach or combination of approaches that comport well with the analytical objectives. The stressed variable, then, becomes the focus of the analysis: either speaker, or message, or situation, or audience—or an appropriate combination of these variables. He argues that "the approaches are not in fundamental opposition to one another. Rather, they arise from different interests or concerns of the rhetorical critic" (Cathcart 1981, 21).

The inclusive considerations of Hart's and Cathcart's philosophies seem most appropriate for the analytical objectives of this current study. The situation, the speaker, and the message all appear to be indispensable considerations for analyses that purport to translate rhetorical acts into a coherent segment of cultural legacy. Certainly the prevailing social-historical climate in which the rhetorical act occurs confers its essence on a medium in which the inherent public orientation is its own defining agent. Thus the rhetorical critic exploring cultural relevance and impact cannot prudently ignore the environmental contours limiting and defining the cultural derivatives of that environment. Analysis of situation also clarifies the rhetorical imperatives of the speakers, the constraints imposed by the political dynamics of the speaking environment that influence critical rhetorical choices.

This critic subscribes also to the premise that the speaker is a thinking, responsive being affected by cultural realities in unique ways because of individual experiences and personalized cognitive mappings. The cultural climate is, therefore, an insufficient—albeit a critically relevant—analytical tool. In view of this insufficiency, biographical factors require consideration since participants in the same culture often interpret their experiences or construct reality variously. Rhetorical analyses in this work will include discussions of personal attributes and environmental influences that suggest relevance to the ideological or philosophical orientation of the speakers. A work of this nature also seems to require consideration of the speaker's influence on and contributions to the general society and the immediate effects of the speech itself.

Socio-political environments and personal constructs represent two significant dimensions of the rhetorical situation. Yet if the claim is made, or inferred, that the public addresses constitute a genre worthy of preservation, certainly a significant component of the analysis should be the intrinsic worth of the messages themselves, the ideational and linguistic features that imbue the work with sufficient intrinsic beauty or universality to justify its inclusion in the historical legacy of a people. A considerable proportion of the analysis focuses on the message itself, the rhetorical features that combine to render a work worthy of continuing consideration.

"Lifting as we climb," the motto adopted by the National Association of Colored Women in the late nineteenth century, dramatizes to an extent the philosophical basis informing the efforts of African American women in this country. The transcendence implied in lifting is tempered by the nature of climbing, an ambiguous concept the dynamics of which at once suggest upward movement and imply continuing hardships and difficulties. Such indeed has been the struggle of women of African descent, and the oratory of the group manifests this dual reality. So the interplay of positive and negative mythic elements that create dialectical tension is relevant here and dramatizes the mixture of pragmatism and transcendence discussed by Hart in *Modern Rhetorical Criticism* (Hart 325-327). That emphasis in this study becomes a central consideration in ascertaining the speakers' perceptions of their challenges and possibilities.

Most of the technical rhetorical heuristics applied in this study derive from the traditional classical canon based on Aristotelian rhetoric. The potential of some of the evolving critical methods has not been lightly dismissed. Several of these approaches may well inform future studies as the genre—necessarily limited for this present study—attains stature and canonical inclusion. In this definitional study, however, the traditional canon seems most appropriate for ferreting out the possibilities and establishing a tenable aesthetic. The rhetorical analysis will encompass lines of argument—or common topics, special topics, arrangement, schemes and tropes, and linguistic features of paragraphs and sentences.

PART ONE

BREAKING THE SHACKLES:
THE STRUGGLE FOR FREEDOM

Chronology and Publication History of Speeches

Maria W. Stewart, "African Rights And Liberty." 1833. Delivered at the African Masonic Hall on 27 February 1833; published in the *Liberator* (27 April 1833).

Frances W. Harper, "Liberty For Slaves." 1857. Delivered on 13 May 1857 before the New York Anti-Slavery Society on their fourth anniversary; published in the *National Anti-Slavery Standard* (23 May 1857).

Sarah P. Remond, "Why Slavery Is Still Rampant." 1859. Delivered at the Athenaeum in Manchester, England; account of speech carried in the *Manchester Times* on 17 September 1859.

Frances E. W. Harper, "The Great Problem To Be Solved." 1875. Delivered 14 April 1885 at the Centennial Anniversary of the Pennsylvania Society For Promoting The Abolition of Slavery in Philadelphia; published in Alice Moore Dunbar's *Masterpieces of Negro Eloquence* (1914).

Ann Julia Cooper, "The Ethics Of The Negro Question." 1902. Delivered at biennial session of Friends General Conference at Asbury, New Jersey in September 1902; text in Anna Julia Cooper Papers at Moorland-Spingarn

Research Center at Howard University in Washington, D. C. (Box 23-4, Folder 32).

Mary Church Terrell, "What It Means To Be Colored In the Capital Of the United States." 1906. Delivered in Washington, D. C. before the United Women's Club on 10 October 1906; published in *The Independent* (24 January 1906).

Mary Church Terrell, "Frederick Douglass." 1908. Delivered at sixtieth anniversary of Seneca Falls Women's Rights Convention. Mary Church Terrell Papers, Library of Congress.

Ida Wells-Barnett, "Lynching, Our National Crime." (1909). Delivered before the founding conference of the National Association for the Advancement of Colored People; published in the organization's *Proceedings* for that year.

Fannie Lee Chaney, "Ben Is Going To Take His Big Brother's Place." 1965. Delivered at Memorial Meeting in New York City for Andrew Goodman, Michael Schwerner, and James Chaney, son of the speaker; published in *Freedomways* (2nd Quarter 1965).

Constance Baker Motley, "Keynote Address." 1965. Delivered before the Southern Christian Leadership Conference in Birmingham, Alabama; published in *The Negro Speaks* (1970).

Alice Walker, "Choice: A Tribute To Martin Luther King, Jr." 1972. Delivered at a restaurant in Jackson, Mississippi; published in Walker's *In Search Of Our Mother's Gardens* (1983).

Lorde, Audre, "Learning From The 60s." 1982. Delivered at the Malcolm X Weekend celebration at Harvard University; published in Lorde's *Sister Outsider: Essays And Speeches* (1984).

Introduction to Part One

The African American's struggle for freedom has been a recursive one, and the oratory of women of the race reflects the upheavals and reversals attending this struggle. Thus when we attempt to explicate the oratory, we must necessarily consider long spans of time because the same battles have been fought more than once. In consequence, we can note some of the same themes in the speeches of the 1960s as those invoked by speakers of the nineteenth century.

Historical reality indeed reveals that at all times during the existence of this republic the rights and privileges gained by African Americans have been precariously maintained, sometimes even reversed. The hope raised by the Civil Rights Bill of 1875, for example, evaporated as a result of the contrary action of the United States Supreme Court which, in 1883, rendered the gains made by that legislation unconstitutional. This reality accounts, at least in part, for the recursive nature of the oratory. Optimistic statements at any given time in the struggle might well give way to lamentations a decade or so later because surreptitious social forces have eroded earlier gains.

The oratory of women, in the documentation and illumination of historical reality, is revelatory of the dynamics at work during significant transition and the reversals that minimized or negated the impact of transition. Speeches included in this division of the work range, chronologically, from 1833 to 1982. Ideologically, they encompass views consistent with the spirit of the times in which they were uttered as well as those that seemed reminiscent of an earlier era, or those that anticipated future emphases and philosophies.

Breaking the shackles was not a one-time victory permanently enshrined and rendered secure forever with the

17

signing of the Emancipation Proclamation by Abraham Lincoln in 1863. African American women and the entire race have never been afforded the luxury of forgetting the price of that victory. That victory has had to be nurtured, fought for, and reclaimed many times since the Emancipation. Even after many decades, forces against equality for the race have rendered necessary militant action and continuing vigilance to anticipate and counteract attempts to restore the shackles binding the physical, emotional, social, and intellectual freedom of African Americans.

As early as 1833, Maria Stewart issued a challenge to the sons of Africa to claim for themselves the dignity and rewards of freedom. Many African Americans were free at this time in history and the outspoken speaker born in Hartford, Connecticut in 1803 anticipated for those of African descent lives of dignity, unencumbered by the degrading restrictions of the institution of slavery. Frances Ellen Watkins Harper reiterated the same themes in 1857, citing freedom as one of the innate yearnings of the human spirit. Her speech "Liberty For Slaves" explores the ironic nature of the slave system in America, a system that communicated a conspicuous difference, an inconsistent symbiosis, with the espoused ideals of America.

During this same period of time Sarah Parker Remond spoke in Manchester, England, noting the continuing practice of slavery in the United States as well as characteristics and manifestations of the slave system. Her speech included here, "Why Slavery Is Still Rampant," was presented in Manchester in 1892. Another speech delivered during that same year was "The Ethics Of The Negro Question" by Anna Julia Cooper, a noted scholar, teacher, and graduate of the Sorbonne in Paris. Cooper explores the problems and possibilities of African Americans and emphasizes the importance of directing the race toward the ideals they sought. Noting the song-loving nature of the race, she nonetheless explains why people of color cannot sing their song in a strange land, an allusion dating back to the Israelites' inability to sing their songs during their enslavement.

Frances E. W. Harper in "The Great Problem To Be Solved" defines the moral contours of justice and injustice, fully cognizant as she was of the injustices continuing to plague people of color in 1875. Despite advances made by the race, extremist white groups were perpetuating acts of terror upon African Americans, this terror sanctioned by some respectable people. Central to her address is the irony of injustice in a land which has as its operative motto respect for individual rights and human dignity. This irony is also evident in Mary Church Terrell's "What It Means To Be Colored In The Capital Of The United States," delivered in 1906. Terrell relates the extensive humiliation endured by African Americans in a city with agencies and institutions essentially synonymous with the concept of liberty—the White House, the capital, and the tomb of the Father of the Country.

During the latter part of the nineteenth century, Ida B. Wells-Barnett began her militant crusade against lynching, amassing numerous statistics dramatizing the prevalence and brutality of this practice. Speaking in 1909 before the National Association for the Advancement of Colored People, Wells questions the conscience of a nation that would tolerate the torture and inhumanity of lynching. The lack of concern demonstrated by the continuation of such inhumane actions is indeed reflective of the many manifestations of racial injustice.

Three other speeches delivered during the twentieth century demonstrate the recursive nature of racial injustice and the necessity of continuing exposure of its presence and consequences. When Constance Baker Motley addressed the annual conference of the Southern Christian Leadership

Conference in 1965, she emphasized the challenges accompanying legislation designed to eliminate overt and legalized discrimination in the country. Implicit in her address is the theme of residual discrimination in America despite racial gains, and she urges members of the race to take advantage of every opportunity made possible by recent legislation. Her primary charge is that African Americans refrain from rendering void the legislative actions taken in their favor by failing to take advantage of every available opportunity.

Mary Church Terrell in "Frederick Douglass" (1908) invokes attributes of a leader from the distant past, extolling Douglass's encouragement of the women's movement but emphasizing the basic virtues possessed by the ex-slave that yielded pivotal changes in the progress of the entire race as well. And Audre Lorde in "Learning From the 60s" (1984) invokes a more recent past in an impassioned plea urging African Americans to look back at the failures and triumphs of the past as they set forth to chart the future. Although Terrell's speech lacks the urgent warning contained in Lorde's speech, both speakers enumerate virtues exhibited by two outstanding race leaders: Frederick Douglass and Malcolm X.

Two other speeches certainly belong in this category designed to capture the nature of the struggle, fought many times over the span of more than a century. Fannie Lee Chaney's "Ben Is Going To Take His Big Brother's Place," delivered in 1965, certainly demonstrates that the shackles had not been broken to the extent that African American citizens could take any dimension of the freedom struggle for granted, that indeed lives were being lost in the cause of freedom, this fact demonstrated poignantly by the death of Chaney's son and his two companions as they worked in behalf of human rights. The speech is not accompanied by an analysis but fully complements the focus of the division. And Alice Walker's speech "Choice: A Tribute to Martin Luther King, Jr." (1972) dramatizes the protracted nature of the struggle and clarifies the extended struggle for freedom so eloquently articulated by courageous women of the nineteenth century.

Introduction to Maria Stewart's
"African Rights and Liberty"

"African Rights and Liberty" is a challenge to the "sons of Africa" to contend actively for the freedom of all people of African descent. While the address contains some appeals to those who govern and wield political power, its primary rhetorical burden seems to be that of exploring the antecedents attending the continuing enslavement of African Americans and provoking sufficient outrage on the part of free African American males to confront the evils of the slave system directly and openly protest its basic inhumanity. As Paula Giddings notes in *When And Where I Enter*, "The role of Blacks in the Revolutionary War, the discontent of a white working class forced to compete with slave labor and infeasibility of slavery at a time of increasing industrialization hastened its [slavery's] abolition in the North by 1830" (Giddings 1984, 41). So at this time the number of free African Americans in the country was increasing. Their role in actively seeking an end to the slave system had been disappointing. Maria Stewart deplored this reticence and in this address employs both logical arguments and emotional appeals in challenging the "sons of Africa" to commit themselves to the freedom of the race.

Maria Stewart, an uneducated woman, was influential in the politics of her time although she delivered only four public speeches. Dorothy Sterling records the following autobiographical statement by Maria Stewart, born Maria Miller in 1803. "I was born in Hartford, Connecticut, in 1803; was left an orphan at five years of age; was bound out in a clergyman's family; had the seeds of piety and virtue early sown in my mind; but was deprived of the advantages of education though my soul thirsted for knowledge. Left them at fifteen years of age; attended Sabbath schools until I was

23

twenty; in 1826 was married to James W. Stewart; was left a widow in 1829" (Sterling 1979, 153). Benjamin Quarles refers to Stewart as "the first native-born American woman to speak in public and leave extant texts of her addresses" (Quarles 1969, 7).

To say that Maria Stewart's activism unfolded in an atmosphere unreceptive to assertive women is certainly an understatement. Women at the time were responding to social and political issues, but their parameters were narrowly defined. Temperance societies and literary clubs became their primary forum, these organizations deemed appropriate by the general populace for the articulation of women's concerns. The *Liberator*, the most liberal journalistic voice of the times, had formally announced the prevailing view of appropriate limits for female participation. In an article entitled "Duty of Females" published on 5 May 1832, the limitations were set: "The voice of a woman should not be heard in public debate, but there are other ways in which her influence would be beneficial" (Giddings 1984, 49-50).

Stewart nonetheless defied cultural mores and, for a short period of time, spoke boldly on behalf of the race and of women. She earned the distinction of presenting the first public lecture by an American woman in 1832 at Boston's Franklin Hall. The theme of that address was "Daughters of Africa, awake! Arise! Distinguishing yourselves" (Sterling 1984, 154). The address analyzed here was delivered at the African Mason Hall in Boston on 23 February 1833.

African Rights and Liberty
Maria W. Stewart
1833

African rights and liberty is a subject that ought to fire the breast of every free man of color in these United States, and excite in his bosom a lively, deep, decided and heart-felt interest. When I cast my eyes on the long list of illustrious names that are enrolled on the bright annals of fame amongst the whites, I turn my eyes within, and ask my thoughts, "Where are the names of our illustrious ones?" It must certainly have been for the want of energy on the part of the free people of color that they have been long willing to bear the yoke of oppression. It must have been the want of ambition and force that has given the whites occasion to say that our natural abilities are not as good, and our capacities by nature inferior to theirs. They boldly assert that, did we possess a natural independence of soul, and feel a love for liberty within our breasts, some one of our sable race, long before this, would have testified it, notwithstanding the disadvantages under which we labor. We have made ourselves appear altogether unqualified to speak in our own defence, and are therefore looked upon as objects of pity and commiseration. We have been imposed upon, insulted and derided on every side; and now, if we complain, it is considered as the height of impertinence. We have suffered ourselves to be considered as dastards, cowards, mean, faint-hearted wretches; and on this account, (not because of our complexion,) many despise us and would gladly spurn us from their presence.

These things have fired my soul with a holy indignation, and compelled me thus to come forward, and endeavor to turn their attention to knowledge and improvement; for knowledge is power. I would ask, is it blindness of mind, or stupidity of soul, or the want of education, that has caused our men who are 60 or 70 years of age, never to let their voices be heard nor their hands be raised in behalf of their color? Or has it been for the fear of offending the whites? If it has, O ye fearful ones, throw off your fearfulness, and come forth in the name of the Lord, and in the strength of the God of Justice, and make yourselves useful and active members in society; for they admire a noble and patriotic spirit in others—and should they not admire it in us? If you are men, convince them that you possess the spirit of men; and as your day, so shall your strength be. Have the sons of Africa no souls? feel they no ambitious desires? shall the chains of ignorance forever confine them? shall the insipid appellation of "clever negroes," or "good creatures," any longer content them? Where can we find amongst ourselves the man of science, or a philosopher, or an able statesman, or a counsellor at law? Show me our fearless and brave, our noble and gallant ones. Where are our lecturers on natural history, and our critics in useful knowledge? There may be a few such men amongst us, but they are rare. It is true, our fathers bled and died in the revolutionary war, and others fought bravely under the command of Jackson, in defence of liberty. But where is the man that has distinguished himself in these modern days by acting wholly in the defence of African rights and liberty? There was one—although he sleeps, his memory lives.

I am sensible that there are many highly intelligent gentlemen of color in these United States, in the force of whose arguments, doubtless, I should discover my inferiority; but if they are blest with wit and talent, friends and fortune, why have they not made themselves men of eminence, by striving to take all the reproach that is cast upon the people of color, and in endeavoring to alleviate the woes of their brethren in bondage? Talk, without effort, is nothing; you are abundantly capable, gentlemen, of making yourselves men of distinction; and this gross neglect, on your part, causes my blood to boil within me. Here is the grand cause which hinders the rise and progress of the people of color. It is their want of laudable ambition and requisite courage.

Individuals have been distinguished according to their genius and talents, ever since the first formation of man, and will continue to be whilst the world stands. The different grades rise to honor and respectability as their merits may deserve. History informs us that we sprung from one of the most learned nations of the whole earth—from the seat, if not the parent of science; yes, poor, despised Africa was once the resort of sages and legislators of other nations, was esteemed the school for learning, and the most illustrious men in Greece flocked thither for instruction. But it was our gross sins and abominations that provoked the Almighty to frown thus heavily upon us, and give our glory unto others. Sin and prodigality have caused the downfall of nations, kings and emperors; and were it not that God in wrath remembers mercy, we might indeed despair; but a promise is left us; "Ethiopia shall again stretch forth her hands unto God."

But it is of no use for us to boast that we sprung from this learned and enlightened nation, for this day a thick mist of moral gloom hangs over millions of our race. Our condition as a people has been low for hundreds of years, and it will continue to be so, unless, by the true piety and virtue, we strive to regain that which we have lost. White Americans, by their prudence, economy and exertions, have sprung up and become one of the most flourishing nations in the world, distinguished for their knowledge of the arts and sciences, for their polite literature. Whilst our minds are vacant and starving for want of knowledge, theirs are filled to overflowing. Most of our color have been taught to stand in fear of the white man from their earliest infancy, to work as soon as they could walk, and call "master" before they scarce could lisp the name of mother. Continual fear and laborious servitude have in some degree lessened in us that natural force and energy which belong to man; or else, in defiance of opposition, our men before this would have nobly and boldly contended for their rights. But give the man of color an equal opportunity with the white, from the cradle to manhood, and from manhood to the grave, and you would discover the dignified statesman, the man of science, and the philosopher. But there is no such opportunity for the sons of Africa, and I fear that our powerful ones are fully determined that there never shall be. Forbid, ye Powers on High, that it should any longer be said that our men possess no force. O ye sons of Africa, when will your voices be heard in our legislative halls, in defiance of your enemies, contending for equal rights and liberty? How can you, when you reflect from what you have fallen, refrain from crying mightily unto God, to turn away from us the fierceness of his anger, and remember our transgressions against us no more forever. But a God of infinite purity will not regard the prayers of those who hold religion in one hand, and prejudice, sin and pollution in the other; he will not regard the prayers of self-righteousness and hypocrisy. Is it possible, I exclaim, that for the want of knowledge, we have labored for thousands of years to support others, and been content to receive what they chose to give us in return? Cast your eyes about—look as far as you can see—all, all is owned by the lordly white, except here and there a lowly dwelling which the man of color, midst deprivations, fraud and opposition, has been scarce able to procure. Like King Solomon, who put neither nail nor hammer to the temple, yet received the praise; so also have the white Americans gained themselves a name, like the names of the great men who are in the earth, whilst in reality we have been their principal foundation and support. We have pursued the shadow, they have obtained the substance; we have performed the labor, they have received the profits; we have planted the vines, they have eaten the fruits of them.

I would implore our men, and especially our rising youth, to flee from the gambling board and the dance hall; for we are poor, and have no money to throw away. I do not consider dancing as criminal in itself, but it is astonishing to me that our young men are so blind to their own interest and the future welfare of their children, as to spend their hard earnings for this frivolous amusement; for it has been carried on among us to such an unbecoming extent that it has become absolutely disgusting. "Faithful are the wounds of a friend, but the kisses of an enemy are deceitful." Had those men amongst us, who have had an opportunity, turned their attention as assiduously to mental and moral improvement as they have to gambling and dancing, I might have remained quietly at home, and they stood contending in my place. These polite accomplishments will never enroll your names on the bright annals of fame, who admire the belle void of intellectual knowledge, or applaud the dandy that talks largely on politics, without striving to assist his fellow in the revolution, when the nerves and muscles of every other man forced him into the field of action. You have a right to rejoice, and to let your hearts cheer you in the days of your youth; yet remember that for all these things God will bring you into judgment. Then, O ye sons of Africa, turn your mind from these perishable objects, and contend for the cause of God and the rights of man. Form yourselves into temperance societies. There are temperate men amongst you; then why will you any longer neglect to strive, by your example, to suppress vice in all its abhorrent forms? You have been told repeatedly of the glorious results arising from temperance, and can you bear to see the whites arising in honor and respectability, without endeavoring to grasp after that honor and respectability also?

But I forbear. Let our money, instead of being thrown away as heretofore, be appropriated for schools and seminaries of learning for our children and youth. We ought to follow the example of the whites in this respect. Nothing would raise our respectability, add to our peace and happiness and reflect so much honor upon us, as to be ourselves the promoters of temperance, and the supporters, as far as we are able, of useful and scientific knowledge. The rays of light and knowledge have been hid from our view; we have been taught to consider ourselves as scarce superior to the brute creation; and have performed the most laborious part of American drudgery. Had we as people received one half the early advantages the whites have received, I would defy the government of these United States to deprive us any longer of our rights.

I am informed that the agent of the Colonization Society has recently formed an association of young men, for the purpose of influencing those of us to go to Liberia who may feel disposed. The colonizationalists are blind to their own interest, for should the nations of the earth make war with America, they would find their forces much weakened by our absence; or should we remain here, can our "brave soldiers" and "fellow citizens," as they were termed in time of calamity, condescend to defend the rights of the whites, and be again deprived of their own, or sent to Liberia in return? O, if the colonizationists are real friends to Africa, let them expend the money which they collect in erecting a college to educate her injured sons in this land of gospel light and liberty; for it would be most thankfully received on our part, and convince us of the truth of their professions, and save time, expense and anxiety. Let them place before us noble objects, worthy of pursuit, and see if we prove ourselves to be those unambitious Negroes they term us. But ah! methinks their hearts are so frozen towards us, they had rather their money should be sunk in the ocean than to administer it to our relief; and I fear, if they dared, like Pharaoh king of Egypt, they would order every male child amongst us to be drowned. But the most high God is still as able to subdue the lofty pride of these white Americans, as He was the heart of that ancient rebel. They say though we are looked upon as things, yet we sprang from a scientific people. Had our men the requisite force and energy, they would soon convince them, by their efforts both in public and private, that they were men, or things in the shape of men. Well may the colonizationists laugh us to scorn for our negligence; well may they cry, "Shame to the sons of Africa." As the burden of the Israelites was too great for Moses to bear, so also is our burden too great for our noble advocate to bear. You must feel interested, my brethren, in what he undertakes, and hold up his hands by your good words, or in spite of himself his soul will become discouraged, and his heart will die within him; for he has, as it were, the strong bulls of Bashan to contend with.

It is of no use for us to wait any longer for a generation of well educated men to arise. We have slumbered and slept too long already; the day is far spent; the night of death approaches; and you have sound sense and good judgment sufficient to begin with, if you feel disposed to make a right use of it. Let every man of color throughout the United States, who possesses the spirit and principles of a man, sign a petition to Congress to abolish slavery in the District of Columbia, and grant you the rights and privileges of common free citizens; for if you had had faith as a grain of mustard seed, long before this the mountains of prejudice might have been removed. We are all sensible that the Anti-Slavery Society has taken hold of the arm of our whole population, in order to raise them out of the mire. Now all we have to do is, by a spirit of virtuous ambition to strive to raise ourselves; and I am happy to have it in my power thus publicly to say that the colored inhabitants of this city, in some respects, are beginning to improve. Had the free people of color in these United States nobly and boldly contended for their rights, and showed a natural genius and talent, although not so brilliant as some; had they held up, encouraged and patronized each other; nothing could have hindered us from being a thriving and flourishing people. There has been a fault amongst us. The reason why our distinguished men have not made themselves more influential is, because they fear the strong current of opposition through which they must pass, would cause their downfall and prove their overthrow. And what gives rise to this opposition? Envy. And what has it amounted to? Nothing. And who are the cause of it? Our whited sepulchres who want to be great, and don't know how; who love to be called of men "Rabbi, Rabbi," who put on false sanctity, and humble themselves to their brethren, for the sake of acquiring the highest place in the synagogue, and the uppermost seats at the feast. You, dearly beloved, who are the genuine followers of our Lord Jesus Christ, the salt of the earth and the light of the world, are not so culpable. As I told you, in the very first of my writing, I tell you again, I am but as one drop in the bucket—as one particle of the small dust of the earth. God will surely raise up those amongst us who will plead the cause of virtue, and the pure principles of morality, more eloquently than I am able to do.

It appears to me that America has become like the great city of Babylon, for she has boasted in her heart,—"I sit a queen, and am no widow, and shall see no sorrow." She is indeed a seller of slaves and the souls of men; she has made the Africans drunk with the wine of her fornication; she has put them completely beneath her feet, and she means to keep them there; her right hand supports the reins of government, and her left hand the wheel of power, and she is determined not to let go her grasp. But many powerful sons and daughters of Africa will shortly arise, who will put down vice and immorality amongst us, and declare by Him that sitteth upon the throne, that they will have their rights; and if refused, I am afraid they will spread horror and devastation around. I believe that the oppression of injured Africa has come up before the majesty of Heaven; and when our cries shall have reached the ears of the Most High, it will be a tremendous day for the people of this land; for strong is the arm of the Lord God Almighty.

Life has almost lost its charms for me; death has lost its sting and the grave its terrors; and at times I have a strong desire to depart and dwell with Christ, which is far better. Let me entreat my white brethren to awake and save our sons from dissipation, and our daughters from ruin. Lend the hand of assistance to feeble merit, and plead the cause of virtue amongst our sable race; so shall our curses upon you be turned into blessings; and though you shall endeavor to drive us from these shores, still we will cling to you the more firmly; nor will we attempt to rise above you; we will presume to be called equals only.

The unfriendly whites first drove the native American from his much loved home. Then they stole our fathers from their peaceful and quiet dwellings, and brought them hither and made bond men and bond women of them and their little ones; they have obliged our brethren to labor, kept them in utter ignorance, nourished them in vice and raised them in degradation; and now that we have enriched their soil, and filled their coffers, they say that we are not capable of becoming like white men, and that we never can rise to respectability in this country. They would drive us to a strange land. But before I go, the bayonet shall pierce me through. African rights and liberty is a subject that ought to fire the breast of every free man of color in these United States, and excite in his bosom a lively, deep, decided and heartfelt interest.

Introduction to Frances Harper's
"Liberty For Slaves"

"Liberty for Slaves" attests to the innate yearning of humankind for freedom and justice. Frances Harper dramatizes the evils of the slave system with all its contradictions and consequences. She enumerates the conditions that had sustained this institution that tolerated the injustice pervading both North and South, denying basic justice to hundreds of thousands. A compelling attribute of her discourse is the discussion of the ironic nature of this kind of enslavement, the presence in America of a system that citizens of other nations would categorically resist. She denounces the materialistic motives that perpetuated the slave system, yet her speech conveys an optimism, a belief that the forces of evil will ultimately be subdued and justice will prevail.

Frances Ellen Watkins Harper was born in Baltimore, Maryland in 1825. She was one of the founders of the National Association of Colored Women. Historian John Hope Franklin lists her among the "prominent Negroes" in the abolition movement as agents and speakers for the various societies (Franklin 1980, 188). Her early work as a servant afforded her access to a library; her overseer, a Baltimore bookseller, permitted her to read in his library during her free time. She received vocational training in dressmaking and later became a teacher. The Antislavery movement provided her the opportunity to pursue challenging, meaningful work after she lost her passion for teaching.

Dorothy Sterling recounts Harper's agonizing over leaving the teaching profession in the following excerpt from one of the speaker's letters written around 1852: "There are no people that need all the benefits resulting from a well-directed education more than we do. The condition of our people, the wants of our children, and the welfare of our race demand the aid of every helping hand. It is a work of time, a labor of patience to become an effective school teacher; and it should be a work of love in which they who engage should not abate heart or hope until it is done" (Sterling 1984, 159). The speech considered here was delivered in 1857 and, according to Dorothy Sterling, serves as a representative illustration of Harper's rhetoric. Sterling quotes a Maine abolitionist's description of Frances Ellen Watkins Harper: "Although Miss W. is slender and gracious both in personal appearance and manners, and her voice soft and musical, yet the deep fervor of feeling and pathos that manifests, together with the choice selection of language which she uses arm her elocution with almost superhuman force and power over her spellbound audience" (Sterling 1984, 161).

Liberty for Slaves
Frances Harper
1857

Could we trace the record of every human heart, the aspirations of every immortal soul, perhaps we would find no man so imbruted and degraded that we could not trace the word liberty either written in living characters upon the soul or hidden away in some nook or corner of the heart. The law of liberty is the law of God, and is antecedent to all human legislation. It existed in the mind of Deity when He hung the first world upon its orbit and gave it liberty to gather light from the central sun.

Some people say, set the slaves free. Did you ever think, if the slaves were free, they would steal everything they could lay their hands on from now till the day of their death—that they would steal more than two thousand millions of dollars? (applause) Ask Maryland, with her tens of thousands of slaves, if she is not prepared for freedom, and hear her answer: "I help supply the coffee gangs of the South." Ask Virginia, with her hundreds of thousands of slaves, if she is not weary with her merchandise of blood and anxious to shake the gory traffic from her hands, and hear her reply: "Though fertility has covered my soil, though a genial sky bends over my hills and vales, though I hold in my hand a wealth of water-power enough to turn the spindles to clothe the world, yet, with all these advantages, one of my chief staples has been the sons and daughters I send to the human market and human shambles." (applause) Ask the farther South, and all the cotton-growing states chime in, "We have need of fresh supplies to fill the ranks of those whose lives have gone out in unrequited toil on our distant plantations."

A hundred thousand new-born babes are annually added to the victims of slavery; twenty thousand lives are annually sacrificed on the plantations of the South. Such a sight should send a thrill of horror through the nerves of civilization and impel the heart of humanity to lofty deeds. So it might, if men had not found out a fearful alchemy by which this blood can be transformed into gold. Instead of listening to the cry of agony, they listen to the ring of dollars and stoop down to pick up the coin. (applause)

But a few months since a man escaped from bondage and found a temporary shelter almost beneath the shadow of Bunker Hill. Had that man stood upon the deck of an Austrian ship, beneath the shadow of the house of the Hapsburgs, he would have found protection. Had he been wrecked upon an island or colony of Great Britain, the waves of the tempest-lashed ocean would have washed him deliverance. Had he landed upon the territory of vine-encircled France and a Frenchman had reduced him to a thing and brought him here beneath the protection of our institutions and our laws, for such a nefarious deed that Frenchman would have lost his citizenship in France. Beneath the feebler light which glimmers from the Koran, the Bey of Tunis would have granted him freedom in his own dominions. Beside the ancient pyramids of Egypt he would have found liberty, for the soil laved by the glorious Nile is now consecrated to freedom. But from Boston harbour, made memorable by the infusion of three-penny taxed tea, Boston in its proximity to the plains of Lexington and Concord, Boston almost beneath the shadow of Bunker Hill and almost in sight of Plymouth Rock, he is thrust back from liberty and manhood and reconverted into a chattel. You have heard that, down South, they keep bloodhounds to hunt slaves. Ye bloodhounds, go back to your kennels; when you fail to catch the flying fugitive, when his stealthy tread is heard in the place where the bones of the revolutionary sires repose, the ready North is base enough to do your shameful service. (applause)

Slavery is mean, because it tramples on the feeble and weak. A man comes with his affidavits from the South and hurries me before a commissioner; upon that evidence *ex parte* and alone he hitches me to the car of slavery and trails my womanhood in the dust. I stand at the threshold of the Supreme Court and ask for justice, simple justice. Upon my tortured heart is thrown the mocking words, "You are a Negro; you have no rights which white men are bound to respect"! (loud and long-continued applause) Had it been my lot to have lived beneath the Crescent instead of the Cross, had injustice and violence been heaped upon my head as a Mohammendan woman, as a member of a common faith, I might have demanded justice and been listened to by the Pasha, the Bey or the Vizier; but when I come here to ask for justice, men tell me, "We have no higher law than the Constitution." (applause)

But I will not dwell on the dark side of the picture. God is on the side of freedom; and any cause that has God on its side, I care not how much it may be trampled upon, how much it may be trailed in the dust, is sure to triumph. The message of Jesus Christ is on the side of freedom, "I come to preach deliverance to the captives, the opening of the prison doors to them that are bound." The truest and noblest hearts in the land are on the side of freedom. They may be hissed at by slavery's minions, their names cast out as evil, their characters branded with fanaticism, but O, *"To side with Truth is noble when we share her humble crust Ere the cause bring fame and profit and it's prosperous to be just."*

May I not, in conclusion, ask every honest, noble heart, every seeker after truth and justice, if they will not also be on the side of freedom. Will you not resolve that you will abate neither heart nor hope till you hear the death-knell of human bondage sounded, and over the black ocean of slavery shall be heard a song, more exulting than the song of Miriam when it floated o'er Egypt's dark sea, the requiem of Egypt's ruined hosts and the anthem of the deliverance of Israel's captive people? (great applause)

Introduction to Sarah Parker Remond's
"Why Slavery Is Still Rampant"

"Why Slavery Is Still Rampant" is Sarah Parker Remond's appeal to the people of England to oppose the slave trade in America in such fashion that its disastrous effects would be appropriately appreciated. The speaker offers descriptive details of slave life, poor whites, Black slaves, free Blacks in the North, and the role of the abolitionists. She chides the English for their retreat from active resistance to the slave trade and solicits their support in publicizing and condemning this despicable practice. Remond notes the respect Americans have for the opinions of the English, thereby increasing the obligation of the latter to condemn openly conditions in the United States. She uses anecdotes to dramatize the respectability the slave trade had received in American circles and obliquely condemns the hypocrisy of the Christian religion in its acquiescence, and sometimes participation, in perpetuating the institution of slavery. Concrete descriptions of slave life lend urgency to her plea that England respond until "its voice reaches the American shore. Aid us thus until the shackles of the American slave melt like dew before the morning sun."

Sarah Parker Remond was born in 1824, the daughter of Nancy Lenox Remond and John Remond. Sarah Remond had three sisters who operated a Ladies' Hair Work Salon in Salem, Massachusetts. Sarah herself, according to a friend, was "dedicated from birth to the cause of freedom" (Sterling 1984, 175). Her preparation for antislavery work received the endorsement of her family. Remond experienced discrimination early in life when she was refused admission to Salem High School in 1835 although she had successfully passed the entrance examinations. Although the Remond family was always dedicated to the cause of freedom and

41

encouraged bravery and adaptability in their children, Remond later remarked, "Our home discipline did not—could not, fit us for the scorn and contempt which met us on every hand when face to face with the world, a world which hated all who were identified with the enslaved race." (Sterling 1984, 175-76).

Remond appeared at the National Women's Rights Convention in 1858, but found the unsegregated life of Great Britain far less restrictive. Dorothy Sterling describes Remond's acceptance in Great Britain: "As the first black woman of culture—"a lady every inch"—that the British had seen, Sarah Remond was warmly welcomed. She toured England, Scotland, and Ireland under the sponsorship of Ladies and Young Men's Anti-Slavery societies, speaking to as many as two thousand people at a time. The speech under consideration here was delivered in Manchester, England in 1892.

Why Slavery Is Still Rampant
Sarah Parker Remond
1892

Although the anti-slavery enterprise was begun some thirty years ago, the evil is still rampant in the land. As there are some young people present—and I am glad to see them here, for it is important that they should understand this subject—I shall briefly explain that that there are thirty-two States, sixteen of which are free and sixteen slave States. The free States are in the North. The political feelings in the North and South are essentially different, so is the social life. In the North, democracy, not what the Americans call democracy, but the true principle of equal rights, prevails—I speak of the white population, mind—which is abundant; the country, in every material sense, flourishes. In the South, aristocratic feelings prevail, labor is dishonorable, and five millions of poor whites live in the most degrading ignorance and destitution. I might dwell long on the miserable condition of these poor whites, the indirect victims of slavery; but I must go on to speak of the four millions of slaves.

The slaves are essentially things, with no rights, political, social, domestic, or religious; the absolute victims of all but irresponsible power. For the slave there is no home, no love, no hope, no help; and what is life without hope? No writer can describe the slave's life; it cannot be told; the fullest description ever given to the world does but skim over the surface of this subject. You may infer something of the state of society in the Southern States when I tell you there are eight hundred thousand mulattoes, nine-tenths of whom are the children of white fathers, and these are constantly sold by their parents, for the slave follows the condition of the mother. Hence we see every shade of complexion amongst the slaves.

To describe to you the miserable poor whites of the South, I need only quote the words of Mr. Helper, a Southerner, in his important work on slavery, and the testimony also of a Virginian gentleman of my acquaintance. The five millions poor whites are most of them in as gross a state of ignorance as Mrs. Stowe's "Topsey," in Uncle Tom's Cabin.

The free colored people of the Northern States are, for no crime but merely the fact of complexion, deprived of all political and social rights. Whatever wealth or eminence in intellect and refinement they may attain to, they are treated as outcasts and white men and women who identify themselves with them are sure to be insulted in the grossest manner. I do not ask your political interference in any way. This is a moral question. Even in America the Abolitionists generally disclaim every other ground but the moral and religious one on which this matter is based. You send missionaries to the heathen; I tell you of professing Christians practising what is worse than any heathenism on record. How is it that we have come to this state of things, you ask. I reply, the whole power of the country is in the hands of the slaveholders. For more than thirty years we have had a slaveholding President, and the Slave Power has been dominant. The consequence has been a series of encroachments, until now at last the slave trade is reopened and all but legitimised in America. It was a sad backward step when England last year fell into the trap laid by America and surrendered the right of search. Now slavers ply on the seas which were previously guarded by your ships. We have, besides, an international slave trade. We have States, where, I am ashamed to say, men and women are reared like cattle, for the market. When I walk through the streets of Manchester and meet load after load of cotton, I think of those eighty thousand cotton plantations on which was grown the one hundred and twenty-five millions of dollars' worth of cotton which supply your market, and I remember that not one cent of that money ever reaches the hands of the laborers. Here is an incident of slave life for you—an incident of common occurrence in the South. In March, 1859, a slave auction took place in the city of Savannah. Three hundred and forty-three slaves, the property of Pierce Butler—the husband of your own Fanny Kemble—were sold, regardless of every tie of flesh and blood; old men and maidens, young men, and babes of fifteen months—there was but one question about them, and that was decided at the auction-block. Pierce Butler, the owner, resides in Philadelphia, and is a highly-respected citizen and a member of a Church. He was reputed a kind master, who rarely separated the families of his slaves. The financial crisis took place, and I have given you the result to his human property. But Mr. Butler has in no wise lost caste among his friends; he still moves in the most respectable society, and his influence in his Church is so great that, with other members, he has procured the removal from the pulpit of the Reverend Dudley Tyng, who had uttered a testimony against slavery, and in that pulpit, the man who now preaches, Mr. Prentice by name, is the owner of a hundred slaves.

Such is the state of public opinion in America, and you find the poison running through everything. With the exception of the Abolitionists, you will find people of all classes thus contaminated. The whole army and navy of the United States are pledged to pursue and shoot down the poor fugitives, who panting for liberty fly to Canada, to seek the security of the British flag. All denominations of professing Christians are guilty of sustaining or defending slavery. Even the Quakers must be included in this rule. Now I ask for your sympathy and your influence, and whoever asked English men and women in vain? Give us the power of your public opinion, it has great weight in America. Words spoken here are read there as no words written in America are read. Lord Broughan's testimony on the first of August resounded through America; your Clarkson and your Wilberforce are names of strength to us! I ask you, raise the moral public opinion until its voice reaches the American shores. Aid us thus until the shackles of the American slave melt like dew before the morning sun. I ask for especial help from the women of England. Women are the worst victims of the Slave Power.

I am met on every hand by the cry "Cotton!" "Cotton!" I cannot stop to speak of cotton while men and women are being brutalized. But there is an answer for the cotton cry too, and the argument is an unanswerable one. Before concluding I shall give you a few passages from the laws of the slave States. By some of these laws, free colored people may be arrested in the discharge of their lawful business; and, if no papers attesting their freedom be found on them, they are committed to jail; and, if not claimed within a limited time, they may be sold to pay the jail fees. By another law, any person who speaks at the bar, bench, on the stage, or in private, to the slaves, so as to excite insurrection, or brings any paper or pamphlet of such nature into the State, shall be imprisoned for not less than three nor more than twenty-one years; or shall suffer death as the judge decides. I could read such laws for hours, but I shall only add that in Maryland there is at present a gentleman in prison, condemned for ten years, because a copy of *Uncle Tom's Cabin* was found in his possession. The laws are equally severe against teaching a slave to read—against teaching even the name of the good God.

Introduction to Francis E.W. Harper's
"The Great Problem To Be Solved"

"The Great Problem To Be Solved" is an eloquent moral appeal to the conscience of America to go beyond the surface acts connoting equality and develop the moral sensibilities that would render it sensitive to the true nature of justice and injustice. In the discourse, the speaker acknowledges the progress made in race relations by enumerating serious violations of justice within the past century. She structures her enumeration to reveal the pattern of progress taking place during that time period. Yet she hastens to call attention to blatant injustices currently meted out by various extremist groups. Harper marvels at the brutality gaining acceptance despite "all the victories and triumphs which freedom and justice [had] won in this country . . ." The essence of her plea is that the consciousness be transformed to incorporate the concept of "simple justice" and a "broader humanity." Her idealistic plea focuses on the brotherhood of all humanity, the seed of a common Father. Overall, she expresses confidence that appropriate attitudes and effort will yield a moral victory commensurate with the promise of America.

Frances Harper brought an impressive legacy of public service to this occasion. She was born in Baltimore, Maryland in 1825. Circumstances forced her to leave school when she was thirteen, but the library of her employer became the informal vehicle of her education. Harper emerged as the most popular African American poet of the time, a lecturer of national prominence, and a founder of the National Association of Colored Women—an organization that fulfilled many significant charitable functions.

When Frances Harper made this appeal before the Pennsylvania Society for Promoting the Abolition of Slavery in 1875, the provocation was indeed concrete. The White

Leagues of Louisiana and Mississippi had terrorized and murdered a large number of African Americans in attempts to restore white supremacy, a status they perceived to be eroding in Reconstruction efforts. Less than two decades following the Emancipation Proclamation, forces of bigotry resurfaced to thwart any efforts designed to secure the precarious freedom of African Americans. Harper had lectured for Antislavery groups since 1845 and, in the process, had seen numerous social barriers yield to the common justice and simple mercy of which she spoke. Yet a full century after its inception, the Pennsylvania Society must now confront the reality that the country had again failed to live up to its professed ideals. The speaker's preparation and experiences were equal to the rhetorical problems inherent at the one hundredth anniversary of this organization. Fully cognizant of the Society's continuing efforts to confront the horrors spawned by bigotry and injustice, she must again bring before this body the sobering reality of continuing atrocities and human rights violations. The challenge was tremendous. But Frances Harper's sustained efforts in race relations provided the wherewithal to articulate the current problems with integrity and determination.

Harper entered the teaching profession but soon found that profession less satisfying than the prospects of devoting full time to the promotion of freedom for African Americans. Implying the hand of fate in her decision, she remarked: "It may be that God himself has written upon both my heart and brain a commission to use time, talent, and energy in the cause of freedom" (Sterling 1984, 159). She identified with every facet of the race struggle and, as active as she was in the cause of women's rights, she subordinated gender issues when they came in conflict with the survival imperatives of the race. At the Equal Rights Association meeting in 1869, she strenuously rebuked white female advocates of women's rights for making derogatory statements about African American men although she did not hesitate to condemn the men herself when they failed to exhibit appropriate respect for women of color. One statement in particular demonstrates her commitment to the racial struggle and her concern for all segments of the race. Referring to the satisfaction attained from the lectures she undertook during the 1860s and 1870s, she explained her commitment:" I belong to this race; and when it is down, I belong to a down race; when it is up, I belong to a risen race" (Sterling 1984, 405).

The Great Problem To Be Solved
Frances Ellen Watkins Harper
1875

Ladies and Gentlemen: The great problem to be solved by
the American people, if I understand it, is this: Whether or
not there is strength enough in democracy, virtue enough in
our civilization, and power enough in our religion to have
mercy and deal justly with four millions of people but lately
translated from the old oligarchy of slavery to the new
commonwealth of freedom; and upon the right solution of
this question depends in a large measure the future strength,
progress and durability of our nation. The most important
question before us colored people is not simply what the
Democratic party may do against us or the Republican party
do for us; but what are we going to do for ourselves? What
shall we do toward developing our character, adding our
quota to the civilization and strength of the country,
diversifying our industry, and practising those lordly virtues
that conquer success, and turn the world's dread laugh into
admiring recognition? The white race has yet work to do in
making practical the political axiom of equal rights, and the
Christian idea of human brotherhood; but while I lift mine
eyes to the future I would not ungratefully ignore the past.
One hundred years ago Africa was the privileged hunting
ground of Europe and America, and the flag of different
nations hung a sign of death on the coasts of Congo and
Guinea, and for years unbroken silence had hung around the
horrors of the African slave-trade. Since then Great Britain
and other nations have wiped the bloody traffic from their
hands, and shaken the gory merchandise from their fingers,
and the brand of piracy has been placed upon the African
slave-trade. Less than fifty years ago mob violence belched
out its wrath against the men who dared to arraign the

51

slaveholder before the bar of conscience and Christendom. Instead of golden showers upon his head, he who garrisoned the front had a halter around his neck. Since, if I may borrow the idea, the nation has caught the old inspiration from his lips and written it in the new organic world. Less than twenty-five years ago slavery clasped hands with King Cotton, and said slavery fights and cotton conquers for American slavery. Since then slavery is dead, the colored man has exchanged the fetters on his wrist for the ballot in his hand. Freedom is king, and cotton a subject.

It may not seem to be a gracious thing to mingle complaint in a season of general rejoicing. It may appear like the ancient Egyptians seating a corpse at their festal board to avenge the Americans for their shortcomings when so much has been accomplished. And yet with all the victories and triumphs which freedom and justice have won in this country, I do not believe there is another civilized nation under Heaven where there are half so many people who have been brutally and shamefully murdered, with or without impunity, as in this Republic within the last ten years. And who cares? Where is the public opinion that has scorched with red-hot indignation the cowardly murderers of Vicksburg and Louisiana? Sheridan lifts up the veil from Southern society, and behind it is the smell of blood, and our bones scattered at the grave's mouth; murdered people; a White League with its "covenant of death and agreement with hell." And who cares? What city pauses one hour to drop a pitying tear over these mangled corpses, or has forged against the perpetrator one thunderbolt of furious protest? But let there be a supposed or real invasion of Southern rights by our soldiers, and our great commercial emporium will rally its forces from the old man in his classic shades, to clasp hands with "dead rabbits" and "plug-uglies" in protesting against military interference. What we need today in the onward march of humanity is a public sentiment in favor of common justice and simple mercy. We have a civilization which has produced grand and magnificent results, diffused knowledge, overthrown slavery, made constant conquests over nature, and built up a wonderful material prosperity. But two things are wanting in American civilization—a keener and deeper, broader and tenderer sense of justice—a sense of humanity, which shall crystallize into the life of the nation the sentiment that justice, simple justice, is the right, not simply of the strong and powerful, but of the weakest and feeblest of all God's children; a deeper and broader humanity, which will teach men to look upon their feeble brethren not as vermin to be crushed out, or beasts of burden to be bridled and bitted, but as the children of the living God; of that God whom we may earnestly hope is in perfect wisdom and in perfect love working for the best good of all. Ethnologists may differ about the origin of the human race. Huxley may search for it in protoplasms, and Darwin send for the missing links, but there is one thing of which we may rest assured—that we all come from the living God and that He is the common Father. The nation that has no reverence for man is also lacking in reverence for God and needs to be instructed.

As fellow citizens, leaving out all humanitarian views—as a mere matter of political economy it is better to have the colored race a living force animated and strengthened by self-reliance and self-respect, than a stagnant mass, degraded and self-condemned. Instead of the North relaxing its efforts to diffuse education in the South, it behooves us for our national life, to throw into the South all the healthful reconstructing influences we can command. Our work in this country is grandly constructive. Some races have come into this world and overthrown and destroyed. But if it is glory to destroy, it is happiness to save, and Oh! what a noble work there is before our nation! Where is there a young man who would consent to lead an aimless life when there are such glorious opportunities before him? Before our young men is another battle—not a battle of flashing swords and clashing steel—but a moral warfare, a battle against ignorance, poverty, and low social condition. In physical warfare the keenest swords may be blunted and the loudest batteries hushed; but in the great conflict of moral and spiritual progress your weapons shall be brighter for their service and better for their use. In fighting truly and nobly for others you win the victory for yourselves.

Give power and significance to your own life, and in the great work of upbuilding there is room for women's work and woman's heart. Oh, that our hearts were alive and our vision quickened, to see the grandeur of the work that lies before. We have some culture among us, but I think our culture lacks enthusiasm. We need a deep earnestness and a lofty unselfishness to round out our lives. It is the inner life that develops the outer, and if we are in earnest the precious things lie all around our feet, and we need not waste our strength in striving after the dim and unattainable. Women, in your golden youth; mother, binding around your heart all the precious ties of life—let no magnificence of culture, or amplitude of fortune, or refinement of sensibilities, repel you from helping the weaker and less favored. If you have ampler gifts, hold them as larger opportunities with which you can benefit others. Oh, it is better to feel that the weaker and feebler our race the closer we will cling to them, than it is to isolate ourselves from them in selfish, or careless unconcern, saying there is a lion without. Inviting you to this work I do not promise you fair sailing and unclouded skies. You may meet with coolness where you expect sympathy; disappointment where you feel sure of success; isolation and loneliness instead of heart support and cooperation. But if your lives are based and built upon these divine certitudes, which are the only enduring strength of humanity, then whatever defeat and discomfiture may overshadow your plans or frustrate your schemes, for a life that is in harmony with God and sympathy for man there is no such word as fail. And in conclusion, permit me to say, let no misfortunes crush you; no hostility of enemies or failure of friends discourage you. Apparent failure may hold in its rough shell the germs of a success that will blossom in time, and bear fruit throughout eternity. What seemed to be a failure around the Cross of Calvary and in the Garden has been the grandest recorded success.

Introduction to Anna J. Cooper's
"The Ethics Of The Negro Question"

"The Ethics of the Negro Question" recounts the history of the race in this country and places in perspective the race's evolving status, the achievements made, and the challenges remaining. Anna J. Cooper emphasizes the importance of education, particularly Christian education, in effecting the transformation that would ultimately confer upon African Americans their rightful place in this society. She notes the complexity and the possibilities of African Americans, yet she repudiates the emotionally incendiary propagandist tactics that create fears of "Negro domination." She attests to the loyalty of the race and articulates the potential pride of African Americans when they can sing "America," noting that "We are a song loving people and that song of all songs we would love to sing, and we challenge the lustiest singer to sing it more lustily and more eloquently than can we."

Anna J. Cooper, the daughter of George Washington Haywood, was born in Raleigh, North Carolina. Her father, a slave, bought his and his children's freedom. *The Evening Star* of 29 February 1964, described Cooper as an educator and "champion of Negro academic rights for more than half a century." Cooper died in 1964 at the age of 105. She earned a master's degree from Oberlin College in 1884 and a Ph.D in Latin from the Sorbonne in 1935. Her eloquent acceptance on that occasion concluded with the following words: "I ask no memorial in bronze. There is nothing in life worth striving for but the esteem of just men founded on a sincere effort to serve to the best of one's powers in the advancement of one's day and generation. I take at your hands, therefore, this diploma, not as a symbol of cold intellectual success, but with the warm pulsing heart throbs of a peoples' satisfaction in my humble efforts to serve them

. . . With all my heart, I thank you" (Anna J. Cooper papers, Moorland Spingarn Research Center).

Cooper was the author of *A Voice From The South By A Black Woman of the South* (1892). The *Parent-Teacher Journal* (May-June 1930) wrote of Cooper's "courageous revolt . . . against a special "colored" curriculum for the M Street High School. The proposal was already in Congress to give the pupils of this school a course of study commensurate with their alleged 'inferior' abilities. . . . Mrs. Cooper at the risk of insubordination, stoutly maintained that her pupils should have equal opportunity to choose whatever subjects might be chosen if they were in one of the other high schools" (p. 13). The speech considered here was presented to the Society of Friends at Asbury Park in 1892.

The Ethics Of The Negro Question
Anna J. Cooper
1892

Where there is no vision, the people perish. Proverbs 29:18.

A nation's greatness is not dependent upon the things it makes and uses. Things without thoughts are mere vulgarities. America can boast her expanse of territory, her gilded domes, her paving stones of silver dollars; but the question of deepest moment in this nation today is its span of the circle of brotherhood, the moral stature of its men and its women, the elevation at which it receives its "vision" into the firmament of eternal truth.

I walked not long since thro the national library at Washington. I confess that my heart swelled and my soul was satisfied; for however overpowering to a subdued individual taste the loud scream of color in the grand hallway may be, one cannot but feel that the magnificence of that pile, the loftiness of sentiment and grandeur of execution here adequately and artistically express the best in American life and aspiration. I have often sat silent in the gallery under the great dome contemplating the massive pillars that support the encircling arches and musing on the texts traced above the head of each heroic figure: science, holding in her hand instruments for the study of Astronomy, proclaims "The heavens declare the glory of God and the firmament showeth His handiwork." Law bears the equal scales with the text: "Of Law there can be no less acknowledged than that her voice is the harmony of the world." Religion stands with firm feet and fearless mien, unequivocally summing up the whole matter: "What doth the Lord require of thee but to do justly, to love mercy and to walk humbly with thy God."

59

Surely if American civilization should one day have to be guessed from a few broken columns and mutilated statues like the present grandeur of Egypt, Greece and Rome, the antiquarian or the historian who shall in future ages, dig from the dust of centuries this single masterpiece, this artistic expression of a people's aspiration and achievement, will yield ready homage to the greatness of the nation which planned and executed such a monument of architectural genius. "Surely here was a Nation" they must conclude, "Whose God was the Lord! A nation whose vision was direct from the Mount of God!"

Whether such an estimate is just, it is our deepest concern to examine. Where there is no vision, the people perish. A nation cannot long survive the shattering of its own ideals. Its doom is already sounded when it begins to write one law on its walls and lives another in its halls. Weighed in the balance and found wanting was not more terribly signed and sealed for the trembling Belshazzar than for us by these handwritings on our walls if they have lost their hold on the thought and conduct of the people.

The civilizations that have flowered and failed in the past did not harvest their fruit and die of old age. A worm was eating at the core even in the heyday of their splendor and magnificence so soon as the grand truths which they professed had ceased to vitalize and vivify their national life.

Rome's religion was pagan, it is true, but for all that it was because Rome had departed from the integrity of her own ideals and was laughing in her sleeve at the gods of her fathers that she found herself emasculated and effete before the virile hordes that plundered and finally superseded her. Thor and Woden had not become to the barbarians a figure to paint a wall or adorn a fountain. Let America beware how she writes on her walls to be seen of men the lofty sentiment *"Give instruction to those who cannot procure it for themselves"*, while she tips a wink at those communities which propose to give her instruction to the poor only that which is wrung from their penury. The vision as pictured on our walls is divine. The American ideal is perfect. A weak or undeveloped race apparently might ask no better fate than the opportunity of maturing under the great wing of this nation and of becoming christianized under its spiritual ministrations.

It is no fault of the Negro that he stands in the United States of America today as the passive and silent rebuke to the Nation's Christianity, the great gulf between its professions and its practices, furnishing the chief ethical element in its politics, constantly pointing with dumb but inexorable fingers to those ideals of our civilization which embody the Nation's highest, truest, and best thought, its noblest and grandest purposes and aspirations.

Amid all the deafening and maddening clamor of expediency and availability among politicians and parties, from tariffs and trusts to free coinage and 16 to 1, from microscopic questions of local sovereignty to the telescopic ones of expansion and imperialism, the Negro question furnishes the one issue that says *ought*. Not what will the party gain by this measure or that, not will this or that experiment bring in larger percentages and cash balances; but who, where, what is my neighbor? Am I my brother's keeper? Are there any limitations or special adaptations of the Golden Rule? If Jesus were among men today, is there a type of manhood veiled wherein, the Divinity whom our civilization calls Captain, would again, coming to His own, be again despised, rejected, because of narrow prejudices and blinding pride of race?

Uprooted from the sunny land of his forefathers by the white man's cupidity and selfishness, ruthlessly torn from all the ties of clan and tribe, dragged against his will over thousands of miles of unknown waters to a strange land among strange peoples, the Negro was transplanted to this continent in order to produce chattels and beasts of burden for a nation "conceived in liberty and dedicated to the proposition that all men are created equal." A nation worshiping as God one who came not to be ministered unto, but to minister; a nation believing in a Savior meek and lowly of heart who, having not where to lay His head, was eyes to the blind, hearing to the deaf, a gospel of hope and joy to the poor and outcast, a friend to all who travail and are heavy laden.

The whites of America revolted against the mother country for a trifling tax on tea, because they were not represented in the body that laid the tax. They drew up their Declaration of Independence, a Magna Carta of human rights, embodying principles of universal justice and equality.

Professing a religion of sublime altruism, a political faith in the inalienable rights of man as man, these jugglers with reason and conscience were at the same moment stealing heathen from their far away homes, forcing them with lash and gun to unrequited toil, making it a penal offense to teach them to read the Word of God,—nay, more, were even begetting and breeding mongrels of their own flesh among these helpless creatures and pocketing the guilty increase, the price of their own blood in unholy dollars and cents. Accursed hunger for gold!

To what dost thou not drive mortal breasts! But God did not ordain this nation to reenact the tragedy of Midas and transmute its very heart's core into yellow gold. America has a conscience as well as a pocket-book, and it comes like a pledge of perpetuity to the nation that she has never yet lost the seed of the prophets, men of inner light and unfaltering courage, who would cry aloud and spare not, against the sin of the nation. The best brain and heart of this country have always rung true and it is our hope today that the petrifying spirit of commercialism which grows so impatient at the Negro question or any other question calculated to weaken the money getting nerve by pulling at the heart and the conscience may still find a worthy protagonist in the reawakened ethical sense of the nation which can take no step backward and which must eventually settle, and settle right this and every question involving the nation's honor and integrity.

It gives me great pleasure to record the historian's testimony to the clear vision and courageous action of the Society of Friends who persisted in keeping alive this ethical sense in some dark days of the past.

"The Quakers have the honor" says Von Holtz "of having begun the agitation of the Slavery Question from the moral standpoint earliest and most radically." Thanks to the fiery zeal of some members of this Society, the religious and moral instruction of the slaves and the struggle against any further importation of the Negroes were begun by the close of the 17th Century. By the middle of the 18th Century the emancipation of slaves had gradually become a matter of action by the whole Quaker body. By a resolution of 1774 all members concerned in importing, selling, purchasing, giving or transferring Negroes or other slaves were directed to be excluded from membership or disowned. Two years later this resolution was extended to cover cases of those who delayed to set their slaves free. In February 1790 the Quaker meeting in Philadelphia and the Quakers in New York sent addresses to Congress requesting it to abolish the African slave trade. Certain representatives from the North urged that the petitions of so respectable a body as that of the Quakers in relation to so great a moral evil, were deserving of special consideration. The representatives of the South replied with provoking irony and mercilessly castigated the Quakers. Year after year the

Friends came indefatigably with new petitions each time, and each time had to undergo the same scornful treatment. In 1797 the yearly meeting at Philadelphia set forth some special wrongs in a petition, a prominent place in which was occupied by a complaint against the law of North Carolina condemning freed slaves to be sold again. Many Southern delegates in Congress expressed in a bullying fashion their scorn for the tenacity with which these men of earnest faith ever constantly came back again and again to their fruitless struggle. Not in America alone, England also witnessed the faith and works of this body of consistent Christians of unimpaired vision and unwavering determination. The first petition to the House of Commons for the abolition of the Slave Trade and Slavery went up from the Friends, and thro out the long agitation which ensued before that prayer was granted, the Society of Friends took an active and prominent part. Their own dear Whittier has sounded the keynote both of their struggle and its reward:

"Whatever in love's name is truly done To free the bound and lift the fallen one Is done to Christ."

And the Master Himself: Inasmuch as ye did it unto one of the least of these my brethren ye did it unto me.

The colored people of America find themselves today in the most trying period of all their trying history in this land of their trial and bondage. As the trials and responsibilities of the man weigh more heavily than do those of the infant, so the Negro under free labor and cutthroat competition today has to vindicate his fitness to survive in face of a colorphobia that heeds neither reason nor religion and a prejudice that shows no quarter and allows no mitigating circumstances.

In the darkest days of slavery, there were always at the North friends of the oppressed and devoted champions of freedom who would go all lengths to wipe out the accursed stain of human slavery from their country's scutcheon; while in the South the slave's close contact with the master class, mothering them in infancy, caring for them in sickness, sorrow and death, resulted as pulsing touch of humanity must ever result, in many warm sympathies and a total destruction of that repulsion to mere color which betokens narrow and exclusive intercourse among provincials.

Today all this is changed. White and black meet as strangers with cold, distant or avowed hostility. The colored domestic who is no longer specially trained for her job or taught to look on it with dignity and appreciation, is barely tolerated in the home till she can do up the supper dishes and get away—when she can go—to the devil if he will have her. The mistress who bemoans her shiftlessness and untidiness does not think of offering her a comfortable room, providing for her social needs and teaching her in the long evenings at home the simple household arts and virtues which our grandmothers found time for. Her vices are set down to the debit account of her freedom, especially if she has attended a public school and learned enough to spell her way thro a street ballad. So generally is this the case that if a reform were attempted suddenly, the girl herself of the average type would misunderstand and probably resent it. The condition of the male laborer is even more hopeless. Receiving 50 cents a day or less for unskilled but laborious toil from which wage he boards himself and is expected to keep a family in something better than a "one room cabin," the Negro workman receives neither sympathy nor recognition from his white fellow laborers. Scandinavians, Poles and Hungarians can tie up the entire country by a strike paralysing not only industry but existence itself, when they are already getting a wage that sounds like affluence to the hungry black man. The union means war to the death against him and the worst of it is he can never be lost in the crowd and have his opprobrium forgotten. A foreigner can learn the language and out-American the American on his own soil. A white man can apply burnt cork and impute his meanness to the colored race as his appointed scapegoat. But the Ethiopian cannot change his skin. On him is laid the iniquity of his whole race and his character is prejudged by formula. Even charity does not study his needs as an individual person but the good that love has planned for him must be labeled and basketed "special" for the Negro. Special kinds of education, special forms of industry, special churches and special places of amusement, special sections of our cities during life and special burying grounds in death. White America has created a *terra cognita* in its midst, a strange dark unexplored waste of human souls from which if one essay to speak out an intelligible utterance, so well known is the place of preferment accorded the mirroring of preconceived notions, that instead of being the revelation of a personality and the voice of a truth, the speaker becomes a phonograph and merely talks back what is talked into him. It is no popular task today to voice the black man's woe. It is far easier and safer to say that the wrong is all in him. The American conscience would like a rest from the black man's ghost. It was always an unpalatable subject but preeminently now is the era of good feeling, and self complacency, of commercial omnipotence and military glorification. It seems an impertinence as did the boldness of Nathan when he caught the conscience of the great king at the pinnacle of victorious prosperity with the inglorious seizure of the ewe lamb from a man of no importance. Has not the nation done and suffered enough for the Negro? Is he worth the blood and treasure that have been spilled on his account, the heartache and bitterness that have racked the country in easing him off its shoulders and out of its conscience. Let us have no more of it. If he is a man let him stand up and prove it. Above all let us have peace. Northern capital is newly wed to Southern industry and the honeymoon must not be disturbed. If southern conventions are ingenious enough to invent a device for disfranchising these unwelcome children of the soil, if it will work, what of it?

On the floor of the most august body in the land, a South Carolina senator said: "Yes; we bull dozed and terrorized niggers and we are not ashamed of it. If you had been in our place you would have done the same."

During the slavery agitation Garrison was mobbed in the streets of Boston for advocating abolition; but he kept right on and would be heard. In our day the simplest narrative in just recognition of the Negro meets with cold disfavor and the narrator is generally frozen into silence. A lecturer on the Spanish War attempted as an eye witness and with the aid of Stereopticon to tell a Richmond audience of the gallant charge up San Juan Hill and the brave part in it by the 10th Cavalry. His words were met by hisses, his lantern slides destroyed and he was obliged to close his entertainment in darkness and confusion.

A professor in a Southern school who in a magazine article condemned the saturnalia of blood and savagery known as lynching arguing that the Negro while inferior, was yet a man and should be accorded the fundamental rights of a man, lost his position for his frankness and fairness. The Negro is being ground to powder between the upper and the nethermillstones. The South, intolerant of interference from either outside or inside, the North too polite or too busy or too gleeful over the promised handshaking to manifest the most distant concern.

But God is not dead neither doth the ruler of the universe slumber and sleep. As a Nation sows so shall it reap. Men do not gather grapes from thorns or figs from thistles. To sow the wind is to reap the whirlwind.

A little over two years ago while the gentlest and kindest of presidents was making a tour of the South bent only on good will to men with a better understanding and the healing of all sectional rancor and ill feeling, there occurred in almost a stone's throw of where he was for the time being domiciled an outburst of diabolism that would shame a tribe of naked savages. A black wretch was to be burned alive. Without court or jury his unshrived soul was to be ushered into eternity and the prospect furnished a holiday festival for the country side.

Excursion trains with banners flying were run into the place and eager children were heard to exclaim: "we have seen a hanging, we are now going to see a burning!"

Human creatures with the behavior of hyenas contended with one another for choice bones of their victim as souvenirs of the occasion. So wanton was the cannibalistic thirst for blood that the Negro preacher who offered the last solace of the Christian to the doomed man was caught in the same mad frenzy and made to share his fate. A shiver ran thro the nation at such demoniacal lawlessness. But a cool analysis of the situation elicited from the Attorney General of the United States the legal opinion that the case "probably had no Federal aspects!"

Just one year ago the same gentle people-loving president was again acting out his instinct of mingling naturally and democratically with his people. Again lawlessness, this time in the form of a single red handed unreasoning ruffian instead of many but the same mad spirit which puts its own will whether swayed by lurid passion or smoldering hate, on the throne of the majesty of law and of duty, made the nation shudder and bleed by striking down unaccused and untried the great head of the nation. A fact may be mentioned here, which was unquestioned at the time by those around, but which was not often repeated afterwards, that it was the burly arm of a Negro that felled the assassin and dealt the first blows in defense of the stricken president.

I will not here undertake an apology for the shortcomings of the American Negro. It goes without saying that the black is centuries behind the white race in material, mental and moral development. The American Negro is today but 37 years removed from chatteldom, not long enough surely to ripen the century plant of a civilization. After 250 years of a most debasing slavery, inured to toil but not to thrift, without home, without family ties, without those habits of self reliant industry by which peoples maintain their struggle for existence, poor, naked, weak, ignorant, degraded even below his pristine state as a savage, the American Negro was at the close of the War of the Rebellion "cut loose" as the slang of the day expressed it, and left to fend for himself. The master class, full of resentment and rage at the humiliations and losses of a grinding war, suffered their old time interest to turn into bitterness or cold indifference and Ku Klux beatings with re-enslaving black codes became the sorry substitute for the overseer's lash and the auction block.

At this juncture the conscience of the Nation asserted itself and the federal constitution was so amended as to bring under the aegis of national protection these helpless babes whom the exigencies of war had suddenly thrown into the maelstrom of remorseless life.

That they are learning to stem the current there is ground for hope; that they have already made encouraging headway even enemies cannot deny. The Negro's productivity as a free laborer is conceded to be greater than formerly as a slave, and the general productivity of the South where he constitutes the chief labor element, has since his emancipation more than doubled. Not having inherited the "business bump" his acquisitive principles have received some shocks and many times have been paralyzed and stunted by the insecurity of his property and the disregard of his rights shown by his powerful white neighbors. Such was the case in the collapse of the Freedman's Savings Bank and the recent Wilmington massacre when the accumulations of a lifetime were wantonly swept away and home loving, law-abiding citizens were forced into exile, their homes and little savings appropriated by others. In spite of this, however, some headway is making in material wealth and the tax lists in former slave states show a credit of several millions to the descendants of the enslaved.

But all his advancement in wealth and education counts for naught, and ought to count for naught, if it be true, as commonly reported in certain quarters, that the Negro is a moral leper and that sexually he is a dangerous animal in any community. It is said that those astounding exhibitions of fury and force which dizzy the head and sicken the heart of civilized people, are necessary to cower his brutish passions and guard the Holy Grail of Saxon civilization. That the sanctity of pure homes, the inviolability of helpless womanhood must be protected at any cost and that nothing short of devastation and war will suffice. That the beast must be kept under a reign of terror to make him know his place and keep his distance. The iteration and reiteration of sharp and swift retribution for the "usual" crime is kept up altho the "crime" has been again and again proved to be unusual by more than 90 per cent and statistics of lynchings and their causes have been published from year to year showing every cause for a black man's being lynched from "being impudent to a white man to Preaching the Gospel of Jesus Christ to a doomed convict, and yet we are told that these things have "probably no federal aspects." Don't you think we would find

a way to give them Federal Aspects if it were poor old Spain
lynching her obstreperous islanders?

Says Prof. Shaler of Harvard:

"When we recall the fact that there are now some five
million Negro men in the South and that not one in ten
thousand is guilty of crime against womanhood, we see how
imperfect is the basis of this judgment. We have also to
remember," he continues, "that this offense when committed
by a Negro is thro action of the mob widely publicized while
if the offender be a white man it is unlikely to be so well
known. I therefore hold to the belief that violence to women
is not proved to be a crime common among the blacks. I am
inclined to believe that on the whole there is less danger to
be apprehended from them in this regard than from an equal
body of whites of like social grade."

Such is the calm testimony of an expert sociologist who
speaks after scientific "investigation and careful analysis."

Is it credible that this race which has under freedom caught
so eagerly on the rungs of progress in other respects has so
shockingly deteriorated in this all important particular as to
reverse all claims to humane consideration which they had
won by patient service during long years of slavery?

Have a race of men to whom masters not over kind were
not afraid to entrust their helpless women and children while
faring forth to rivet the fetters more firmly on their dumb
driven bodies and who without one single exception
demonstrated remarkable fidelity, trustworthiness, reverence
for women and kindness toward children, suddenly become
such monsters of lust and vindictiveness that a woman is not
safe on the same highway with them?

A noble army of Christian workers and helpers have gone
to the South ever since the War, have lived with these people
on terms of christian sympathy and perfect social equality.
Have you ever heard of one of these pure minded

missionaries who was insulted or outraged and her delicate sensibilities shocked by the unconquerable instincts and baser passions of the men they came to help?

You ask what is the need of today.

How can the Negro be best helped?

What can be done by the man who loves his fellowmen and needs not to be convinced of duties but only to be assured of methods? What is the best means of the Negro's uplift and amelioration?

In a word I answer: Christian Education. This is nothing new you say. That experiment has been tried and tried and there are even those whose faith in the efficacy of this expedient is beginning to wane and we are looking around to see if there be not some other, some quicker and surer way of doing the job. Is it not a mistake to suppose that the same old human laws apply to these people? Is there not after all something within that dark skin not yet dreamt of in our philosophy? Can we seriously take the Negro as a man "endowed by his Creator with certain unalienable rights such as Life, Liberty, Pursuit of Happiness" and the right to grow up, to develop, to reason and to live his life. In short can we hope to apply the key that unlocks all other hearts and by a little human sympathy and putting ourselves in his place learn to understand him and let him understand us? Assuredly, yes!

The black man is not a saint, neither can he be reduced to an algebraic formula. His thirty or forty checkered years of freedom have not transfigured *en masse* ten million slaves into experienced, thrifty, provident, law abiding members of society. There are some criminal, some shiftless, some provokingly intractable and seemingly uneducable classes and individuals among blacks as there are still unless I am misinformed, also among whites. But our philosophy does not balk at this nor do we lose our belief in the efficacy of Christian teaching and preaching. Turn on the light! Light, more light! There will always be some who do not live up to the light they have. But the Master has left us no alternative. Ye are the light of the world.

We cannot draw lines where He recognized none. We cannot falter so long as there is a human soul in need of the light. We owe it, and owe it independently of the worthiness or unworthiness of that soul. Does any one question that Jesus' vision would have pierced to the heart and marrow of our national problem. And what would be His teaching in America today as to *who is my* neighbor?

For after all the Negro Question in America today is the white man's problem—Nay it is humanity's problem. The past, in which the Negro was mostly passive, the white man active, has ordained that they shall be neighbors, permanently and unavoidably. To colonize or repatriate the blacks on African soil or in any other continent is physically impossible even if it were generally desired, and no sane man talks of deportation now except as an exploded chimera. For weal or for woe the lots of these two are unified, indissolubly, eternally, and thinking people on both sides are convinced that each race needs the other. The Negro is the most stable and reliable factor today in American industry. Patient and docile as a laborer, conservative, law abiding, totally ignorant of the anarchistic, socialistic radicalism and nihilism of other lands, the American Negro is capable of contributing not only of his brawn and sinew but also from brain and character a much needed element in American civilization, and here is his home. The only home he has ever known. His blood has mingled with the bluest and the truest on every battle field that checkers his country's history. His sweat and his toil have, more than any other's, felled its forests, drained its swamps, plowed its fields and opened up its highways and waterways.

From the beginning was he here, a strong, staunch and not unwilling worker and helper. His traditions, his joys, his sorrows are all here. He has imbibed the genius and spirit of its institutions, growing with their growth, gathering hope and strength with their strength and depth. Alien neither in language, religion nor customs, the educated colored American is today the most characteristic growth of the American soil, its only genuinely indigenous development. He is the most American of Americans for he alone has no other civilization than what America has to offer. Its foibles are his foibles. Its youthful weaknesses and pompous self-confidence are all found here imitated or originating, as between sitter and portrait. Here in the warp and woof of his character are photographed and writ large even the grotesque caricatures, the superficial absurdities and social excrescences of "Get-rich-quick" and "Pike's Peak-or-bust" America. Nor is it too much to hope that America's finer possibilities and promise also prefigure his ultimate struggle and achievement in evolving his civilization. As the character of Uncle Tom is rated the most unique in American literature, so the plantation melodies and corn songs form the most original contribution to its music. Homogeneous or not, the national web is incomplete without the African thread that glints and ripples thro it from the beginning.

In a description of the Rough Riders' charge on the Block House at El Caney a recent columnist has this to say: "Over against the scene of the Rough Riders set the picture of the 10th U. S. Cavalry—the famous colored regiment side by side with Roosevelt's men they fought—these black men. Scarce used to freedom themselves they are dying that Cuba may be free. Their marksmanship was magnificent; their courage was superb. They bore themselves like veterans and gave proof positive that from nature's congenitally peaceful, carefree and playful, military discipline and an inspiring cause can make soldiers worthy to rank with Caesar's legions or Cromwell's Army.

Mr. Bryce in his study of the American Commonwealth says: "The South is confronted by a peculiar and menacing problem in the presence of a mass of Negroes larger than was the whole population of the union in 1800, persons who tho they are legally and industrially members of the nation are still virtually an alien element, unabsorbed and unabsorbable."

A similar judgment was passed by the gifted author of the Bonnie Briar Bush in his "Impressions of America" who thought that the Negroes were like the Chinese in constituting the sole exception to an otherwise homogeneous population. This misapprehension is common. The explanation obvious. Social cleavage in America is strictly along the lines of color only. Jim Crow cars are not for the unwashed of all races, not for the drunken rowdy and the degraded, ignorant, vicious rabble,—not even for the pauper classes who cannot pay for superior comforts in traveling. Quite simply the only question is "What is the tinge of pigment in your epidermal cells, or in the epidermis of your mother's grandmother? The colored man or woman of culture and refinement is shoved into the same box with the filthy and the degraded no matter what his ability to pay for and his desire to secure better accommodations. He cannot eat a sandwich in one of the "white" hotels nor set down his luggage in one of their waiting rooms at a railway station. The result is that students of American society like Bryce and Ian McClaren never see or suspect the existence of intelligent aspiring thinking men and women of color in the midst of this social system. Men and women who are pondering its adjustment chafing it may be under its rule and crude incongruities and gathering strength no doubt to snap asunder one of these days its issue beltings and couplings.

The American traveler sees and can account for only the
black porter and colored boot black, the waiter and barber
and scullion. And these only as automatons in a passing
show. He cannot know them as human beings capable of
human emotions, human aspirations, human suffering, defeats
and triumphs. Our traveler is then introduced by design to the
criminal records wherein the Negro, because the poorest,
weakest, least shielded class in the community figures, of
course, at his full strength. Taken for a drive thro what would
in New York or Philadelphia constitute a slum appealing only
to the Christ spirit in good men to send out their light and
their love, to start a mission to provide wholesome living
conditions for healthy living and clean thinking. But here
both the Priest and the Levite pass by on the other side. The
missions are to seek and to save the lost who are already
fortunate enough to be born white.

Come unto me all ye *whites* who are heavy laden. The
Poor (*whites*) have the Gospel preached unto them. Suffer the
little *white* children to come unto me! for of such is the
kingdom of heaven. Love the Lord they God with all they
heart, soul, and strength and thy *white* neighbor as thyself!"

But these Negro quarters, these submerged souls, this
"darkest America"—Ah this is our terrible "Problem!" This
mass that menaces Anglo Saxon civilization "unabsorbed and
unabsorbable!"

But this time our traveler is wholly inoculated. "It is truly
a *peculiar* problem to be sure. He does not quite see how the
question can be solved. He is disposed with Mr. Bryce to
trust much to the *vis medicatrix naturae* and to hope that
somehow, somewhere, and some when the Sphinx will
answer its own riddle, and yet I am no pessimist regarding
the future of my people in America. God reigns and the good
will prevail. It must prevail. While these are times that try
men's souls, while a weak and despised people are called

upon to vindicate their right to exist in the face of a race of hard, jealous, intolerant, all—subduing instincts, while the iron of their wrath and bitter prejudice cuts into the very bones and marrow of my people, I have faith to believe that God has not made us for naught and He has not ordained to wipe us out from the face of the earth. I believe, moreover, that America is the land of destiny for the descendants of the enslaved race, that here in the house of their bondage are the seeds of promise for their ultimate enfranchisement and development. This I maintain in full knowledge of what at any time may be wrought by a sudden paroxysm of rage caused by the meaningless war whoop of some obscure politicians such as the rally word of "Negro domination" which at times deafens and bemuddles all ears.

Negro domination! Think of it! The great American eagle, soaring majestically sun-ward, eyes ablaze with conscious power, suddenly screaming and shivering in fear of a little mouse colored starling, which he may crush with the smallest finger of his great claw. Yet this mad shriek is allowed to unbridle the worst passions of wicked men, to stifle and seal up the holiest instincts of good men. In dread of domination by a race whom they outnumber five to one, with every advantage in civilization, wealth, culture, with absolute control of every civil and military nerve center, Anglo Saxon America is in danger of forgetting how to deal justly, to love mercy, to walk humbly with its God.

In the old days, I am told that two or three Negroes gathered together in supplication and prayer, were not allowed to present their petition at the throne of Grace without having it looked over and revised by a white man for fear probably that white supremacy and its "peculiar" system might be endangered at the Court of the Almighty by these faltering lips and uncultured tongues! The same fear cowers the white man's heart today. He dare not face his God with a lie on his lips.

These "silent sullen peoples" (so called because sympathetically unknown and unloved) are the touchstone of his conscience. America with all her wealth and power, with her pride of inventions and mastery of the forces of nature, with all her breadth of principles and height of ideals, will never be at peace with herself till this question is settled and settled right. It is the conscience in her throat that is "unabsorbed and unabsorbable!"

The despairing wail of Macbeth's blood-stained queen in all her gilded misery at the moment of her sickening success, is profoundly and everlastingly true: "Better be that which we destroy!" It is in the power of this mighty nation to turn upon us in a St. Bartholomew's Massacre and in one bloody day reckon us among the extinct races of history. A governor of Georgia is reported to have declared that "a dead Negro in the back yard" was his suggestion for settling this question, and another has recommended that a reward be offered for every one so disposed of.

But the Negro's blood on this great Nation becomes a heavier burden than the Negro's education and Christianization. His extermination will weigh more than all the weight of his uplift and regeneration. A nation's dishonor is a far more serious problem to settle than the extension of a brother's hand and a Christian's grip by a favored race bearing the torch, as a sacred trust from the source of All light to lead, enlighten and lift. Ye who have the light *owe it* to the least of these my brethren.

> "Is your God a wooden fetish
> To be hidden out of sight,
> That his block eyes may not see you
> Do the thing that is not right?

But the Destinies think not so;
To their judgment chamber lone
Comes no voice of popular clamor
There Fame's trumpet is not blown
But their silent way they keep.
Where empires towered that were not just,
To the skulking wild fox scratches
in a little heap of dust."

This it were well for great powers to ponder. The right to
rule entails the obligation to rule right. Righteousness and
Righteousness only exalteth a nation and the surest guarantee
of the perpetuity of our institutions is alliance with God's
eternal forces that make for rightness and justness in His
world.

As for the Negro there can be no doubt that these trials are
God's plan for refinement of the good gold to be found in
him. The dross must be purged out. There is no other way
than by fire. If the great Refiner sees that a stronger, truer,
purer racial character can be evolved from His crucible by
heating the furnace seven times, He can mean only good.

With hearty earnestness the million and half colored boys
and girls in the public schools South repeat on June 14 the
salute to their country's flag:

"I pledge allegiance to my flag and to the country for
which it stands." I commend these boys and girls to you for
as staunch and loyal a yeomanry as any country can boast.
They are Americans, true and bona fide citizens—not by
adoption or naturalization but by birth and blood
incontestable.

Whatever may be problematical about us, our citizenship
is beyond question. We have owned no other allegiance, have
bowed before no other sovereign. Never has hand of ours

been raised either in open rebellion or secret treachery against the Fatherland.

Our proudest aspiration has been but to serve her, the crown of our glory to die for her. We were born here thro no choice of our own or of our ancestors; we cannot expatriate ourselves, even if we would. When the wild forces of hate and unholy passion are unleashed to run riot against us our hearts recoil not more in dread of such a catastrophe for ourselves than in grief and shame at the possibility of such a fall and such a failure for our country's high destiny. It is inconceivable that we should not feel the unnatural prejudice environing us and our children. It is like stones between our teeth and like iron in the marrow of our bones. If at such times we cannot sing America it is not because of any treason lurking in our hearts. Our harps are hung on the willows and in the Babylon of our sorrow we needs must sit down and weep. But no dynamite plots are hatching amongst us. No vengeful uprising brewing. We are a song-loving people and that song of all songs we would love to sing, and we challenge the lustiest singer to sing it more lustily and more eloquently than we. But when the wound is festering and the heart is so sore we can only suffer and be silent, praying God to change the hearts of our misguided countrymen and help them to see the things that make for righteousness.

Then pray we shall that come it may for come it will for a 'that'.

That man to man the world o'er shall brothers be for a 'that'."

Introduction to Mary Church Terrell's
"What It Means To Be Colored in the Capital of the United States"

"What It Means To Be Colored in the Capital of the United States" enumerates a myriad of racially discriminatory practices in the nation's capital. Mary Church Terrell comments on the irony of the city being called "the Colored Man's Paradise," noting that it had never been a paradise for people of color and that conditions were deteriorating rather than improving. Her categorization of discriminatory practices is expansive and encompasses almost every facet of African American life. The speaker exposes political, social, and educational inequities, providing anecdotal proof of each category of injustice. Her argument gains force as she reveals that the array of injustices cited do not exhaust the realities. She closes the address with an observation, compelling in its irony, "And surely nowhere in the world do oppression and persecution based solely on the color of the skin appear more hateful and hideous than in the capital of the United States, because the chasm between the principles upon which this Government was founded, in which it still professes to believe, and those which are daily practiced under the protection of the flag, yawns so wide and deep" (Par. 20).

Mary Church Terrell was born in Memphis, Tennessee, to Louisa and Robert Reed Church, newly-emancipated slaves on 23 September 1863. She died at her summer home in Maryland on 24 July 1954. A graduate of Oberlin College, Terrell taught at Wilberforce University and at high schools in Washington. The first woman of African descent appointed to the Washington, D.C. Board of Education (1895), Terrell assumed the presidency of the National Association of Colored Women in 1896 and served in this capacity for three terms. During the twentieth century Terrell remained active,

81

serving as a delegate to the International Congress of Women at Zurich, directing the organization of Black Republican voters, and lecturing on Black life and history.

Terrell delivered "What It Means To Be Colored in the Capital of the United States" before the Washington D. C.'s United Women's Club on 10 October 1906. African American women's clubs played a prominent role in the racial activism of the late nineteenth century, this activism continuing in various local and national groups during the twentieth century. Fannie Barrier Williams commented that "Among colored women the club is the effort of the few competent in behalf of the many incompetent" (Williams 1900, 379). But, as Terrell astutely observed, public sentiment placed the fortunate in the same category as the lesser fortunate. In most instances, their education and money made little difference in the way they were viewed by the majority culture.

What It Means To Be Colored
in the Capital of the United States
Mary Church Terrell
1906

Washington, D.C., has been called "The Colored Man's Paradise." Whether this sobriquet was given to the national capital in bitter irony by a member of the handicapped race, as he reviewed some of his own persecutions and rebuffs, or whether it was given immediately after the war by an ex-slave-holder who for the first time in his life saw colored people walking about like freemen, minus the overseer and his whip, history saith not. It is certain that it would be difficult to find a worse misnomer for Washington than "The Colored Man's Paradise" if so prosaic a consideration as veracity is to determine the appropriateness of a name.

For fifteen years I have resided in Washington, and while it was far from being a paradise for colored people, when I first touched these shores it has been doing its level best ever since to make conditions for us intolerable. As a colored woman I might enter Washington any night, a stranger in a strange land, and walk miles without finding a place to lay my head. Unless I happened to know colored people who live here or ran across a chance acquaintance who could recommend a colored boarding-house to me, I should be obliged to spend the entire night wandering about. Indians, Chinamen, Filipinos, Japanese and representatives of any other dark race can find hotel accommodations, if they can pay for them. The colored man alone is thrust out of the hotels of the national capital like a leper.

As a colored woman I may walk from the Capitol to the White House, ravenously hungry and abundantly supplied with money with which to purchase a meal, without finding a single restaurant in which I would be permitted to take a morsel of food, if it was patronized by white people, unless I were willing to sit behind a screen. As a colored woman I cannot visit the tomb of the Father of this country, which owes its very existence to the love of freedom in the human heart and which stands for equal opportunity to all, without being forced to sit in the Jim Crow section of an electric car which starts from the very heart of the city—midway between the Capitol and the White House. If I refuse thus to be humiliated, I am cast into jail and forced to pay a fine for violating the Virginia laws. Every hour in the day Jim Crow cars filled with colored people, many of whom are intelligent and well to do, enter and leave the national capital.

As a colored woman I may enter more than one white church in Washington without receiving that welcome which as a human being I have a right to expect in the sanctuary of God. Sometimes the color blindness of the usher takes on that peculiar form which prevents a dark face from making any impression whatsoever upon his retina, so that it is impossible for him to see colored people at all. If he is not so afflicted, after keeping a colored man or woman waiting a long time, he will ungraciously show these dusky Christians who have had the temerity to thrust themselves into a temple where only the fair of face are expected to worship God to a seat in the rear, which is named in honor of a certain personage, well known in this country, and commonly called Jim Crow.

Unless I am willing to engage in a few menial occupations, in which the pay for my services would be very poor, there is no way for me to earn an honest living, if I am not a trained nurse or a dressmaker or can secure a position as teacher in the public schools, which is exceedingly difficult to do. It matters not what my intellectual attainments may be or how great is the need of the services of a competent person, if I try to enter many of the numerous vocations in which my white sisters are allowed to engage, the door is shut in my face.

From one Washington theater I am excluded altogether. In the remainder certain seats are set aside for colored people, and it is almost impossible to secure others. I once telephoned to the ticket seller just before a matinee and asked if a neat-appearing colored nurse would be allowed to sit in the parquet with her little white charge, and the answer rushed quickly and positively thru the receiver—NO. When I remonstrated a bit and told him that in some of the theaters colored nurses were allowed to sit with the white children for whom they cared, the ticket seller told me that in Washington it was very poor policy to employ colored nurses, for they were excluded from many places where white girls would be allowed to take children for pleasure. If I possess artistic talent, there is not a single art school of repute which will admit me. A few years ago a colored woman who possessed great talent submitted some drawings to the Corcoran Art School, of Washington, which were accepted by the committee of awards, who sent her a ticket entitling her to a course in this school. But when the committee discovered that the young woman was colored they declined to admit her, and told her that if they had suspected that her drawings had been made by a colored woman they would not have examined them at all. The efforts of Frederick Douglass and a lawyer of great repute who took a keen interest in the affair were unavailing. In order to cultivate her talent this young woman was forced to leave her comfortable home in Washington and incur the expense of going to New York. Having entered the Woman's Art School of Cooper Union, she graduated with honor, and then went to Paris to continue her studies, where she achieved signal success and was complimented by some of the greatest living artists in France.

With the exception of the Catholic University, there is not

a single white college in the national capital to which colored people are admitted, no matter how great their ability, how lofty their ambition, how unexceptionable their character or how great their thirst for knowledge may be.

A few years ago the Columbian Law School admitted colored students, but in deference to the Southern white students the authorities have decided to exclude them altogether.

Some time ago a young woman who had already attracted some attention in the literary world by her volume of short stories answered an advertisement which appeared in a Washington newspaper, which called for the services of a skilled stenographer and expert typewriter. It is unnecessary to state the reasons why a young woman whose literary ability was so great as that possessed by the one referred to should decide to earn money in this way. The applicants were requested to send specimens of their work and answer certain questions concerning their experience and their speed before they called in person. In reply to her application the young colored woman, who, by the way, is very fair and attractive indeed, received a letter from the firm stating that her references and experience were the most satisfactory that had been sent and requesting her to call. When she presented herself there was some doubt in the mind of the man to whom she was directed concerning her racial pedigree, so he asked her point-blank whether she was colored or white. When she confessed the truth the merchant expressed great sorrow and deep regret that he could not avail himself of the services of so competent a person, but frankly admitted that employing a colored woman in his establishment in any except a menial position was simply out of the question.

Another young friend had an experience which, for some reasons, was still more disheartening and bitter than the one just mentioned. In order to secure lucrative employment she left Washington and went to New York. There she worked her way up in one of the largest dry goods stores till she was placed as saleswoman in the cloak department. Tired of being separated from her family she decided to return to Washington, feeling sure that, with her experience and her fine recommendation from the New York firm, she could easily secure employment. Nor was she overconfident, for the proprietor of one of the largest dry goods stores in her native city was glad to secure the services of a young woman who brought such hearty credentials from New York. She had not been in this store very long, however, before she called upon me one day and asked me to intercede with the proprietor in her behalf, saying that she had been discharged that afternoon because it had been discovered that she was colored. When I called upon my young friend's employer he made no effort to avoid the issue, as I feared he would. He did not say he had discharged the young saleswoman because she had not given satisfaction, as he might easily have done. On the contrary, he admitted without the slightest hesitation that the young woman he had just discharged was one of the best clerks he had ever had. In the cloak department, where she had been assigned, she had been a brilliant success, he said. "But I cannot keep Miss Smith in my employ," he concluded. "Are you not master of your own store?" I ventured to inquire. The proprietor of this store was a Jew, and I felt that it was particularly cruel, unnatural and cold-blooded for the representative of one oppressed and persecuted race to deal so harshly and unjustly with a member of another. I had intended to make this point when I decided to intercede for my young friend, but when I thought how a reference to the persecution of his own race would wound his feelings, the words froze on my lips. "When I first heard your friend was colored," he explained, "I did not believe it and said so to the clerks who made the statement. Finally, the girls who had been most pronounced in their opposition to working in a store with a colored girl came to me in a body and threatened to strike. 'Strike away,' said I, 'your places will be easily filled.' Then they started on another tack. Delegation after delegation began to file down to my office, some of the women my very best customers, to protest against my employing a colored girl. Moreover, they threatened to boycott my store if I did not discharge her at once. Then it became a question of bread and butter and I yielded to the inevitable—that's all." "Now," said he, concluding, "if I lived in a great, cosmopolitan city like New York, I should do as I pleased, and refuse to discharge a girl simply because she was colored." But I thought of a similar incident that happened in New York. I remembered that a colored woman, as fair as a lily and as beautiful as a madonna, who was the head saleswoman in a large department store in New York, had been discharged, after she had held this position for years, when the proprietor accidentally discovered that a fatal drop of African blood was percolating somewhere thru her veins.

Not only can colored women secure no employment in the Washington stores, department and otherwise, except as menials, and such positions, of course, are few, but even as customers they are not infrequently treated with discourtesy both by the clerks and the proprietor himself. Following the trend of the times, the senior partner of the largest and best department store in Washington, who originally hailed from Boston, once the home of Wm. Lloyd Garrison, Wendell Phillips and Charles Sumner, if my memory serves me right, decided to open a restaurant in his store. Tired and hungry after her morning's shopping a colored school teacher, whose relation to her African progenitors is so remote as scarcely to be discernible to the naked eye, took a seat at one of the tables in the restaurant of this Boston store. After sitting unnoticed a long time the colored teacher asked a waiter who passed her by if she would not take her order. She was quickly informed that colored people could not be served in that restaurant and was obliged to leave in confusion and shame, much to the amusement of the waiters and the guests who had noticed the incident. Shortly after that a teacher in Howard University, one of the best schools for colored youth in the country, was similarly insulted in the restaurant of the same store.

In one of the Washington theaters from which colored people are excluded altogether, members of the race have been viciously assaulted several times, for the proprietor well knows that colored people have no redress for such discriminations against them in the District courts. Not long ago a colored clerk in one of the departments who looks more like his paternal ancestors who fought for the lost cause than his grandmothers who were victims of the peculiar institution, bought a ticket for the parquet of this theater in which colored people are nowhere welcome, for himself and mother, whose complexion is a bit swarthy. The usher refused to allow the young man to take the seats for which his tickets called and tried to snatch from him the coupons. A scuffle ensued and both mother and son were ejected by force. A suit was brought against the proprietor and the damages awarded the injured man and his mother amounted to the munificent sum of one cent. One of the teachers in the Colored High School received similar treatment in the same theater.

Not long ago one of my little daughter's bosom friends figured in one of the most pathetic instances of which I have ever heard. A gentleman who is very fond of children promised to take six little girls in his neighborhood to a matinee. It happened that he himself and five of his little friends were so fair that they easily passed muster, as they stood in judgment before the ticket seller and the ticket taker.

Three of the little girls were sisters, two of whom were very fair and the other a bit brown. Just as this little girl, who happened to be last in the procession, went by the ticket taker, that argus-eyed sophisticated gentleman detected something which caused a deep, dark frown to mantle his brow and he did not allow her to pass. "I guess you have made a mistake," he called to the host of this theater party. "Those little girls," pointing to the fair ones,"may be admitted, but this one," designating the brown one, "can't." But the colored man was quite equal to the emergency. Fairly frothing at the mouth with anger he asked the ticket taker what he meant, what he was trying to insinuate about that particular little girl. "Do you mean to tell me," he shouted in rage, "that I must go clear to the Philippine Islands to bring this child to the United States and then I can't take her to the theater in the National Capital?" The little ruse succeeded brilliantly, as he knew it would. "Beg your pardon," said the ticket taker, "don't know what I was thinking about. Of course she can go in."

"What was the matter with me this afternoon mother?" asked the little brown girl innocently, when she mentioned the affair at home. "Why did the man at the theater let my two sisters and the other girls in and try to keep me out?" In relating this incident the child's mother told me her little girl's question which showed such blissful ignorance of the depressing, cruel conditions which confronted her, completely unnerved her for a time.

Altho white and colored teachers are under the same Board of Education and the system for the children of both races is said to be uniform, prejudice against the colored teachers in the public schools is manifested in a variety of ways. From 1870 to 1900 there was a colored superintendent at the head of the colored schools. During all that time the directors of the cooking, sewing, physical culture, manual training, music and art departments were colored people. Six years ago a change was inaugurated. The colored superintendent was legislated out of office and the directorships, without a single exception, were taken from colored teachers and given to the whites. There was no complaint about the work done by the colored directors no more than is heard about every officer in every school. The directors of the art and physical culture departments were particularly fine. Now, no matter how competent or superior the colored teachers in our public schools may be, they know that they can never rise to the height of a directorship, can never hope to be more than an assistant and receive the meager salary therefore, unless the present regime is radically changed.

Not long ago one of the most distinguished kindergartners in the country came to deliver a course of lectures in Washington. The colored teachers were eager to attend, but they could not buy the coveted privilege for love or money. When they appealed to the director of kindergartens, they were told that the expert kindergartners had come to Washington under the auspices of private individuals, so that she could not possibly have them admitted. Realizing what a loss colored teachers had sustained in being deprived of the information and inspiration which these lectures afforded, one of the white teachers volunteered to repeat them as best she could for the benefit of her colored co-laborers for half the price she herself had paid, and the proposition was eagerly accepted by some.

Strenuous efforts are being made to run Jim Crow street cars in the national capital. "Resolved, that a Jim Crow law should be adopted and enforced in the District of Columbia," was the subject of a discussion engaged in last January by the Columbian Debating Society of the George Washington University in our national capital, and the decision was rendered in favor of the affirmative. Representative Heflin, of

Alabama, who introduced a bill providing for Jim Crow street cars in the District of Columbia last winter, has just received a letter from the president of the East Brookland Citizens' Association "Endorsing the movement for separate street cars and sincerely hoping that you will be successful in getting this enacted into law as soon as possible." Brookland is a suburb of Washington.

The colored laborer's path to a decent livelihood is by no means smooth. Into some of the trade unions here he is admitted, while from others he is excluded altogether. By the union men this is denied, altho I am personally acquainted with skilled workmen who tell me they are not admitted into the unions because they are colored. But even when they are allowed to join the unions they frequently derive little benefit, owing to certain tricks of the trade. When the word passes round that help is needed and colored laborers apply, they are often told by the union officials that they have secured all the men they needed, because the places are reserved for white men, until they have been provided with jobs, and colored men must remain idle, unless the supply of white men is too small.

I am personally acquainted with one of the most skillful laborers in the hardware business in Washington. For thirty years he has been working for the same firm. He told me he could not join the union, and that his employer had been almost forced to discharge him, because the union men threatened to boycott his store if he did not. If another man could have been found at the time to take his place he would have lost his job, he said. When no other human being can bring a refractory chimney or stove to its senses, this colored man is called upon as the court of last appeal. If he fails to subdue it, it is pronounced a hopeless case at once. And yet this expert workman receives much less for his services than do white men who cannot compare with him in skill.

And so I might go on citing instance after instance to show the variety of ways in which our people are sacrificed on the altar of prejudice in the Capital of the United States and how almost insurmountable are the obstacles which block his path to success. Early in life many a colored youth is so appalled by the helplessness and the hopelessness of his situation in this country that in a sort of stoical despair he resigns himself to his fate. "What is the good of our trying to acquire an education? We can't all be preachers, teachers, doctors and lawyers. Besides those professions there is almost nothing for colored people to do but engage in the most menial occupations, and we do not need an education for that." More than once such remarks, uttered by young men and women in our public schools who possess brilliant intellects, have wrung my heart. It is impossible for any white person in the United States, no matter how sympathetic and broad, to realize what life would mean to him if his incentive to effort were suddenly snatched away. To the lack of incentive to effort, which is the awful shadow under which we live, may be traced the wreck and ruin of scores of colored youth. And surely nowhere in the world do oppression and persecution based solely on the color of the skin appear more hateful and hideous than in the capital of the United States, because the chasm between the principles upon which this Government was founded, in which it still professes to believe, and those which are daily practiced under the protection of the flag, yawns so wide and deep.

Introduction to Ida M. Wells-Barnett's
"Lynching, Our National Crime"

"Lynching, Our National Crime" is Ida B. Wells' appeal to the National Association For the Advancement of Colored People to organize a systematic attack against the wave of lynching that had terrorized African Americans for more than two decades. The appeal is not emotional in its presentation, but the speaker's logical analysis of the history and causes for these atrocities result in a compelling appeal to a group of influential citizens wielding sufficient political power to affect public policy. The speaker clarifies the hypocrisy surrounding justifications for the crimes, questions the conscience of a nation that permits such atrocities, and challenges the host organization to use its influence to investigate and stop the lynchings.

Ida B. Wells was born on 16 July 1862, in Hollysprings, Mississippi, the daughter of slave parents—Elizabeth and James Wells. Ida Wells attended Rust College, read widely, and "formed a picture of a world outside of Mississippi—a world where good people were rewarded while evil doers were always punished. This youthful faith in a well-ordered world in which justice prevailed never entirely left her; it enabled her to keep on struggling even when the odds seemed unsurmountable" (Sterling 1979, 65).

She lost her parents to a yellow fever epidemic and assumed the support of five brothers and sisters. She went to Memphis to teach in 1883, later attending Fisk University and Lemoyne College. In 1884 she published an article about her experience of being ejected from a first-class car on a train ride, the subject of a lawsuit. Her outspoken nature created numerous problems for her across time.

When Ida B. Wells came before the National Association for The Advancement of Colored People in 1909, she was

well prepared to discuss lynching. Sterling describes Well's
motivation to come before this group: "In 1909 Wells went
to New York for the founding conference of the National
Association for the Advancement of Colored People, in the
hope that it would become the fighting organization that the
Afro-American Council had once promised to be" (Sterling
1979, 104). After the lynching of Tom Moss in 1892, Well's
life was changed forever. Tom Moss was a person whom
Wells had known since her first days in Memphis, and his
lynching motivated her relentless campaign against lynching.
She conscientiously recorded incidents of lynching and spoke
out boldly against this atrocity in *Free Speech* and *The Age*,
the former a weekly black newspaper in which Wells
reported.

Lynching, Our National Crime
Ida M. Wells-Barnett
1909

The lynching record for a quarter of a century merits the thoughtful study of the American people. It presents three salient facts:

First: Lynching is color-line murder.

Second: Crimes against women is the excuse, not the cause.

Third: It is a national crime and requires a national remedy.

Proof that lynching follows the color line is to be found in the statistics which have been kept for the past twenty-five years. During the few years preceding this period and while frontier lynch law existed, the executions showed a majority of white victims. Later, however, as law courts and authorized judiciary extended into the far West, lynch law rapidly abated, and its white victims became few and far between.

Just as the lynch-law regime came to a close in the West, a new mob movement started in the South. This was wholly political, its purpose being to suppress the colored vote by intimidation and murder. Thousands of assassins banded together under the name of Ku Klux Klans, "Midnight Raiders," "Knights of the Golden Circle," et cetera, et cetera, spread a reign of terror, by beating, shooting and killing colored people by the thousands. In a few years, the purpose was accomplished, and the black vote was suppressed. But mob murder continued.

From 1882, in which year fifty-two were lynched, down to the present, lynching has been along the color line. Mob murder increased yearly until in 1892 more than two hundred victims were lynched and statistics show that 3,284 men, women and children have been put to death in this quarter of a century. During the last ten years from 1899 to 1908 inclusive the number lynched was 959. Of this number 102 were white, while the colored victims numbered 857. No other nation, civilized or savage, burns its criminals; only under the Stars and Stripes is the human holocaust possible. Twenty-eight human beings burned at the stake, one of them a woman and two of them children, is the awful indictment against American civilization—the gruesome tribute which the nation pays to the color line.

Why is mob murder permitted by a Christian nation? What is the cause of this awful slaughter? This question is answered almost daily—always the same shameless falsehood that "Negroes are lynched to protect womanhood." Standing before a Chautauqua assemblage, John Temple Graves, at once champion of lynching and apologist for lynchers, said: "The mob stands today as the most potential bulwark between the women of the South and such a carnival of crime as would infuriate the world and precipitate the annihilation of the Negro race." This is the never-varying answer of lynchers and their apologists. All know that it is untrue. The cowardly lyncher revels in murder, then seeks to shield himself from public execration by claiming devotion to woman. But truth is mighty and the lynching record discloses the hypocrisy of the lyncher as well as his crime.

The Springfield, Illinois, mob rioted for two days, the militia of the entire state was called out, two men were lynched, hundreds of people driven from their homes, all because a white woman said a Negro assaulted her. A mad mob went to the jail, tried to lynch the victim of her charge and, not being able to find him, proceeded to pillage and burn the town and to lynch two innocent men. Later, after the police had found that the woman's charge was false, she published a retraction, the indictment was dismissed and the intended victim discharged. But the lynched victims were dead. Hundreds were homeless and Illinois was disgraced.

As a final and complete refutation of the charge that lynching is occasioned by crimes against women, a partial record of lynchings is cited; 285 persons were lynched for causes as follows:

Unknown cause, 92; no cause, 10; race prejudice, 49; miscegenation, 7; informing, 12; making threats, 11; keeping saloon, 3; practicing fraud, 5; practicing voodooism, 2; bad reputation, 8; unpopularity, 3; mistaken identity, 5; using improper language, 3; violation of contract, 1; writing insulting letter, 2; eloping, 2; poisoning horse, 1; poisoning well, 2; by white caps, 9; vigilantes, 14; Indians, 1; moonshining, 1; refusing evidence, 2; political causes, 5; disputing, 1; disobeying quarantine regulations, 2; slapping a child, 1; turning state's evidence, 3; protecting a Negro, 1; to prevent giving evidence, 1; knowledge of larceny, 1; writing letter to white woman, 1; asking white woman to marry, 1; jilting girl, 1; having smallpox, 1; concealing criminal, 2; threatening political exposure, 1; self-defense, 6; cruelty, 1; insulting language to woman, 5; quarreling with white man, 2; colonizing Negroes, 1; throwing stones, 1; quarreling, 1; gambling, 1.

Is there a remedy, or will the nation confess that it cannot protect its protectors at home as well as abroad? Various remedies have been suggested to abolish the lynching infamy, but year after year, the butchery of men, women and children continues in spite of plea and protest. Education is suggested as a preventive, but it is as grave a crime to murder an ignorant man as it is a scholar. True, few educated men have been lynched, but the hue and cry once started stops at no bounds, as was clearly shown by the lynchings in Atlanta, and in Springfield, Illinois.

Agitation, though helpful, will not alone stop the crime. Year after year statistics are published, meetings are held, resolutions are adopted and yet lynchings go on. Public sentiment does measurably decrease the sway of mob law, but the irresponsible blood-thirsty criminals who swept through the streets of Springfield, beating an inoffensive law-abiding citizen to death in one part of the town and in another torturing and shooting to death a man who for three score years had made a reputation for honesty, integrity and sobriety, had raised a family and had accumulated property, were not deterred from the heinous crimes by either education or agitation. The only certain remedy is an appeal to law. Law-breakers must be made to know that human life is sacred and that every citizen of this country is first a citizen of the United States and secondly a citizen of the state in which he belongs. This nation must assert itself and protect its federal citizenship at home as well as abroad. The strong men of the government must reach across state lines whenever unbridled lawlessness defies state laws and must give to the individual under the Stars and Stripes the same measure of protection it gives to him when he travels in foreign lands. Federal protection of American citizenship is the remedy for lynching. Foreigners are rarely lynched in America; if, by mistake, one is lynched the national government quickly pays the damages. The recent agitation in California against the Japanese compelled this nation to recognize that federal power must yet assert itself to protect the nation from the treason of sovereign states. Thousands of American citizens have been put to death and no president has yet raised his hand in effective protest. But a simple insult to a native of Japan was quite sufficient to stir the government in Washington to prevent the threatened wrong. If the government has power to protect a foreigner from insult certainly it has the power to save a citizen's life.

The practical remedy has been more than once suggested in Congress; Senator Gallinger of New Hampshire in a resolution introduced in Congress called for an investigation with the view of ascertaining whether there is a remedy for lynching which Congress may apply. The Senate committee has under consideration a bill drawn by A. E. Pillsbury, former Attorney General of Massachusetts, providing for federal prosecution of lynchers in cases where the state fails to protect citizens or foreigners. Both of these resolutions indicate that the attention of the nation has been called to this phase of the lynching question.

As a final word it would be a beginning in the right direction if this conference can see its way clear to establish a bureau for the investigation and publication of the details of every lynching, so that the public could know that an influential body of citizens has made it a duty to give the widest publicity to the facts in each case, that it will make an effort to secure expressions of opinion all over the country against lynching for the sake of the country's fair name; and lastly, but by no means least, to try to influence the daily papers of the country to refuse to become accessory to mobs either before or after the fact. Several of the greatest riots and the most brutal burnt offerings of the mobs have been suggested and incited by the daily papers of the offending community. If the newspaper which suggests lynching in its accounts of an alleged crime, could be held legally as well as morally responsible for reporting that "threats of lynching were heard"; or, "it is feared that if the guilty one is caught, he will be lynched"; or, "there were cries of 'lynch him,' and the only reason the threat was not carried out was because no leader appeared," a long step toward a remedy will have been taken.

In a multitude of counsel there is wisdom. Upon the grave question presented by the slaughter of innocent men, women and children there should be an honest, courageous conference of patriotic, law-abiding citizens anxious to punish crime promptly, impartially and by due process of law, also to make life, liberty and property secure against mob rule.

Time was when lynching appeared to be sectional, but now it is national—a blight upon our nation, mocking our laws and disgracing our Christianity. "With malice toward none but with charity for all" let us undertake the work of making the "law of the land" effective and supreme upon every foot of American soil—a shield to the innocent; and to the guilty, punishment swift and sure.

Ben Is Going To Take His Big Brother's Place
Fannie Lee Chaney
1965

I am here to tell you about Meridian, Mississippi. That's my home. I have been there all of my days. I know the white man; I know the black man. The white man is not for the black man—we are just there. Everything to be done, to be said, the white man is going to do it; he is going to say it, right or wrong. We hadn't, from the time that I know of, been able to vote or register in Meridian. Now, since the civil-rights workers have been down in Mississippi working, they have allowed a lot of them to go to register. A lot of our people are scared, afraid. They are still backward, "I can't do that; I never have," they claimed. "I have been here too long. I will lose my job; I won't have any job." So, that is just the way it is. My son, James, when he went out with the civil-rights workers around the first of '64 felt it was something he wanted to do, and he enjoyed working in the civil-rights movement. He stayed in Canton, Mississippi, working on voter registration from February through March. When he came home he told me how he worked and lived those few weeks he was there; he said, "Mother, one half of the time, I was out behind houses or churches, waiting to get the opportunity to talk to people about what they needed and what they ought to do." He said, "Sometime they shunned me off and some would say, 'I want you all to stay away from here and leave me alone.'" But he would pick his chance and go back again. That is what I say about Mississippi right now. There is one more test I want to do there. I am working with the civil-rights movement, my whole family is, and my son, Ben, here, he is going to take his big brother's place.

He has been working for civil rights. Everything he can do, he does it. For his activities, he had been jailed twice before he was twelve years old. He told me when he was in jail he wasn't excited. He is not afraid; he would go to jail again! I am too, because we need and we've got to go to jail and we've got to get where the white man is. The white man has got Mississippi and we are just there working for the white man. He is the one getting rich. And when he gets rich, we can be outdoors or in old houses and he is going to knock on the door and get his rent money.

This is not something that has just now started, it has been going on before my time and I imagine before my parents' time. It is not just NOW the white man is doing this; it was borne from generation to generation. So, as I say, Ben is going to take his big brother's place, and I am with him and the rest of the family also. You all read about Mississippi—all parts of Mississippi—but I just wish it was so you could just come down there and be able to see; just try to live there just for one day, and you will know just how it is there.

Introduction to Constance Baker Motley's
Keynote Address before
The Southern Christian Leadership Conference

Constance Baker Motley's Keynote address before the Southern Christian Leadership Conference in 1965 acknowledged the singular contributions of Rosa L. Parks, principal honoree of the occasion, to the civil rights movement. This recognition served as an example of the direct action characterizing the agenda of the Southern Christian Leadership Conference. Much of the discourse focuses on the significance and implications of the Civil Rights Act of 1964 and the Voting Rights Act of 1965. The speaker explores the challenges evolving from this legislation, noting particularly the increased responsibility devolving upon the beneficiaries of these two landmark legislative actions. She outlines remaining challenges and emphasizes the residual resistance from the general population that would continue to threaten the implementation of the two laws.

Constance Baker was born in 1921 in New Haven, Connecticut. Judge Motley was educated at New York University and Columbia University, receiving her law degree from the latter in 1946. Her work with the National Association for the Advancement of Colored People spanned more than a decade. Initially an assistant, Motley emerged as associate counsel for the organization and principal trial attorney for the NAACP Legal Defense and Education Fund. She successfully argued nine discrimination cases before the United States Supreme Court. In 1964, she was elected to the New York State Senate, the first woman of African descent to have been thus honored. And on 25 January 1966, she was appointed to the Federal District Court in New York City by President Lyndon B. Johnson, becoming the first federal judge among African American women.

The speech considered here was delivered in Birmingham, Alabama, at the 1965 annual convention of the Southern Christian Leadership Conference. This organization, ironically, grew out of dissatisfaction with the political methodology of the NAACP, the organization to which Motley had devoted extended and distinguished service. Motley, as an NAACP attorney, had been pivotal in the integration of previously segregated universities in the South, "gaining academic admission to the University of Alabama for Autherine Lucy, to the University of Georgia for Charlayne Hunter and Hamilton Holmes, and to the University of Mississippi for James Meredith . . ." Williams and Williams 1970, 192). The conservative politics of the NAACP motivated the organization of groups like the SCLC that emphasized direct action.

Keynote Address To The Annual Convention Of The Southern Christian Leadership Conference
Constance Baker Motley
1965

First, I want to say how pleased I am to have this opportunity to address the Southern Leadership Conference (SCLC) on its return to desegregated Birmingham. Your coveted invitation to be the guest speaker at this opening night banquet is, indeed, a high compliment.

No city in America owes more to the SCLC than Birmingham. Your crusade for freedom has placed Birmingham on the civil rights map and has assured it a place in the history of our fight for freedom.

I am especially proud to be here tonight to honor the movement's most celebrated daughter, Rosa Parks.

We do honor tonight to Mrs. Parks, the freedom fighter whose proud refusal to move to the back of the bus in Montgomery, Alabama, ten years ago was an act of courage comparable in importance to that of the Yankee militiaman at Concord who "fired the shot heard round the world." No Emerson has as yet given Mrs. Park's historic act the poetic commemoration which it deserves, but when the history of the second half of this century is written, there is no doubt in my mind that Montgomery, 1955, will rank with Fort Sumter, 1861, and Concord, Massachusetts, 1775, as a turning point in our nation's history.

It is, of course, always a pleasure to see Martin King, but especially on a memorable occasion such as this. The record Dr. King has compiled in the last ten years has established him not only as America's most widely acclaimed freedom fighter but as a spokesman for the entire country. He is an American hero of authentic distinction who has achieved an unprecedented position of respect and prestige throughout the world. His inspiring oratory, his doctrine of aggressive restraint, his sweeping influence for good over the entire American scene, has made him a leader of unique importance. Every great cause requires great leadership. We are fortunate indeed that, at this time in history, Dr. King came to us to serve and to lead.

The Civil Rights Act of 1964, that historic declaration of human equality, would have been thought impossible ten years ago, at the time Mrs. Parks first refused to obey the order to move to the back of the bus. Yet, today, we find that momentous Act significantly strengthened and implemented by the Voting Rights Act of 1965. The Voting Rights Act will rewrite what otherwise might have been the political history of the southern United States in the next few decades. Nevertheless, its passage through Congress was relatively tranquil. It is a measure of the strength of the civil rights forces that such significant legislation—this pioneer involvement by the federal government in an area previously left to state misrule—was passed with such near unanimity.

Notably, most of the opposition to the New Voting Rights Act came from states where people are denied the right to vote. That opposition, we hope, has been now put down for all time by the passage of this new Act. Consequently, we can all well understand the newfound fear and trembling on the part of Jim Crow governors and legislators as they contemplate the future expansion of their constituencies. Let the new voters of the 1960s remember at the polls officials whose racist appeals kept them in political bondage, but let them never forget those civil rights martyrs who laid down their lives for this new day.

The importance of the Voting Rights Act was illustrated by the historic manner in which it was signed last Friday by President Johnson. The President and the entire cabinet assembled and went to the Rotunda of the Capitol. There the

President spoke on this second great landmark in civil rights legislation passed during the current administration. With unprecedented speed, the Justice Department has moved toward implementation of the Voting Rights Act by the filing of a suit in Mississippi to bar enforcement of that state's poll tax law.

I believe that wise exercise of the right to vote is now the keystone to actual equality, legal equality having been won. It is through the ballot that the great social changes which transformed America in the past have been authorized. The voting strength of Negroes does not only mean civil rights legislation and the complete destruction of state-supported segregation and discrimination. It means an equal share in the state's revenues for all communities and individuals regardless of race. It means paved streets in the Negro communities as well as in the white communities. And it means the harnessing of the power and resources of the state to provide the economic changes required for the elimination of poverty and illiteracy. The gains achieved in the area of civil rights thus provide hope for gains in other areas. All this will be part of the impact of the Voting Rights Act of 1965.

Another important gain which has been won in recent years is the ruling of the United States Supreme Court in support of that ancient but often ignored principle, "one man, one vote." The elimination of malapportionment and rural domination of state legislatures has enfranchised city voters and brought legislators closer to the realities of the twentieth century.

In this connection we should be thankful for the recent defeat in the United States Senate of the Dirksen Amendment, which would have allowed for the reapportionment of one house of the state legislature on a basis other than population, actually received a majority of the votes of the Senate. It received fifty-seven votes, while only thirty-nine were cast against it. Needless to say, every Senator from the states where Negroes were denied the right to vote supported this amendment. It was only defeated because a two-thirds vote is required for a constitutional amendment. We cannot be secure when, in the most heavily democratic and liberal senate of this century, such a proposal could come within seven votes of adoption.

Another result of the "one man, one vote" decision has been the end of the State of Georgia's county unit system, under which a candidate who receives a majority of votes could actually be defeated by overweighted rural ballots in a statewide primary. As if it were not bad enough that Negroes were not allowed to vote in Georgia, when they did vote the votes were not counted equally. But the fact that such an utter perversion of majority rule could have persisted for so long, and the fact that it took federal intervention to destroy it, shows how fragile our liberties are.

Today, in 1965, ten Negroes sit in the Georgia legislature—two senators and eight representatives. Some day the legislatures of all southern states will contain Negroes in substantially larger numbers. This day cannot come too soon. I should say at this time that as many of you know, I hold the office of President of the Borough of Manhattan. In this, an elective office, I represent 1,700,000 residents in the heart of New York City. My jurisdiction includes black Harlem and Park Avenue, Wall Street and Chinatown, and Manhattan's newly created Puerto Rican ghettos and the famous Lower East Side. I am the twentieth person to hold the office of Borough President since the position was established with the consolidation of five boroughs (counties) into New York City on 1 January 1988. In the beginning, most of the Borough Presidents were Irish-Americans. In the 1930s, there was a string of Jewish borough presidents. In November 1953, A Negro was elected to this position for the first time.

When the borough presidency was held by a member of a white minority group, one did not hear racist charges or complaints. Historically, in New York as in many areas, candidates had been nominated for office for many different reasons, one of which was their ethnic appeal. The tradition of the balanced ticket in a melting-pot society is an old custom that has been adhered to by reformers and traditionalists alike. Yet, when this rotation of office brings a succession of Negroes into a high position, there is an undercurrent of dissatisfaction. The quality of the candidate is ignored, and the feeling is piously expressed that race should not be a factor in the selection of candidates. Where were all these critics when Negroes were excluded from candidacy or public office because of their race? I believe that full equality demands treatment of the Negro community the same way that our society treats its other communities, and that includes the political recognition of the Negro.

I believe in electing people without regard to their race, and I am aware that those who cry "race"—on both sides—are often those who have no more worthy arguments to present. But I do not believe that all the merit and all the fitness to govern can be found in people of one color. I look forward to the day when race will be relegated to obscurity as a criterion in the selection of candidates for high office. But until that happy day, we must all remain aware of our long-standing struggle to prevent discrimination and to gain first-class citizenship for the Negro. And I know, as you know, that first-class citizenship means not only the right to vote but the right to run for office and the right to hold office. In order to do this, it will be necessary for Negroes by the hundreds of thousands to take advantage of the new federal laws and to register and vote.

A Negro who does not vote is ungrateful to those who already have died in the fight for freedom. A Negro who does not vote is not helping to make a better world for his or her children. A Negro who does not vote is lending aid and support to the racists who argue that Negroes will not assume the responsibilities of citizenship. Any person who does not vote is failing to serve the cause of freedom—his own freedom, his people's freedom, and his country's freedom.

In its struggle for the achievement for these social goals, the Alliance should use all the time-honored methods which Americans have used to seek freedom. I am reminded of a statement made just six days ago by President Johnson at the White House. The President said, "So, free speech, free press, free religion, and . . . teach-ins and sit-ins and parades and marches and demonstrations—well, they're still radical ideas." And so are secret ballots, and so are free elections, and so is the principle of equal dignity, and so is the principle of equal rights for all the sons and daughters of man. But all of these things are what America stands for, and all of these things are what you and all other Americans need to stand up for today.

President Johnson thus encouraged the fullest range of expression for Americans anxious to improve social conditions and to implement court decisions already won. I think we should consider his remarks carefully and be guided by his words. We should not be weary. We must move toward full equality for our children's sake. Let us not forget them.

In pursuit of this goal, now is the time to finish the task of integrating our schools. In this struggle, we have a strong new ally in the Department of Health, Education, and Welfare, which has the responsibility for withholding federal funds from school districts that refuse to desegregate. Tonight, we are dining in a white hotel in Birmingham—several hundred of us.

But how many Negroes will go to school with whites in Birmingham come September 1965? How many Negro teachers who will teach white children are now teaching Negro children? The Department of Health, Education, and Welfare has its responsibility, but we also have ours. Our responsibility is to secure for our children all the rights for which the civil rights revolution of the last decade was fought. There are today no more Jim Crow buses—there are only Negroes who are afraid to ride up front. There are no more segregated public recreational facilities—only Negroes who are afraid to take advantage of their rights. There are no more legally segregated schools—only Negro parents who fail their children. I believe that the only way the segregated schools of the South will now be desegregated is for Negro parents, en masse, to take their children by the hand to a white school in September 1965. I predict that such a demonstration by Negro parents—coupled with the new federal determination to require compliance with the school desegregation decision as a condition of federal financial assistance—will bring a swift end to segregated school systems in the South. Just as Rosa Parks's courageous refusal to be segregated brought about the end of Jim Crow travel, so every Negro mother has it within her power to end school segregation.

Rosa Parks, we honor you tonight because yours is the kind of courage and determination and nonviolent spirit we all need for the future. Your name will be remembered as long as freedom is abroad in this land. My prayer in Birmingham tonight is that Negro women everywhere will follow your example and hasten the day when all of our hard won legal rights are secure in practice—here and throughout the land.

Introduction to Mary Church Terrell's
Frederick Douglass

Mary Church Terrell's "Frederick Douglass" delivered at the sixtieth anniversary of the Seneca Falls Women's Convention, lends an additional dimension to the famous race leader, an ex-slave and relentless advocate of equality. Many recall his "Fourth of July Speech" at Rochester, New York (1905) in which he chided his hosts for having the audacity to invite a man of color to participate in their celebration of independence, considering the status of the race in this society. In this excerpt from Terrell's speech considered here, she extols the basic human virtues that rendered Douglass's contributions invaluable both to the women of America and African Americans.

Terrell understood well the ambivalence deriving from relative assessments of gender and race. Her conclusion, however, was indeed a poignant one as she reflected: ". . . I assure you that nowhere in the United States have my feelings been so lacerated, my spirit so crushed, my heart so wounded; nowhere have I been more humiliated on account of my sex as I have been on account of my race."

The closing paragraphs omitted in this volume recount the speaker's regret at having declined Douglass's invitation to lunch on the day of his death. In that section the speaker notes: "How often since that memorable day have I regretted that I did not remain in that inspiring, kingly, kindly presence another short hour." Her tribute to his fearless support of women underscores his intrepid pursuit of freedom for the entire race. He was one who literally broke the shackles to emerge as a renowned advocate of freedom.

Frederick Douglass
Mary Church Terrell
1908

There are two reasons why I look back upon the meeting of which this is the sixtieth anniversary with genuine pleasure and glowing pride. In the first place, I am a woman like Elizabeth Cady Stanton. In the second place, I belong to the race of which Frederick Douglass was such a magnificent representative. Perhaps I should be too modest to proclaim from the housetops that I think I have a decided advantage over everybody else who participates in this anniversary today. Perhaps I should be too courteous and generous to call attention to the fact that I have one more reason of being proud of that record-breaking history making meeting, which was held in this city 60 years ago, than anybody else who takes part in these exercises today. But I simply cannot resist the temptation to show that this is one occasion which a colored woman really has good and sufficient reasons for feeling several inches taller than her sisters in the more favored race. It so rarely happens that a colored woman in the United States can prove by convincing, indisputable facts that she has good reasons for being proud of the race with which she is identified that you will pardon me for the pride I feel on this occasion, I am sure.

The incomparable Frederick Douglass did many things of which I as a member of that race which he served so faithfully and well am proud. But there is nothing he ever did in his long and brilliant career in which I take keener pleasure and greater pride than I do in his ardent advocacy of equal political rights for women and the effective service he rendered the cause of woman suffrage sixty years ago. Even though some of us have passed that period in our lives, when we take much pleasure in those romances which describe in such deliciously· thrilling details those days of old, when knights were bold and had a chronic habit of rescuing fair ladies in high towers in distress, still I am sure there is nobody here today with soul so dead and heart so cold who, in the everyday affairs of this prosaic world, rushes gallantly to the assistance of a woman fighting to the death for a principle as dear to her as life and actually succeeds in helping her establish and maintain it, in spite of the opposition of even faithful coadjutors and her most faithful friends. This is precisely the service which Frederick Douglass rendered Elizabeth Cady Stanton at that Seneca Falls meeting sixty years ago.

When the defeat of that resolution which demanded equal political rights for women seemed imminent, because some of the most ardent advocates of woman suffrage deemed it untimely and unwise, when even dear, broad, brave Lucretia Mott tried to dissuade Mrs. Stanton, to whom it was the very heart and soul of the movement from insisting upon it by declaring "Lizzie, thee will make us all ridiculous." I am glad that it was to a large extent due to Frederick Douglass' masterful arguments and matchless eloquence that it was carried in spite of the opposition of its equally conscientious and worthy foes. And I am as proud of Elizabeth Cady Stanton, as a woman, as I am of Frederick Douglass, the Negro. Try as hard as we may, it is difficult for women of the present day to imagine what courage and strength of mind it required for Elizabeth Cady Stanton to demand equal political rights for her sex at that time. . . .

But if Elizabeth Cady Stanton manifested sublime courage and audacious contempt for the ridicule and denunciation she knew would be heaped upon her as a woman, how much more were such qualities displayed by Frederick Douglass, the ex-slave. It is doubtful if Frederick Douglass' independence of spirit and sense of justice were ever put to severer test than they were on that day, when for the first time in his life, he publicly committed himself to the cause of woman suffrage. I have always extracted great pleasure from the thought not only that Frederick Douglass, and he alone of all men present at the Seneca Falls meeting, was conspicuous for his enthusiastic advocacy of equal political rights for women, but that he found in his heart to advocate it ever afterward with such ardor and zeal.

In no half-hearted way did he lay hold of the newly-proclaimed doctrine,nor did he ever try to conceal his views. When nearly all the newspapers, big and little, good, bad and indifferent were hurling jibes and jeers at the women and the men who participated in the Seneca Falls meeting, there was one newspaper, published in Rochester, N. Y., which not only heartily commended the leaders, in the new movement, but warmly espoused their cause. This was Frederick Douglass' *North Star*, in the leading editorial 28 July 1848, after declaring, "we could not do justice to our own convictions nor to the excellent persons connected with the infant movement, if we did not in this connection offer a few remarks on the general subject which the convention met to consider and objects it seeks to attain." As editor of the *North Star*, Mr. Douglass expresses his views as follows: " A discussion of the rights of animals would be regarded with far more complacency by many of what are called the wise and good of the land than would be a discussion of the rights of women. Many who have at last made the discovery that Negroes have some rights as well as other members of the human family have yet to be convinced that women have any. Standing as we do upon the watch tower of human freedom, we cannot be deterred from expression of our approbation of any movement, however humble, to improve and elevate any member of the human family."

If at any time Mr. Douglass seemed to waver in his allegiance to the cause of political enfranchisement of women, it was he realized as no white person,no matter how broad and sympathetic he may be, has ever been able to feel or can possibly feel today just what it means to belong to my despised, handicapped and persecuted race. I am woman and I know what it means to be circumscribed, deprived, handicapped and fettered on account of my sex. But I assure you that nowhere in the United States have my feelings been so lacerated, my spirit so crushed, my heart so wounded, nowhere have I been so humiliated on account of my sex as I have been on account of my race. I can readily understand, therefore, what feelings must have surged through Frederick Douglass' heart, and I can almost feel the intensity of the following words he uttered, when he tried to explain why he honestly thought it was more necessary and humane to give the ballot to the Negro than to women, for the law makers of this country were too narrow and ungenerous to deal justly both by the oppressed race and the handicapped, disfranchised sex at one and the same time. "I must say,"declared Mr. Douglass, "that I cannot see how anyone can pretend that there is the same urgency in giving the ballot to woman as to the Negro. With us,"he said, "the matter is a question of life and death at best in fifteen states of the union. When women, because they are women, are hunted down through the streets of New York and New Orleans; their children torn from their arms and their brains dashed out on the pavement; when they are objects of insult and outrage at every turn; when they are in danger of having their houses burnt down over their heads; when their children are not allowed to enter school; then they will have an urgency to obtain the ballot to our own." "Is that not also true about black women?" somebody in the audience inquired. "Yes, yes, yes," replied Mr. Douglass, "But not because they are women, but because they are black. . . ."

Choice: A Tribute To
Dr. Martin Luther King, Jr.
Alice Walker
1972

My great-great-great-grandmother walked as a slave from Virginia to Eatonton, Georgia—which passes for the Walker ancestral home—with two babies on her hips. She lived to be a hundred and twenty-five years old and my own father knew her as a boy. (It is in memory of this walk that I choose to keep and to embrace my "maiden" name, Walker.)

There is a cemetery near our family church where she is buried; but because her marker was made of wood and rotted years ago, it is impossible to tell exactly where her body lies. In the same cemetery are most of my mother's people, who have lived in Georgia for so long nobody even remembers when they came. And all of my great-aunts and uncles are there, and my grandfather and grandmother, and, very recently, my own father.

If it is true that land does not belong to anyone until they have buried a body in it, then the land of my birthplace belongs to me, dozens of times over. Yet the history of my family, like that of all black Southerners, is a history of dispossession. We loved the land and worked the land, but we never owned it; and even if we bought land, as my great-grandfather did after the Civil War, it was always in danger of being taken away, as his was, during the period following Reconstruction.

My father inherited nothing of material value from his father, and when I came of age in the early sixties I awoke to the bitter knowledge that in order just to continue to love the land of my birth, I was expected to leave it. For black people—including my parents—had learned a long time ago that to stay willingly in a beloved but brutal place is to risk losing the love and being forced to acknowledge only the brutality.

It is a part of the black Southern sensibility that we treasure memories; for such a long time, that is all of our homeland those of us who at one time or another were forced away from it have been allowed to have.

I watched my brothers, one by one, leave our home and leave the South. I watched my sisters do the same. This was not unusual; abandonment, except for memories, was the common thing, except for those who "could not do any better," or those whose strength or stubbornness was so colossal they took the risk that others could not bear.

In 1960, my mother bought a television set, and each day after school I watched Hamilton Holmes and Charlayne Hunter as they struggled to integrate—fair-skinned as they were—the University of Georgia. And then, one day, there appeared the face of Dr. Martin Luther King, Jr. What a funny name, I thought. At the moment I first saw him, he was being handcuffed and shoved into a police truck. He had dared to claim his rights as a native son, and had been arrested. He displayed no fear, but seemed calm and serene, unaware of his own extraordinary courage. His whole body, like his conscience, was at peace.

At the moment I saw his resistance I knew I would never be able to live in this country without resisting everything that sought to disinherit me, and I would never be forced away from the land of my birth without a fight.

He was The One, The Hero, The One Fearless Person for whom we had waited. I hadn't even realized before that we *had* been waiting for Martin Luther King, Jr., but we had. And I knew it for sure when my mother added his name to the list of people she prayed for every night.

I sometimes think that it was literally the prayers of people like my mother and father, who had bowed down in the struggle for such a long time, that kept Dr. King alive until five years ago. For years we went to bed praying for his life, and awoke with the question "Is the 'Lord' still here?"

The public acts of Dr. King you know. They are visible all around you. His voice you would recognize sooner than any other voice you have heard in this century—this in spite of the fact that certain municipal libraries, like the one in downtown Jackson, do not carry recordings of his speeches, and the librarians chuckle cruelly when asked why they do not.

You know, if you have read his books, that his is a complex and revolutionary philosophy that few people are capable of understanding fully or have the patience to embody in themselves. Which is our weakness, which is our loss.

And if you know anything about good Baptist preaching, you can imagine what you missed if you never had a chance to hear Martin Luther King, Jr., preach at Ebeneezer Baptist Church.

You know of the prizes and awards that he tended to think very little of. And you know of his concern for the disinherited: the American Indians, the Mexican-American, and the poor American white—for whom he cared much.

You know that this very room, in this very restaurant, was closed to people of color not more than five years ago. And that we eat here together tonight largely through his efforts and his blood. We accept the common pleasures of life, assuredly, in his name.

But add to all of these things the one thing that seems to me second to none in importance: He gave us back our heritage. He gave us back our homeland; the bones and dust of our ancestors, who may now sleep within our caring and our hearing. He gave us the blueness of the Georgia sky in autumn as in summer; the colors of the Southern winter as well as glimpses of the green of vacation-time spring. Those of our relatives we used to invite for a visit we now can ask to stay . . . He gave us full-time use of our own woods, and restored our memories to those of us who were forced to run away, as realities we might each day enjoy and leave for our children.

He gave us continuity of place, without which community is ephemeral. He gave us home.

Introduction to Audre Lorde's
"Learning From The 60's"

"Learning from the 60s" is both a summary and an evaluation of the politics and ideology during that decade. The address focuses particularly on the contributions and influence of Malcolm X. Throughout the speech, Lorde explores the implications of the Muslim leader's influence on the political thought of the race. She analyzes the forces that militated against unity, and therefore progress, during the sixties and suggests corrective attitudinal adjustments. Strongly emphasized in the speech is the centrality of individual responsibility in effecting social change since the past has shown that the lives of great or charismatic leaders cannot be automatically assumed. Central to the discourse is the dynamics of time, the impossibility of neatly dividing efforts into past, present, and future. Respect for diversity and individual responsibility are prominent themes that explicate the possibilities for African Americans.

Audre Lorde, prominent poet and essayist, was born in Harlem in 1934. Lorde graduated from Hunter College with a bachelors in literature in 1959 and later received degrees from the Columbia University School of Library Science and the University of Mexico. Much of her career has been spent as professor of English at Hunter College. Joan Martin commented on the nature of Lorde's work: "Her themes cross continents, wind through city streets, lavish color and form over seasons . . . She is favored companion to African gods. Defender of Black women suffering the injustice of white America" (Martin 1984, 277). Lorde herself articulated her "duty" to write: " . . . I have a duty to speak the truth as I see it and to share not just my triumphs, not just the things that felt good, but the pain, the intense, often unmitigating pain. If what I have to say is wrong, then there will be some woman who will stand up and say Audre Lorde was in error. But my words will be there" (Evans 1984, 261).

This speech was delivered at Harvard University in February 1982 at the Malcolm X Weekend. John Hope Franklin describes Malcolm X as "the ablest and most eloquent spokesman" of the Black Muslims (Franklin 1980, 413). Malcolm X, born Malcolm Little, changed his name to dramatize his rejection of white America. Following the assassination of President John F. Kennedy, Malcolm X spoke of the assassination as "chickens coming home to roost" and was publicly repudiated for the inappropriate statement and subsequently expelled from the pulpit of the Black Muslims. He later embraced a philosophical stance contrary to that held by the traditional body of Muslims and advocated the necessity of interacting with all races in achieving social and economic advancement, a stance that opposed the separatist emphasis of the group. Malcolm X was assassinated at a New York mass meeting in 1965 as he met with a newly organized group espousing his altered philosophy.

Learning from the 60s
Audre Lorde
1982

Malcolm X is a distinct shape in a very pivotal period of my life. I stand here now—Black, Lesbian, Feminist—an inheritor of Malcolm and in his tradition, doing my work, and the ghost of his voice through my mouth asks each one of you here tonight: Are you doing yours?

There are no new ideas, just new ways of giving those ideas we cherish breath and power in our own living. I'm not going to pretend that the moment I first saw or heard Malcolm X he became my shining prince, because it wouldn't be true. In February 1965 I was raising two children and a husband in a three-room flat on 149th Street in Harlem. I had read about Malcolm X and the Black Muslims. I became more interested in Malcolm X after he left the Nation of Islam, when he was silenced by Elijah Muhammad for his comment, after Kennedy's assassination, to the effect that the chickens had come home to roost. Before this I had not given much thought to the Nation of Islam because of their attitude toward women as well as because of their nonactivist stance. I'd read Malcolm's autobiography, and I liked his style, and I thought he looked a lot like my father's people, but I was one of the ones who didn't really hear Malcolm's voice until it was amplified by death.

I had been guilty of what many of us are still guilty of—letting the media, and I don't mean only the white media —define the bearers of those messages most important to our lives.

When I read Malcolm X with careful attention, I found a man much closer to the complexities of real change than anything I had read before. Much of what I say here tonight was born from his words.

In the last year of his life, Malcolm X added a breadth to this essential vision that would have brought him, had he lived, into inevitable confrontation with the question of difference as a creative and necessary force for change. For as Malcolm X progressed from a position of resistance to, and analysis of, the racial status quo, to more active considerations of organizing for change, he began to reassess some of his earlier positions. One of the most basic Black survival skills is the ability to change, to metabolize experience, good or ill, into something that is useful, lasting, effective. Four hundred years of survival as an endangered species has taught most of us that if we intend to live, we had better become fast learners. Malcolm knew this. We do not have to live the same mistakes over again if we can look at them, learn from them, and build upon them.

Before he was killed, Malcolm had altered and broadened his opinions concerning the role of women in society and the revolution. He was beginning to speak with increasing respect of the connection between himself and Martin Luther King, Jr., whose policies of nonviolence appeared to be so opposite to his own. And he began to examine the societal conditions under which alliances and coalitions must indeed occur.

He had also begun to discuss those scars of oppression which lead us to war against ourselves in each other rather than against our enemies.

As Black people, if there is one thing we can learn from the 60s, it is how infinitely complex any move for liberation must be. For we must move against not only those forces which dehumanize us from the outside, but also against those oppressive values which we have been forced to take into ourselves. Through examining the combination of our triumphs and errors, we can examine the dangers of an incomplete vision. Not to condemn that vision but to alter it, construct templates for possible futures, and focus our rage for change upon our enemies rather than upon each other. In the 1960s, the awakened anger of the Black community was often expressed, not vertically against the corruption of power and true sources of control over our lives, but horizontally toward those closest to us who mirrored our own impotence.

We were poised for attack, not always in the most effective places. When we disagreed with one another about the solution to a particular problem, we were often far more vicious to each other than to the originators of our common problem. Historically, difference had been used so cruelly against us that as a people we were reluctant to tolerate any diversion from what was externally defined as Blackness. In the 60s, political correctness became not a guideline for living, but a new set of shackles. A small and vocal part of the Black community lost sight of the fact that unity does not mean unanimity—Black people are not some standardly digestible quantity. In order to work together we do not have to become a mix of indistinguishable particles resembling a vat of homogenized chocolate milk. Unity implies the coming together of elements which are, to begin with, varied and diverse in their particular natures. Our persistence in examining the tensions within diversity encourages growth toward our common goal. So often we either ignore the past or romanticize it, render the reason for unity useless or mythic. We forget that the necessary ingredient needed to make the past work for the future is our energy in the present, metabolizing one into the other. Continuity does not happen automatically, nor is it a passive process.

The 60s were characterized by a heady belief in instantaneous solutions. They were vital years of awakening, of pride, and of error. The civil rights and Black power movements rekindled possibilities for disenfranchised groups within this nation. Even though we fought common enemies, at times the lure of individual solutions made us careless of

each other. Sometimes we could not bear the face of each
other's differences because of what we feared those
differences might say about ourselves. As if everybody can't
eventually be too Black, too White, too man, too woman.
But any future vision which can encompass all of us, by
definition, must be complex and expanding, not easy to
achieve. The answer to cold is heat, the answer to hunger is
food. But there is no simple monolithic solution to racism, to
sexism, to homophobia. There is only the conscious focusing
within each of my days to move against them, wherever I
come up against these particular manifestations of the same
disease. By seeing who the we is, we learn to use our
energies with greater precision against our enemies rather
than against ourselves.

In the 60s, white america—racist and liberal alike—was
more than pleased to sit back as spectator while Black
militant fought Black Muslim, Black Nationalist badmouthed
the non-violent, and Black women were told that our only
useful position in the Black Power movement was prone.
The existence of Black lesbian and gay people was not even
allowed to cross the public consciousness of Black america.
We know in the 1980s, from documents gained through the
Freedom of Information Act, that the FBI and CIA used our
intolerance of difference to foment confusion and tragedy in
segment after segment of Black communities of the 60s.
Black was beautiful, but still suspect, and too often our
forums for debate became stages for playing who's-Blacker-
than-who or who's-poorer-than-who games, ones in which
there can be no winners.

The 60s for me was a time of promise and excitement, but
the 60s was also a time of isolation and frustration from
within. It often felt like I was working and raising my
children in a vacuum, and that it was my own fault—if I was
only Blacker, things would be fine. It was a time of much

wasted energy, and I was often in a lot of pain. Either I denied or chose between various aspects of my identity, or my work and my Blackness would be unacceptable. As a Black lesbian mother in an interracial marriage, there was usually some part of me guaranteed to offend everybody's comfortable prejudices of who I should be. That is how I learned that if I didn't define myself for myself, I would be crunched into other people's fantasies for me and eaten alive. My poetry, my life, my work, my energies for struggle were not acceptable unless I pretended to match somebody else's norm. I learned that not only couldn't I succeed at that game, but the energy needed for that masquerade would be lost to my work. And there were babies to raise, students to teach. The Vietnam War was escalating, our cities were burning, more and more of our school kids were nodding out in the halls, junk was overtaking our streets. We needed articulate power, not conformity. There were other strong Black workers whose visions were racked and silenced upon some imagined grid of narrow Blackness. Nor were Black women immune. At a national meeting of Black women for political action, a young civil rights activist who had been beaten and imprisoned in Mississippi only a few years before, was trashed and silenced as suspect because of her white husband. Some of us made it and some of us were lost to the struggle. It was a time of great hope and great expectation; it was also a time of great waste. That is history. We do not need to repeat these mistakes in the 80s.

The raw energy of Black determination released in the 60s powered changes in Black awareness and self-concepts and expectations. This energy is still being felt in movements for change among women, other peoples of Color, gays, the handicapped—among all the disenfranchised peoples of this society. That is a legacy of the 60s to ourselves and to others. But we must recognize that many of our high expectations of rapid revolutionary change did not in fact occur. And many of the gains that did are even now being dismantled. This is not a reason for despair, nor for rejection of the importance of those years. But we must face with clarity and insight the lessons to be learned from the oversimplification of any struggle for self-awareness and liberation, or we will not rally the force we need to face the multidimensional threats to our survival in the 80s.

There is no such thing as a single-issue struggle because we do not live single-issue lives. Malcolm knew this. Martin Luther King, Jr. knew this. Our struggles are particular, but we are not alone. We are not perfect, but we are stronger and wiser than the sum of our errors. Black people have been here before us and survived. We can read their lives like signposts on the road and find, as Bernice Reagon says so poignantly, that each one of us is here because somebody before us did something to make it possible. To learn from their mistakes is not to lessen our debt to them, nor to the hard work of becoming ourselves, and effective.

We lose our history so easily, what is not predigested for us by the *New York Times*, or the *Amsterdam News*, or *Time magazine*. Maybe because we do not listen to our poets or to our fools, maybe because we do not listen to our mamas in ourselves. When I hear the deepest truths I speak coming out of my mouth sounding like my mother's, even remembering how I fought against her, I have to reassess both our relationship as well as the sources of my knowing. Which is not to say that I have to romanticize my mother in order to appreciate what she gave me—Woman, Black. We do not have to romanticize our past in order to be aware of how it seeds our present. We do not have to suffer the waste of an amnesia that robs us of the lessons of the past rather than permit us to read them with pride as well as deep understanding.

We know what it is to be lied to, and we know how important it is not to lie to ourselves.

We are powerful because we have survived, and that is what it is all about—survival and growth.

Within each one of us there is some piece of humanness that knows we are not being served by the machine which orchestrates crisis after crisis and is grinding all our futures into dust. If we are to keep the enormity of the forces aligned against us from establishing a false hierarchy of oppression, we must school ourselves to recognize that any attack against Blacks, any attack against women, is an attack against all of us who recognize that our interests are not being served by the systems we support. Each one of us here is a link in the connection between antipoor legislation, gay shootings, the burning of synagogues, street harassment, attacks against women, and resurgent violence against Black people. I ask myself as well as each one of you, exactly what alteration in the particular fabric of my everyday life does this connection call for? Survival is not a theory. In what way do I contribute to the subjugation of any part of those who I define as my people? Insight must illuminate the particulars of our lives: who labors to make the bread we waste, or the energy it takes to make nuclear poisons which will not biodegrade for one thousand years; or who goes blind assembling the microtransistors in our inexpensive calculators?

We are women trying to knit a future in a country where an Equal Rights Amendment was defeated as subversive legislation. We are Lesbians and gay men who, as the most obvious target of the New Right, are threatened with castration, imprisonment, and death in the streets. And we know that our erasure only paves the way for erasure of other people of Color, of the old, of the poor, of all of those who do not fit that mythic dehumanizing norm.

Can we really still afford to be fighting each other?

We are Black people living in a time when the consciousness of our intended slaughter is all around us. People of Color are increasingly expendable, our government's policy both here and abroad. We are functioning under a government ready to repeat in El Salvador and Nicaragua the tragedy of Vietnam, a government which stands on the wrong side of every single battle for liberation taking place upon this globe; a government which has invaded and conquered (as I edit this piece) the fifty-three square mile sovereign state of Grenada, under the pretext that her 110,000 people pose a threat to the U. S. Our papers are filled with supposed concern for human rights in white communist Poland while we sanction by acceptance and military supply the systematic genocide of apartheid in South Africa, of murder and torture in Haiti and El Salvador. American advisory teams bolster repressive governments across Central and South America, and in Haiti, while advisory is only a code name preceding military aid.

Decisions to cut aid for the terminally ill, for the elderly, for dependent children, for food stamps, even school lunches, are being made by men with full stomachs who live in comfortable houses with two cars and umpteen tax shelters. None of them go hungry to bed at night. Recently, it was suggested that senior citizens be hired to work in atomic plants because they are close to the end of their lives anyway.

Can any one of us here still afford to believe that efforts to reclaim the future can be private or individual? Can any one here still afford to believe that the pursuit of liberation can be the sole and particular province of any one particular race, or sex, or age, or religion, or sexuality, or class?

Revolution is not a one-time event. It is becoming always vigilant for the smallest opportunity to make a genuine change in established, outgrown responses; for instance, it is learning to address each other's difference with respect.

We share a common interest, survival, and it cannot be pursued in isolation from others simply because their differences make us uncomfortable. We know what it is to be lied to. The 60s should teach us how important it is not to lie to ourselves. Not to believe that revolution is a one-time event, or something that happens around us rather than inside of us. Not to believe that freedom can belong to any one group of us without the others also being free. How important it is not to allow even our leaders to define us to ourselves, or to define our sources of power to us.

There is no Black person here who can afford to wait to be led into positive action for survival. Each one of us must look clearly and closely at the genuine particulars (conditions) of his or her life and decide where action and energy is needed and where it can be effective. Change is the immediate responsibility of each of us, wherever and however we are standing, in whatever arena we choose. For while we wait for another Malcolm, another Martin, another charismatic Black leader to validate our struggles, old Black people are freezing to death in tenements, Black children are being brutalized and slaughtered in the streets, or lobotomized by television, and the percentage of Black families living below the poverty line is higher today than in 1963.

And if we wait to put our future into the hands of some new messiah, what will happen when those leaders are shot, or discredited, or tried for murder, or called homosexual, or otherwise disempowered? Do we put our future on hold? What is that internalized and self-destructive barrier that keeps us from moving, that keeps us from coming together?

We who are Black are at an extraordinary point of choice within our lives. To refuse to participate in the shaping of our future is to give it up. Do not be misled into passivity either by false security (they don't mean me) or by despair (there's nothing we can do). Each of us must find our work and do it.

Militancy no longer means guns at high noon, if it ever did. It means actively working for change, sometimes in the absence of any surety that change is coming. It means doing the unromantic and tedious work necessary to forge meaningful coalitions, and it means recognizing which coalitions are possible and which coalitions are not. It means knowing that coalition, like unity, means the coming together of whole, self-actualized human beings, focused and believing, not fragmented automatons marching to a prescribed step. It means fighting despair.

And in the university, that is certainly no easy task, for each one of you by virtue of your being here will be deluged by opportunities to misname yourselves, to forget who you are, to forget where your real interests lie. Make no mistake, you will be courted; and nothing neutralizes creativity quicker than tokenism, that false sense of security fed by a myth of individual solutions. To paraphrase Malcolm—a Black woman attorney driving a Mercedes through Avenue Z in Brooklyn is still a "nigger bitch," two words which never seem to go out of style.

You do not have to be me in order for us to fight alongside each other. I do not have to be you to recognize that our wars are the same. What we must do is commit ourselves to some future that can include each other and to work toward that future with the particular strengths of our individual identities. And in order to do this, we must allow each other our differences at the same time as we recognize our sameness.

If our history has taught us anything, it is that action for change directed only against the external conditions of our oppressions is not enough. In order to be whole, we must recognize the despair oppression plants within each of us—that thin persistent voice that says our efforts are useless, it will never change, so why bother, accept it. And we must fight that inserted piece of self-destruction that lives and flourishes like a poison inside of us, unexamined until it makes us turn upon ourselves in each other. But we can put our finger down upon that loathing buried deep within each one of us and see who it encourages us to despise, and we can lessen its potency by the knowledge of our real connectedness, arching across our differences.

Hopefully, we can learn from the 60s that we cannot afford to do our enemies' work by destroying each other.

What does it mean when an angry Black ballplayer—this happened in Illinois—curses a white heckler but pulls a knife on a Black one? What better way is there to police the streets of a minority community than to turn one generation against the other?

Referring to Black lesbians and gay men, the student president at Howard University says, on the occasion of a Gay Student Charter on campus, "The Black community has nothing to do with such filth—we will have to abandon these people." Abandon? Often without noticing, we absorb the racist belief that Black people are fitting targets for everybody's anger. We are closest to each other, and it is easier to vent fury upon each other than upon our enemies.

Of course, the young man at Howard was historically incorrect. As part of the Black community, he has a lot to do with "us." Some of our finest writers, organizers, artists and scholars in the 60s as well as today, have been lesbian and gay, and history will bear me out.

Over and over again in the 60s I was asked to justify my existence and my work, because I was a woman, because I was a Lesbian, because I was not a separatist, because some piece of me was not acceptable. Not because of my work but because of my identity. I had to learn to hold on to all the parts of me that served me, in spite of the pressure to express only one to the exclusion of all others. And I don't know

what I'd say face to face with that young man at Howard
University who says I'm filth because I identify women as
my primary source of energy and support, except to say that
it is my energy and the energy of other women very much
like me which has contributed to his being where he is at this
point. But I think he would not say it to my face because
name-calling is always easiest when it is removed, academic.
The move to render the presence of lesbians and gay men
invisible in the intricate fabric of Black existence and survival
is a move which contributes to fragmentation and weakness
in the Black community.

In academic circles, as elsewhere, there is a kind of name-
calling increasingly being used to keep young Black women
in line. Often as soon as any young Black woman begins to
recognize that she is oppressed as a woman as well as a
Black, she is called a lesbian no matter how she identifies
herself sexually. "What do you mean you don't want to make
coffee take notes wash dishes go to bed with me, you a
lesbian or something?" And at the threat of such a dreaded
taint, all too often she falls meekly into line, however
covertly. But the word lesbian is only threatening to those
Black women who are intimidated by their sexuality, or who
allow themselves to be defined by it and from outside
themselves. Black women in struggle from our own
perspective, speaking up for ourselves, sharing close ties with
one another politically and emotionally, are not the enemies
of Black men. We are Black women who seek our own
definitions, recognizing diversity among ourselves with
respect. We have been around within our communities for a
very long time, and we have played pivotal parts in the
survival of those communities: from Hat Shep Sut through
Harriet Tubman to Daisy Bates and Fannie Lou Hamer to
Lorraine Hansberry to your Aunt Maydine to some of you
who sit before me now.

In the 60s Black people wasted a lot of our substance fighting each other. We cannot afford to do that in the 80s, when Washington, D.C. has the highest infant mortality rate of any U.S. city, 60 percent of the Black community under twenty is unemployed and more are becoming unemployable, lynchings are on the increase, and less than half the registered Black voters voted in the last election.

How are you practicing what you preach—whatever you preach, and who exactly is listening? As Malcolm stressed, we are not responsible for our oppression, but we must be responsible for our own liberation. It is not going to be easy, but we have what we have learned and what we have been given that is useful. We have the power those who came before us have given us, to move beyond the place where they were standing. We have the trees, and water, and sun, and our children. Malcolm X does not live in the dry texts of his words as we read them; he lives in the energy we generate and use to move along the visions we share with him. We are making the future as well as bonding to survive the enormous pressures of the present, and that is what it means to be a part of history.

PART TWO

CONTENDING FOR EQUALITY: THE STRUGGLE FOR WOMEN'S RIGHTS AND PROGRESS

Chronology and Publication History of Speeches

Maria W. Stewart, "What If I Am A Woman?" 1833. Delivered before her friends in Boston on 21 September 1833; Published in transcript of *What If I Am A Woman* by Folkway Records (1977).

Sojourner Truth, "Woman's Rights." 1851. Delivered before the Woman's Rights Convention in Akron, Ohio; published in Volume 1 of *History of Woman Suffrage*, edited by E. C. Stanton, S. B. Anthony, and M. Gage (1887).

Sojourner Truth, "When Woman Gets Her Rights Man Will Be Right." 1867. Delivered at the annual meeting of the American Equal Rights Association in New York City in May of 1967; published in *National Anti-Slavery Standard* (1 June 1867).

Lucy Laney, "The Burden of the Educated Colored Woman." 1899. Delivered at the third Hampton Negro Conference in Virginia; published in *Proceedings of Hampton Negro Conference*, (July 1899). Courtesy of Hampton University Archives.

Fanny J. Coppin, "A Plea For Industrial Opportunity." N.D. Delivered circa the end of the nineteenth century at a fair in Philadelphia; published in Alice Moore Dunbar's *Masterpieces Of Negro Eloquence* (1914).

Georgia Washington, "The Condition Of The Women In The Rural Districts of Alabama: What Is Being Done To Remedy That Condition." 1902. Delivered at the Hampton Negro Conference and published in the Conference *Proceedings* (July 1902). Courtesy of Hampton University Archives.

Fannie Barrier Williams, "The Problem Of Employment For Negro Women." 1903. Delivered at the Hampton Negro Conference and published in the Conference *Proceedings* (July 1903). Courtesy of Hampton University Archives.

Mary Church Terrell, "The Progress Of Negro Women." 1904. Delivered before the Congregational Association of Maryland and the District of Columbia; published in *The Voice Of The Negro* (July 1904).

Mary McLeod Bethune, "A Century of Progress Of Negro Women." 1933. Delivered in Chicago before the Chicago Women's Federation on 30 June 1933. Typescript in Mary McLeod Bethune papers at Amistad Research Center at Tulane University, New Orleans, Louisiana.

Shirley Chisholm, "For The Equal Rights Amendment." 1970. Delivered on 10 August 1970 to the United States House of Representatives; published in the *Congressional Record* (91st Congress, 2nd Session).

Angela Davis, "Let Us All Rise Together: Radical Perspectives On Empowerment For Afro-American Women." 1987. Delivered at Spelman College in Atlanta, Georgia on 25 June 1987; published in *Harvard Educational Review* 25.3 (August 1988) under the title "Radical Perspectives On Empowerment For Afro-American Women" and in Davis's *Women, Culture, and Politics* (1989).

Alice Walker, "The Right To Life: What Can The White Man Say To The Black Woman?" 1989. Delivered before the Pro-Choice/Keep Abortion Legal Rally at the Mayflower Hotel, Washington, D. C.; published in Walker's *Her Blue Body Everything We Know: Earthling Poems 1965-1990* (1991).

Introduction to Part Two

African American women have actively engaged in the struggle for equal rights since the inception of the women's movement in the nineteenth century. No less vigorously than did Susan B. Anthony and Elizabeth Cady Stanton, they joined in the protracted struggle for women's suffrage and efforts that led eventually to the passage of the Nineteenth Amendment. Ironically, the passage of that amendment yielded no political benefits for women of color. Giddings describes the results of the movement: " . . . the suffrage amendment was finally ratified by two thirds of the states, making this country the twenty-second nation to enfranchise women. But Black women understood that for them, the struggle to be able to cast their votes was just beginning . . particularly in the South . . . " (Giddings, *when* 164). Educational tests and other restrictions placed upon women of color rendered the nineteenth amendment essentially meaningless.

Speeches selected for inclusion in "Contending for Equality" represent an amalgam of concerns affecting the dignity and progress of African American women. The speeches span more than a century, the first one delivered in 1833 and the last one included in this section presented in 1989. The women's struggle, as did the race struggle, suffered numerous reversals. Thus, in many instances, the speeches of the latter years differ little in substance and intensity from those of the late nineteenth and early twentieth century. Overall, however, they encompass the evolving aspirations of a group working under what Mary Church Terrell termed "the double cross," the burdens of both race and gender.

The atmosphere of the 1830s is evident in Maria Stewart's "What If I Am A Woman?" delivered in 1833. Stewart uses

Biblical and historical examples to document the centrality of women in major movements and causes. She emphasizes the possibilities for women in rendering more concrete the promise of America. Although Stewart's public career was cut short by public protest based on her gender, she argued eloquently for the cause of women. Another speech, delivered late in the nineteenth century, deplores the limitations placed on women and the possible benefits to be gained through liberation and fair treatment. Sojourner Truth's "When Woman Gets Her Rights Man Will Be Right," delivered in 1867, is an affirmation of the potential of women and a declaration of her commitment to contend for equality.

Three speeches in this section emphasize the issue of access and make appeals for an improved status for African American women. In 1899 Lucy C. Laney addressed the Annual Hampton Conference exploring the responsibilities devolving upon educated women of color. In "The Burden Of The Educated Colored Woman," Laney enumerated the challenges confronting the more fortunate African American women in elevating the masses through actions extending opportunities to those who lacked the advantages of those to whom she spoke. Fanny Jackson Coppin in "A Plea For Industrial Opportunity" delivered in the late nineteenth century and Georgia Washington in "The Condition Of Women In The Rural Districts Of Alabama" delivered in 1902 both addressed efforts designed to improve the quality of life for women of the race.

Coppin emphasized industrial education, valuing productive service more than prestige in relation to employment opportunities. Espousing an emphasis that was not universally accepted, she sought to demonstrate how, through self-help and industry, African Americans in general could achieve greater dignity and economic independence. Although Coppin's address concerns African Americans of both sexes, it is included under women's rights and progress because the tone of her address assumes equal interest in meaningful employment on the part of women. At this time in history, such an assumption was indeed noteworthy and represents a significant advancement in women's quest for equality and dignity. In her speech, Washington enumerated positive efforts underway to remedy the pathetic condition of women in rural Alabama, citing the success of the People's Village School in Mt. Meigs, Alabama, and outreach programs designed to elevate the standard of living and enhance the future prospects of women in this area of the country.

Another speech with thematic similarity to Coppin's and Washington's speeches is "The Problem Of Employment For Negro Women" delivered by Fannie Barrier Williams in 1903 before the Hampton Conference. Willams attempted to confer dignity on domestic work and urged women of color to prepare diligently for opportunities in this occupation. Emphasizing the monopoly that African American women currently held in the area of domestic work, Williams challenged them to take pride in their duties and establish a reputation for the occupation that would not penalize or ostracize socially the women who chose domestic service as a satisfying and an honorable occupation.

The year following Williams' speech, Mary Church Terrell in "The Progress Of Colored Women" gave an optimistic account of the gains made by African American women. Terrell challenged unfavorable stereotypes by identifying successful women of color and enumerating the diverse areas in which women of color excelled. Her presentation is revelatory of the versatility and perseverance demonstrated by women of the race, the burden of the double cross rendering their achievements even more spectacular.

More than two decades later, Mary McLeod Bethune continued this adulatory pattern. In a speech entitled "A

Century of Progress Of Negro Women" delivered in 1933, Bethune chronicled the evolving respectability earned by women of the race. She cited a range of activities and efforts that demonstrate the elevation of women of color. The progress made by these women, Bethune argued, should be measured by the obstacles overcome on their journey to a more satisfying and respectable status. Her claim of the African American woman as one of the "modern miracles of the New World" received confirmation in her enumeration of their achievements.

Although movements initiated during intervening decades produced significant gains for women, several factors affected their efforts. Alarming sociological factors creating more demands impinged on the prospects of African American women, and the chaotic alliance with white women in the feminist movement illuminated the peculiar plight of women of color in this country. In addition, a divisive gender battle between men and women of color further complicated the struggle of women toward the elusive equality so vigorously pursued by the group.

Shirley Chisholm's "For The Equal Rights Amendment," delivered in 1970, explicated the prejudice and bias militating against the progress of women. Her primary challenge was that the country complete the task left undone by the founding fathers and confer upon women an equality commensurate with their contributions and basic human rights. And the concluding speech analyzed in this section, Angela Davis' "Let Us All Rise Together," outlined one of the forces deferring empowerment for women. Noting the similarity between racial and gender bias, she called for multiracial unity as a corrective to the divisive forces that threatened empowerment.

Two speeches presented in this section without analysis typify the nature and duration of women's struggle for equality. One of these works is Sojourner Truth's 1851 speech, known variously as "Woman's Rights" or "And Ain't I A Woman?" Often referred to as the first truly feminist address by a woman of color, "And Ain't I a Woman?" challenges the stereotypes invoked to keep women in their places. The address, delivered in compelling colloquial language, demonstrates the courage and insight of this pioneer in the area of equal rights for women. Another speech included in this section provides some appreciation for the texture of efforts designed to secure and maintain empowerment for women. Alice Walker's compelling address before a pro-choice rally in Washington, D. C. on 8 April 1989, "The Right To Life: What Can The White Man Say To The Black Woman?" is an emotionally moving address, eloquently argued by the Pulitzer prize winning novelist, poet, and essayist. The speeches in this section dramatize effectively the character and essence of women's efforts in contending for equality. As with the struggle of the race, women's struggle for equality has been uneven and fraught with reversals. The speeches reveal as well the often disparate themes attending this struggle, but the unity of purpose remains intact. Across time, women have contended for equality of treatment and opportunity, an ideal that remains elusive. But, as the addresses clearly indicate, the perseverance and commitment of women of all classes and interests have not declined with time or with acceptance as joint heirs of America's opportunities and promise.

Introduction to Maria W. Stewart's
"What If I Am A Woman?"

"What If I Am A Woman?" speaks to the historical and current influence of women. Beginning with Biblical examples, Maria Stewart catalogues the contributions of women across time. She uses this cataloguing of illustrious women to support her thesis that influential women can again come to the forefront in participation and leadership. The speaker uses an historical perspective to document the initiative and courage characterizing women of various localities and eras. Her address is essentially an affirmation of the possibilities of women and an articulation of the belief that future contributions are not only possible but probable.

Maria Stewart was born in Hartford, Connecticut in 1803. Her education was limited essentially to what she learned in the Sabbath Schools, yet she attained a sophistication that lent eloquence and wisdom to her espousal of race and gender rights. After leaving the public speaking scene, Stewart taught black children in Baltimore, New York, and Washington, D. C. She died in Washington, D. C. in 1879.

This address is Stewart's farewell one. Dorothy Sterling refers to the hostility directed toward Stewart, particularly after she began to speak out in behalf of women's rights. Opposition to her speaking could be categorized as inevitable since women of that time were not expected to speak publicly. Although Stewart is leaving her public speaking career behind her, she eloquently defends the right of women to speak.

What If I Am A Woman?
Maria W. Stewart
1833

To begin my subject. "Ye have heard that it hath been said whoso is angry with his brother without cause shall be in danger of the judgment; and whoso shall say to his brother Raca, shall be in danger of the council. But whosoever shall say, thou fool, shall be in danger of hell fire." For several years my heart was in continual sorrow. Then I cried unto the Lord my troubles. And thus for wise and holy purposes best known to himself, he has raised me in the midst of my enemies to vindicate my wrongs before this people, and to reprove them for sin as I have reasoned to them of righteousness and judgment to come. "For as the heavens are higher than the earth, so are his ways above our ways, and his thoughts above our thoughts. I believe, that for wise and holy purposes best known to himself, he hath unloosed my tongue and put his word into my mouth in order to confound and put all those to shame that rose up against me. For he hath clothed my face with steel and lined my forehead with brass. He hath put his testimony within me and engraven his seal on my forehead. And with these weapons I have indeed set the fiends of earth and hell at defiance."

What if I am a woman; is not the God of ancient times the God of these modern days? Did he not raise up Deborah to be a mother and a judge in Israel? Did not Queen Esther save the lives of the Jews? And Mary Magdalene first declare the resurrection of Christ from the dead?

Again: Holy women ministered unto Christ and the apostles; and women of refinement in all ages, more or less, have had a voice in moral, religious, and political subjects.

Again: Why the Almighty hath imparted unto me the power
of speaking thus I cannot tell.

But to convince you of the high opinion that was formed
of the capacity and ability of woman by the ancients, I would
refer you to "Sketches of the Fair Sex." Read to the fifty-first
page, and you will find that several of the northern nations
imagined that women could look into futurity, and that they
had about them an inconceivable something approaching to
divinity. A belief that the Deity more readily communicates
himself to women, has at one time or other prevailed in every
quarter of the earth: not only among the Germans and the
Britons, but all the people of Scandinavia were possessed of
it. Among the Greeks, women delivered the oracles. The
respect the Romans paid to the Sybils is well known. The
Jews had their prophetesses. The prediction of the Egyptian
women obtained much credit at Rome, even unto the
emperors. And in most barbarous nations all things that have
the appearance of being supernatural, the mysteries of
religion, the secrets of physic, and the rights of magic, were
in the possession of women.

If such women as are here described have once existed, be
no longer astonished, then, my brethren and friends, that God
at this eventful period should raise up your own females to
strive by their example, both in public and private, to assist
those who are endeavoring to stop the strong current of
prejudice that flows so profusely against us at present. No
longer ridicule their efforts; it will be counted for sin. For
God makes use of feeble means sometimes to bring about his
most exalted purposes.

In the fifteenth century, the general spirit of this period is
worthy of observation. We might then have seen women
preaching and mixing themselves in controversies. Women
occupying the chairs of philosophy and justice; women
haranguing in Latin before the Pope; women writing in Greek

and studying in Hebrew; we were poetesses and women of quality divine. Women in those days devoted their leisure hours to contemplation and study.) The religious spirit which has animated women in all ages showed itself at this time. It has made them, by turns, martyrs, apostles, warriors, and concluded in making them divines and scholars.

Why cannot a religious spirit animate us now? Why cannot we become divines and scholars? Although learning is somewhat requisite, yet recollect that those great apostles, Peter and James, were ignorant and unlearned. They were taken from the fishing-boat, and made fishers of men.

In the thirteenth century, a young lady of Bologne devoted herself to the study of the Latin language and of the laws. At the age of twenty-three she pronounced a funeral oration in Latin in the great church of Bologne; and to be admitted as an orator, she had neither need of indulgence on account of her youth or of her sex. At the age of twenty-six she took the degree of doctor of laws, and began publicly to expound the Institutes of Justinian. At the age of thirty-four, her great reputation raised her to a chair (where she taught the law to a prodigious concourse of scholars from all nations.) She joined the charms and accomplishments of a woman to all the knowledge of a man. And such was the power of her eloquence, that her beauty was only admired when her tongue was silent.

What if such women as are here described should rise among our sable race? And it is not impossible, for it is not the color of the skin that makes the man or the woman, but the principle formed in the soul. Brilliant wit will shine, come from whence it will; and genius and talent will not hide the brightness of its lustre.

Woman's Rights
Sojourner Truth
1851

Wall, chilern, whar dar is so much racket dar must be somethin' out of' kilter. I tink dat 'twixt de niggers of de Souf and de womin at de Norf, all talkin' 'bout rights, de white men will be in a fix pretty soon. But what's all dis here talkin' 'bout?

Dat man ober dar say dat womin needs to be helped into carriages and lifted ober ditches, and to hab de best place everywhar. Nobody eber helps me into carriages, or ober mud puddles, or gibs me any best place! And a'n't I a woman? Look at my arm! I have ploughed, and planted and gathered into barns, and no man could head me! And a'n't I a woman? I could work as much and eat as much as a man—when I could get it—and bear de lash as well! And a'n't I a woman? I have borne thirteen chilern, and seen 'em mos' all sold off to slavery, and when I cried out with my mother's grief, none but Jesus heard me! And a'n't I a woman?

Den dey talks 'bout dis ting in de head; what dis dey call it? ('Intellect," whispered some one near.) Dat's it, honey. What dat got to do wid womin's rights or nigger's rights? If my cup won't hold but a pint, and yourn holds a quart, wouldn't ye be mean not to let me have my little half-measure full?

Den dat little man in black dar, he say women can't have as much rights as men, 'cause Christ wan't a woman! Whar did your Christ come from? Whar did your Christ come from? From God and a woman! Man had nothin' to do wid Him!

If de fust woman God ever made was strong enough to turn de world upside down all alone, dese women togedder (and she glanced her eye over the platform) ought to be able

157

to turn it back, and get it right side up again! And now dey is asking to do it, de men better let 'em.

Introduction to Sojourner Truth's
"When Woman Gets Her Rights Man Will Be Right"

"When Woman Gets Her Rights Man Will Be Right" is a moving explication, rendered in colloquial language, of the social and economic advantages separating men from women. Sojourner Truth discusses her commitment to contend for equal rights for women and suggests that her role in the struggle is somehow preordained. More than eighty years old at the time this speech was delivered, Truth comments, "But I suppose I am kept here because something remains for me to do; I suppose I am yet to help break the chain." She offers commentary on women's limited legal rights, restrictions that prevent them from voting, discrepancies between women's occupational opportunities in relation to those for men, and unequal pay for comparable work. She closes with an emotional exhortation to women: "Be strong women! Blush not! Tremble not! I want you to keep a good faith and good courage." She then reiterates her own determination to pursue the struggle for human rights and equality.

Sojourner Truth was born Isabella Baumfree around 1797. Born a slave, she was emancipated by New York State Law in 1827. According to her own testimony, she heard "voices" in 1843 instructing her to change her name and was known thereafter as Sojourner Truth. Harriet Beecher Stowe offered the following description of this influential woman who never learned to read or write: "I do not recollect ever to have been conversant with any one who had more of that silent and subtle power which we call personal presence than this person . . . She seemed perfectly self-possessed and at her ease; in fact there was almost an unconscious superiority, not unmixed with a solemn twinkle of humor in the odd composed manner in which she looked down on me . . . " (Sterling 1984, 150).

"When Woman Gets Her Rights Man Will Be Right" was delivered before the National Convention of the American Equal Rights Association on 9 May 1867. The group met at the Church of the Puritans in New York. Sojourner Truth was an activist in more than one dimension of the social-political struggle. She raised money and assembled clothing for African American men who volunteered for duty in the Civil War. In addition, she took many speaking tours across the country. Judith Anderson notes that "interwoven in her central message were appeals for black rights, women suffrage, and temperance" (Anderson 1984, 197). Truth died on 26 November 1883.

When Woman Gets Her Rights Man Will Be Right
Sojourner Truth
1867

My Friends, I am rejoiced that you are glad, but I don't know how you will feel when I get through. I come from another field—the country of the slave. They have got their rights—so much good luck. Now what is to be done about it? I feel that I have got as much responsibility as anybody else. I have as good rights as anybody. There is a great stir about colored men getting their rights, but not a word about the colored women; and if colored men get their rights, and not colored women get theirs, there will be a bad time about it. So I am for keeping the thing going while things are stirring; because if we wait till it is still, it will take a great while to get it going again. White women are a great deal smarter and know more than colored women, while colored women do not know scarcely anything. They go out washing, which is about as high as a colored woman gets, and their men go about idle, strutting up and down; and when the women come home, they ask for their money and take it all, and then scold because there is no food. I want you to consider on that, chil'n. I want women to have their rights. In the courts women have no right, no voice; nobody speaks for them. I wish woman to have her voice there among the pettifoggers. If it is not a fit place for women, it is unfit for men to be there. I am above eighty years old; it is about time for me to be going. But I suppose I am kept here because something remains for me to do; I suppose I am yet to help break the chain. I have done a great deal of work—as much as a man, but did not get so much pay. I used to work in the field and bind grain, keeping up with the cradler; but men never doing no more, got twice as much pay. So with the German women. They work in the field and do as much work, but do not get the pay. We do as much, we eat as much, we want as much. I suppose I am about the only colored woman that goes about to speak for the rights of the colored woman, I want to keep the thing stirring, now that the ice is broken. What we want is a little money. You men know that you get as much again as women when you write, or for what you do. When we get our rights, we shall not have to come to you for money, for then we shall have money enough of our own. It is a good consolation to know that when we have got this we shall not be coming to you any more. You have been having our right so long, that you think, like a slaveholder, that you own us. I know that it is hard for one who has held the reins for so long to give up; it cuts like a knife. It will feel all better when it closes up again. I have been in Washington about three years, seeing about those colored people. Now colored men have a right to vote; and what I want is to have colored women have the right to vote. There ought to be equal rights more than ever, since colored people have got their freedom.

I know that it is hard for men to give up entirely. They must run in the old track. I was amused how men speak up for one another. They cannot bear that a woman should say anything about the man, but they will stand here and take up the time in man's cause. But we are going, tremble or no tremble. Men are trying to help us. I know that all—the spirit they have got; and they cannot help us much until some of the spirit is taken out of them that belongs among the women. Men have got their rights, and women has not got their rights. That is the trouble. When woman gets her rights man will be right. How beautiful that will be. Then It will be peace on earth and good will to men. But it cannot be until it be right . . . It will come . . . Yes, it will come quickly. It must come. And now when the waters is troubled, and now is the time to step into the pool. There is a great deal now with the minds, and now is the time to start forth . . . The great fight was to keep the rights of the poor colored people. That made a great battle. And now I hope that this will be the last battle that will be in the world. Let us finish up so that there be no more fighting. I have faith in God and there is truth in humanity. Be strong women! Blush not! Tremble not! I want you to keep a good faith and good courage. And I am going round after I get my business settled and get more equality. People in the North, I am going round to lecture on human rights. I will shake every place I go to.

Introduction to Lucy C. Laney's
"The Burden Of The Educated Colored Woman"

"The Burden of the Educated Colored Woman" is Lucy C. Laney's analysis of the societal responsibilities incumbent on women of color. In the speech, she recounts the evolving status of the African American woman since 1620, differentiating between the privileged few and the masses. She addresses the legacy of marriage as an institution in the African American community and analyzes the circumstances that militated against stability and moral purity in its strictest form. The address contains an enumeration of the tasks that should engage the energies of the women and concludes with a series of rhetorical questions implicitly eliciting the commitment of African American women to take social responsibility for the "burdens" that only women of their caliber could address.

Paula Giddings presents a short biographical sketch of Lucy C. Laney, a member of Atlanta University's first graduating class. Laney's father, a minister, "purchased his own and his wife's manumission from slavery." In 1886 Laney established the Haines Normal and Industrial School and operated the school for more than half a century. An instructive segment of information about Laney also appears in *Portraits Of Color*: "Everybody knows of Booker T. Washington and of how he went from Hampton Institute in 1883 and founded a school for Negroes at Tuskegee. But only a few know that three years later Lucy Laney, graduate of Atlanta University, started in Augusta, Georgia, what was to be known as Haines Institute, a secondary school for Negro boys and girls" (*Portraits* 53). Laney's school had a greater academic emphasis than did Tuskegee at the time because of her perceived need for thorough preparation for college. The author of *Portraits Of Color* describes Laney and her efforts:

165

" . . . when Lucy Laney, dark-skinned, stocky, with cropped hair and plain dress, taught her class to decline Latin nouns and conjugate Latin verbs, she was regarded as foolish and obstinate. But this did not alter her purpose. She knew the value of the education she had had at Atlanta, and she knew also how extremely difficult it was for colored boys and girls in the South to prepare for college" (*Portraits* 54).

The speech considered here was delivered at the third Hampton Negro Conference. Cynthia Neverdon-Morton recounts the history of the Hampton Negro Conferences, noting their inception and objectives. She writes that "Beginning in 1897, annual conferences brought together Hampton graduates and others to consider the plight of Afro-Americans as a race and to suggest ways to further their collective goals" (Neverdon-Morton 1989, 112). Morton discusses the separate meetings of men and women at these conferences and comments on the restrictive effects of the separate meetings, speculating that "the invisible wall assumed to exist between men's and women's duties kept the two groups from working together on causes of direct importance to both" (Neverdon-Morton 1989, 113).

The Burden Of The Educated Colored Woman
Lucy C. Laney
1899

If the educated colored woman has a burden,—and we believe she has—what is that burden? How can it be lightened, how may it be lifted? What it is can be readily seen perhaps better than told, for it constantly annoys to irritation; it bulges out as did the load of Bunyan's Christian—ignorance—with its inseparable companions, shame and crime and prejudice.

That our position may be more readily understood, let us refer to the past; and it will suffice for our purpose to begin with our coming to America in 1620, since prior to that time, we claim only heathenism. During the days of training in our first mission school—slavery—that which is the foundation of right training and good government, the basic rock of all true culture—the home, with its fire-side training, mother's moulding, woman's care, was not only neglected but utterly disregarded. There was no time in the institution for such teaching. We know that there were, even in the first days of that school, isolated cases of men and women of high moral character and great intellectual worth, as Phillis Wheatley, Sojourner Truth, and John Chavers, whose work and lives should have taught, or at least suggested to their instructors, the capabilities and possibilities of their dusky slave pupils. The progress and the struggles of these for noble things should have led their instructors to see how the souls and minds of this people then yearned for light—the real life. But alas! these dull teachers, like many modern pedagogues and school-keepers, failed to know their pupils—to find out their real needs, and hence had no cause to study methods of better and best development of the boys and girls under their care. What other result could come from such training or want of training than a conditioned race such as we now have?

For two hundred and fifty years they married, or were given in marriage. Oft times marriage ceremonies were performed for them by the learned minister of the master's church; more often there was simply a consorting by the master's consent, but it was always understood that these unions for cause, or without cause, might be more easily broken, than a divorce can be obtained in Indiana or Dakota. Without going so long a distance as from New York to Connecticut, the separated could take other companions for life, for a long or short time; for during those two hundred and fifty years there was not a single marriage legalized in a single southern state, where dwelt the mass of this people. There was something of the philosopher in the plantation preacher, who, at the close of the marriage ceremony, had the dusky couple join their right hands, and then called upon the assembled congregation to sing, as he lined it out, "Plunged in a gulf of dark despair," for well he knew the sequel of many such unions. If it so happened that a husband and wife were parted by those who owned them, such owners often consoled those thus parted with the fact that he could get another wife; she, another husband. Such was the sanctity of the marriage vow that was taught and held for over two hundred and fifty years. Habit is indeed second nature. This is the race inheritance. I thank God not of all, for we know, each of us, of instances, of holding most sacred the plighted love and keeping faithfully and sacredly the marriage vows. We know of pure homes and of growing old together. Blessed heritage! If we only had the gold there might be many "Golden Weddings." Despair not; the crushing burden of immorality which has its root in the disregard of the marriage vow, can be lightened. It must be, and the educated colored woman can and will do her part in lifting this burden.

In the old institution there was no attention given to homes and to home-making. Homes were only places in which to sleep, father had neither responsibility nor authority; mother, neither cares nor duties. She wielded no gentle sway nor influence. The character of their children was a matter of no concern to them; surroundings were not considered. It is true, house cleaning was sometimes enforced as a protection to property, but this was done at stated times and when ordered. There is no greater enemy of the race than these untidy and filthy homes; they bring not only physical disease and death, but they are very incubators of sin; they bring intellectual and moral death. The burden of giving knowledge and bringing about the practice of the laws of hygiene among a people ignorant of the laws of nature and common decency, is not a slight one. But this, too, the intelligent women can and must help to carry.

The large number of young men in the state prison is by no means the least of the heavy burdens. It is true that many of these are unjustly sentenced; that longer terms of imprisonment are given Negroes than white persons for the same offences; it is true that white criminals by the help of attorneys, money, and influence, oftener escape the prison, thus keeping small the number of prisoners recorded, for figures never lie. It is true that many are tried and imprisoned for trivial causes, such as the following, clipped from the *Tribune*, of Elberyon, Ga.: "Seven or eight Negroes were arrested and tried for stealing two fish-hooks last week. When the time of our courts is wasted in such a manner as this, it is high time to stop and consider whither we are driving. Such picaunyish cases reflect on the intelligence of a community. It is fair to say the courts are not to blame in this matter." Commenting on this, *The South Daily* says: "We are glad to note that the sentiment of the paper is against the injustice. Nevertheless these statistics will form the basis of some lecturer's discourse." This fact remains, that many of our youth are in prison, that large numbers of our young men are serving out long terms of imprisonment, and this is a very sore burden. Five years ago while attending a Teacher's Institute at Thomasville, Georgia, I saw working on the streets in the chain gang, with rude men and ruder women, with ignorant, wicked, almost naked men, criminals, guilty of all the sins named in the decalogue, a large number of boys from ten to fifteen years of age, and two young girls between the ages of twelve and sixteen. It is not necessary that prison statistics be quoted, for we know too well the story, and we feel most sensibly this burden, the weight of which will sink us unless it is at once made lighter and finally lifted.

Last, but not least, is the burden of prejudice, heavier in that it is imposed by the strong, those from whom help, not hindrance, should come. They are making the already heavy burden of their victims heavier to bear, and yet they are commanded by One who is even the Master of all: "Bear ye one another's burdens, and thus fulfill the law." This is met with and must be borne everywhere. In the South, in public conveyances, and at all points of race contact; in the North, in hotels, at the baptismal pool, in cemeteries; everywhere, in some shape or form, it is to be borne. No one suffers under the weight of this burden as the educated Negro woman does; and she must help to lift it.

Ignorance and immorality, if they are not the prime causes, have certainly intensified prejudice. The forces to lighten and finally to lift this and all of these burdens are true culture and character, linked with that most substantial coupler, cash. We said in the beginning that the past can serve no further purpose than to give us our present bearings. It is a condition that confronts us. With this we must deal, it is this we must change. The physician of today inquires into the history of his patient, but he has to do especially with diagnosis and cure. We know the history; we think a correct diagnosis has often been made—let us attempt a cure. We would prescribe:

homes—better homes, clean homes, pure homes; schools—better schools; more culture; more thrift; and work in large doses; put the patient at once on this treatment and continue through life. Can woman do this work? She can; and she must do her part, and her part is by no means small.

Nothing in the present century is more noticeable than the tendency of women to enter every hopeful field of wage earning and philanthropy, and attempt to reach a place in every intellectual arena. Women are by nature fitted for teaching very young children; their maternal instinct makes them patient and sympathetic with their charges. Negro women of culture, as kindergartners and primary teachers, have a rare opportunity to lend a hand to the lifting of these burdens, for here they may instill lessons of cleanliness, truthfulness, loving kindness, love for nature, and love for Nature's God. Here they may daily start aright hundreds of our children; here, too, they may save years of time in the education of the child; and may save many lives from shame and crime by applying the law of prevention. In the kindergarten and primary school is the salvation of the race.

For children of both sexes from six to fifteen years of age, women are more successful as teachers than men. This fact is proven by their employment. Two-thirds of the teachers in the public schools of the United States are women. It is the glory of the United States that good order and peace are maintained not by a large, standing army of well trained soldiers, but by the sentiment of her citizens, sentiments implanted and nourished by her well trained army of four hundred thousand school teachers, two-thirds of whom are women.

The educated Negro woman, the woman of character and culture, is needed in the schoolroom not only in the kindergarten, and in the primary and the secondary school; but she is needed in high school, the academy, and the college. Only those of character and culture can do successful lifting, for she who would mould character must herself possess it. Not alone in the schoolroom can the intelligent woman lend a lifting hand, but as a public lecturer she may give advice, helpful suggestions, and important knowledge that will change a whole community and start its people on the upward way. To be convinced of the good that can be done for humanity by this means one need only recall the names of Lucy Stone, Mary Livermore, Frances Harper, Frances Willard and Julia Ward Howe. The refined and noble Negro woman may lift much with this lever. Women may also be most helpful as teachers of sewing schools and cooking classes, not simply in the public schools and private institutions, but in classes formed in neighborhoods that sorely need this knowledge. Through these classes girls who are not in school may be reached; and through them something may be done to better their homes, and inculcate habits of neatness and thrift. To bring the influence of the schools to bear upon these homes is the most needful thing of the hour. Often teachers who have labored most arduously, conscientiously, and intelligently have become discouraged on seeing that society had not been benefited, but sometimes positively injured by the conduct of their pupils.

The work of the schoolroom has been completely neutralized by the training of the home. Then we must have better homes, and better homes mean better mothers, better fathers, better born children. Emerson says, "To the well-born child all the virtues are natural, not painfully acquired."

But "The temporal life which is not allowed to open into the eternal life becomes corrupt and feeble even in its temporalness." As a teacher in the Sabbath School, as a leader in young people's meetings and missionary societies, in women's societies and Bible classes our cultured women are needed to do a great and blessed work. Here they may cause many budding lives to open into eternal life. Froebel urged teachers and parents to see to the blending of the temporal and divine life when he said, "God created man in his own image; therefore man should create and bring forth like God." The young people are ready and anxiously await intelligent leadership in Christian work. The less fortunate women, already assembled in churches, are ready for work. Work they do and work they will; that it may be effective work, they need the help and leadership of their more favored sisters.

A few weeks ago this country was startled by the following telegram of southern women of culture sent to ex-Governor Northen of Georgia, just before he made his Boston speech: "You are authorized to say in your address tonight that the women of Georgia, realizing the great importance to both races of early moral training of the Negro race, stand ready to undertake this work when means are supplied." But more startled was the world the next day, after cultured Boston had supplied a part of the means, $20,000, to read the glaring headlines of the southern press, "Who Will Teach the Black Babies?" because some of the cultured women who had signed the telegram had declared when interviewed, that Negro women fitted for the work could not be found, and no self-respecting southern white woman would teach a colored kindergarten. Yet already in Atlanta, Georgia, and in Athens, Georgia, southern women are at work among Negroes. There is plenty of work for all who have the proper conception of the teacher's office, who know that all men are brothers, God being their common father. But the educated Negro women must teach the "Black Babies;" she must come forward and inspire our men and boys to make a successful onslaught upon sin, shame, and crime.

The burden of the educated colored woman is not diminished by the terrible crimes and outrages that we daily hear of, but by these very outrages and lawlessness her burdens are greatly increased.

Somewhere I read a story, that in one of those western cities built in a day, the half-dozen men of the town labored to pull a heavy piece of timber to the top of a building. They pushed and pulled hard to no purpose, when one of the men on the top shouted to those below: "Call the women." They called the women; the women came; they pushed; soon the timber was seen to move, and ere long it was in the desired place. Today not only the men on top call, but a needy race,—the whole world, calls loudly to the cultured Negro women to come to the rescue. Do they hear? Are they coming? Will they push?

Introduction to Fanny Jackson Coppin's "A Plea for Industrial Opportunity"

"A Plea for Industrial Opportunity" speaks to the possibilities within the African American community for economic independence through trades and vocational skills. The speaker extols the benefits of self help, which she characterizes as "the best help that any man can have next to God's" (Par. 1). She criticizes the preference among African Americans for the more prestigious professions, teaching and preaching, when more practical and immediate benefits derive from industrial preparation.

Central to Coppin's plan is co-operative effort that would expand the opportunities and more clearly reflect the race's diversity of talent. Coppin assures no expectation of preference on the part of African Americans; rather, her appeal is for opportunities in business and industry inasmuch as previous efforts, and indeed the occasion which her speech celebrates, is adequate confirmation of the African American's ability to produce.

The occasion of her address was a fair held in Philadelphia in the interest of the *Christian Recorder*, a weekly publication of the African Methodist Episcopal Church initiated in 1847 as the *Christian Herald*. Coppin used the occasion to argue her case for industrial education, an emphasis that traditionally failed to gain unanimous acceptance by African Americans. Cynthia Nerverdon-Morton cites a rationale offered by some proponents of industrial education". . . "Some Africans asserted that an educational focus other than trades would cause Afro-Americans to lose respect for public officials, labor, and the home" (Neverdon-Morton 1989, 113).

Coppin's views seem to differ little from the views articulated by Booker T. Washington: "I would set no limits to the attainments of the Negro in arts, in letters or statesmanship, but I believe the surest way to reach those ends is by laying the foundation in the little things of life that lie immediately about one's door. I plead for industrial education and development for the Negro not because I want to cramp him, but because I want to free him. I want to see him enter the all-powerful business and commercial world" (Franklin 1980, 286).

Fanny Jackson Coppin was born a slave in Washington, D. C. in 1837. She graduated from Rhode Island State Normal School in 1860, having been purchased by an aunt "and sent to live with another aunt in Massachusetts" (Sterling 1984, 203). She later graduated from Oberlin College and served as Principal of the Institute for Colored Youth in Philadelphia from 1869 until 1902. The speaker was a persistent advocate of industrial education and, in a letter to Frederick Douglass in 1876, explained the nature of her motivation in behalf of African American youth. "I feel sometimes like a person to whom in childhood was entrusted some sacred flame," she wrote, "It has burned more dimly sometimes than at others, but it always has and always will, burn steadily and persistently for it will never go out but with my life" (Sterling 1984, 205).

A Plea For Industrial Opportunity
Fanny Jackson Coppin
c. 1895

The great lesson to be taught by this Fair is the value of co-operative effort to make our cents dollars, and to show us what help there is for our selves in ourselves. That the colored people of this country have enough money to materially alter their financial condition, was clearly demonstrated by the millions of dollars deposited in the Freedmen's Bank; that they have the good sense, and the unanimity to use this power, are now proved by this industrial exhibition and fair.

It strikes me that much of the recent talk about the exodus has proceeded upon the high-handed assumption that, owing largely to the credit system of the South, the colored people there are forced to the alternative, to "curse God, and die," or else "go West." Not a bit of it. The people of the South, it is true, cannot at this time produce hundreds of dollars, but they have millions of pennies; and millions of pennies make tens of thousands of dollars. By clubbing together and lumping their pennies, a fund might be raised in the cities of the South that the poorer classes might fall back upon while their crops are growing; or else, by the opening of co-operative stores, become their own creditors and so effectually rid themselves of their merciless extortioners. "Oh, they won't do anything; you can't get them united on anything!" is frequently expressed. The best way for a man to prove that he can do a thing is to do it, and that is what we have shown we can do. This fair, participated in by twenty four States in the Union, and gotten up for a purpose which is of no pecuniary benefit to those concerned in it, effectually silences all slanders about "we won't or we can't do," and teaches its own instructive and greatly needed lessons of self-help,—the best help that any man can have, next to God's.

Those in charge, who have completed the arrangements for the Fair, have studiously avoided preceding it with noisy and demonstrative babblings, which are so often the vapid precursors of promises as empty as those who make them; therefore, in some quarters, our Fair has been overlooked. It is not, we think, a presumptuous interpretation of this great movement, to say, that the voice of God now seems to utter "Speak to the people that they go forward." "Go forward" in what respect? Teach the millions of poor colored laborers of the South how much power they have in themselves, by co-operation of effort, and by a combination of their small means, to change the despairing poverty which now drives them from their homes, and makes them a mill-stone around the neck of any community, South or West. Secondly, that we shall go forward in asking to enter the same employments which other people enter. Within the past ten years we have made almost no advance in getting our youth into industrial and business occupations. It is just as hard for instance, to get a boy into a printing-office now as it was ten years ago. It is simply astonishing when we consider how many of the common vocations of life colored people are shut out of. Colored men are not admitted to the printers' trade-union, nor, with very rare exceptions, are they employed in any city of the United States in a paid capacity as printers or writers; one of the rare exceptions being the employment of H. Price Williams, on the *Sunday Press* of this city. We are not employed as salesmen or pharmacists, or saleswomen, or bank clerks, or merchants' clerks, or tradesmen, or mechanics, or telegraph operators, or to any degree as State or government officials, and I could keep on with the string of "ors" until tomorrow morning, but the patience of an audience has its limit.

Slavery made us poor, and its gloomy, malicious shadow tends to keep us so. I beg to say, kind hearers, that this is not spoken in a spirit of recrimination. We have no quarrel with our fate, and we leave your Christianity to yourselves. Our faith is firmly fixed in that "Eternal Providence," that in its own good time will "justify the ways of God to man." But, believing that to get the right men into the right places is a "consummation most devoutly to be wished," it is a matter of serious concern to us to see our youth with just as decided diversity of talent as any other people, herded together into but three or four occupations.

It is cruel to make a teacher or a preacher of a man who ought to be a printer or a blacksmith, and that is exactly the condition we are now obliged to submit to. The greatest advance that has been made since the War has been effected by political parties, and it is precisely the political positions that we think it least desirable our youth should fill. We have our choice of the professions, it is true, but, as we have not been endowed with an overwhelming abundance of brains, it is not probable that we can contribute to the bar a great lawyer except once in a great while. The same may be said of medicine; nor are we able to tide over the "starving time," between the reception of a diploma and the time that a man's profession becomes a paying one.

Being determined to know whether this industrial and business ostracism lay in ourselves or "in our stars," we have from time to time, knocked, shaken, and kicked, at these closed doors of employment. A cold, metallic voice from within replies, "We do not employ colored people." Ours not to make reply, ours not to question why. Thank heaven, we are not obliged to do and die; having the preference to do or die, we naturally prefer to do.

But we cannot help wondering if some ignorant or faithless steward of God's work and God's money hasn't blundered.

It seems necessary that we should make known to the good men and women who are so solicitous about our souls, and our minds, that we haven't quite got rid of our bodies yet, and until we do, we must feed and clothe them; and this attitude of keeping us out of work forces us back upon charity.

That distinguished thinker, Mr. Henry C. Carey, in his valuable works on political economy, has shown by the truthful and forceful logic of history, that the elevation of all peoples to a higher moral and intellectual plane, and to a fuller investiture of their civil rights, has always steadily kept pace with the improvement in their physical condition. Therefore we feel that resolutely and in unmistakable language, yet in the dignity of moderation, we should strive to make known to all men the justice of our claims to the same employments as others under the same conditions. We do not ask that any one of our people shall be put into a position because he is a colored person, but we do most emphatically ask that he shall not be kept out of a position because he is a colored person. "An open field and no favors" is all that is requested. The time was when to put a colored girl or boy behind a counter would have been to decrease custom; it would have been a tax upon the employer, and a charity that we were too proud to accept; but public sentiment has changed. I am satisfied that the employment of a colored clerk or a colored saleswoman wouldn't even be a "Nine days' wonder." It is easy of accomplishment, and yet it is not. To thoughtless and headstrong people who meet duty with impertinent dictation I do not now address myself; but to those who wish the most gracious of all blessings, a fuller enlightment as to their duty,—to those I beg to say, think of what is suggested in this appeal.

Introduction to Georgia Washington's
"The Condition of the Women
in the Rural Districts of Alabama:
What is Being Done to Remedy That Condition"

"The Condition of the Women in the Rural Districts of Alabama" is essentially a report of the hardships and restrictions confronting women of color in Mt. Meigs, near Montgomery, Alabama. Washington's establishment of the school there necessitated her continuing struggle for funds and support that would benefit the citizens of the community and ensure the best education possible for the black youngsters in that area. In her address, she emphasizes the nature and extent of efforts of the women in this section of Alabama and suggested some concrete measures that could be implemented to reward their tremendous sacrifices. She gives concrete examples of the quality of the daily existence of these women, lamenting the reality that their condition could still be compared to that of women before the war. She appealed to Tuskegee and Hampton, schools committed to her own school's philosophy of emphasis on the work ethic, closing her speech with the appeal: "We need Tuskegee's and Hampton's idea of work rooted in the hearts and minds of these young people . . . Then, and not until then will a real change take place in the condition of our women of the rural districts of Alabama."

Cynthia Neverdon-Morton in *Afro-American Women Of The South* (1989) presents the following biographical information about Georgia Washington: "Georgia Washington, former slave and an 1892 graduate of Hampton Institute, in 1893 founded a private school for black children, the People's Village School, in Mt. Meigs Village, Montgomery County, Alabama. Washington spearheaded a campaign to purchase a plantation, which was divided into lots for individual family homes and continued her efforts in education. By 1910 Mt. Meigs Village School served 800 black boys and girls, with a state supplement of $750. Teachers at the school went for several months without pay, a situation that embarrassed Washington who, nonetheless, continued to fight for funds. She often solicited assistance from Hampton Institute, her alma mater, understanding Hampton's commitment to her struggling efforts.

At 9:40 A.M. on Friday, 18 July 1902, Georgia Washington delivered "The Condition of The Colored Women in The Country Districts of Alabama" before the Hampton Negro Conference. These conferences were held annually, convening Hampton graduates and supporters to explore methods of elevating the race. The 1902 conference convened under the "general conference Division of Domestic Economy" with an emphasis on domestic science. Interest in the proceedings was sufficiently strong that the next annual conference continued the discussion of issues initiated at the 1902 conference.

The Condition of the Women
in the Rural Districts of Alabama:
What is Being Done to Remedy That Condition
Georgia Washington
1902

For nine years my interest has been centered in building a school on one of the old plantations in Montgomery county, Ala. Most of the seven hundred children who have been reached by the school during that time have come from the surrounding plantations, and the only women with whom I have come in contact have been the mothers of these children. I beg leave then to confine myself to the plantation women of my community at Mt. Meigs Village, Alabama.

Many of these women, born before the war, grew up, married the man picked out for them by master and mistress, and lived on these same old plantations. Large families of children were reared in what is called "Quarters," long distances from the "Big House," in which master and mistress lived. Some of the boys and girls were half grown before ever seeing the face of a white man. The mothers left home with their husbands to work in the fields long before it was day. Women, side by side with the men, cleared new ground, cut down big trees, rolled logs, dug ditches, plowed, hoed, and picked cotton. From those women came the mothers of the present generation.

The mother born on free soil and breathing free air, what is her condition to-day? She is on the same old plantation, perhaps still in the "Quarters." The "Big House," once owned by master and mistress, is now occupied by a dozen or more Negro families. The grandchildren of the original owners of these plantations still hold them and rent the places out to Negroes, taking the crops made for rent and food.

The women are all field hands and still leave home very early for the day's work. At noon each day the women carry home on their backs the wood to cook the dinner, the husband hurries to get under a shady tree and sleep until dinner is ready, then eats and afterward has a smoke. The wife must be ready to go back to the field with him when the noon hour is out. The house was left out of order in the morning, the cooking things scattered about the hearth just as they were used, and the few dishes on the old table are unwashed too. Where the mother takes all the children to the field, the house is locked up and the one window barred, but thanks to the builder the cracks are still there and the air will play through all day.

At dinner no time yet is given to washing dishes or making beds, so after sunset the wife brings wood to cook supper and a light-wood knot to give light. No lamps or oil are used unless some one is sick. Next the woman drags up the cow and milks, brings water for the night, then begins the supper. Perhaps the dishes will get washed for supper. After this nature overcomes the strongest and sleep is sought by all the family, in those same unmade beds or pallets.

Girls grow up in such homes, marry early and in turn make others just like them in which to rear their children. Such a woman is a real drudge, not only for her children, but for her husband, and one of the most surprising things to me is that he grows tired of her and quits, leaving six or eight children to be cared for by the mother.

The mother before the war had no time to rear children, or chance to send them to school or church. She, with the children, belonged to master body and soul. The free woman with the church, school, teachers, preachers and the Bible, what is her excuse for her present condition? This woman too has a large family of children, a worthless husband, a one-roomed log house and no kitchen. The mortgage for food and a few clothes is still made. The wife and children are worked very hard every year to pay it off. Where the family is large they are only half fed and clothed; the mother has to hustle all through the winter, in order to get anything. These people handle very little money; whenever they work by the day or month a written order is given by their employers to some store in the village, and they get their food and their clothing too on this. The great excuse of the mother is that it takes all of her time and money to get food, so she cannot educate the children, but she is trying.

The real condition of the women in the rural districts is beyond my power of description. It is worse than anything I ever heard of. There is hardly any bright side to their lives to be seen, even if we searched with a lighted candle. Within a radius of ten miles from our school, hardly a half-dozen families own their own homes.

What is being done to remedy the present condition of these women? Perhaps you will be interested to hear of some of the things attempted, and judge for yourself how far they reach the end in view.

At Mt. Meigs, and in fact all over the state, as far as I can learn, are a great many organizations, whose object is to care for the sick members and bury the dead members. Some of these societies number over two hundred members, and one in the city of Montgomery reaches over four hundred. The women outnumber the men in almost every case. Members are cared for by a good doctor when sick. He is paid from their treasury. Whenever a member dies, the whole society turns out in uniform and gives a very nice burying. These societies are kept up by a monthly fee from each member. Our women will always find money to pay these fees. Everything at home, and even church dues are sacrificed to the societies. The woman who is not a member of one of these is pitied and considered rather out of date.

The Woman's District Association is purely a Baptist church organization, and has for its object the support of Selma University, the great Baptist school of the state. Every loyal Baptist woman is a member and, however poor, is obliged to pay a monthly fee which is given entirely to this one school.

The Southern Federation of Colored Women, of which Mrs. B. T. Washington is president, is an organization devoted to the uplifting of women all over the South. This organization is made up of the federation of the several states. The State federation is made up of women's clubs, organized by leading women in both cities and rural districts all over the State. The state officers are a president, several vice presidents and other officers. The states hold an annual meeting to which delegates go from the different clubs, and carry donations. At this meeting reports are brought from the different clubs telling of work done and results. Ways are suggested for work and the organizing of clubs. The last meeting, held the third and fourth of July, 1902, at the city of Selma, was the best we have had. The Southern Federation also holds an annual meeting to which delegates from the several states go. The plan of the State Federation of Alabama is to use the money donated by clubs towards building and supporting a reformatory for boys and girls.

The club at Mt. Meigs, was made up at first of just the mothers who had children in our school, and as so was called a mothers' meeting. It was no easy task to get hold of these women, but I waked up to the fact that time was being wasted on this crowd of children who came to school each day with dirty faces, uncombed hair, ragged clothes, and that in order to get to the bottom of things I must get hold of the mothers. The mothers, on the other hand, wondered what the school-teachers wanted with them. They had never been asked to come to the schoolhouse except at closing exercises, so they decided not to come. But after repeated messages sent by the children from school, six or seven came. We talked things over together, they opened up their hearts to me. This was nine years ago, and we have been friends ever since. I found out that those mothers were dissatisfied themselves and anxious to change things at home and do better, but had no idea how or where to begin. Some of these women looked pretty rough on the outside, but strong mother-hearts beat in their bosoms, and the key-note was struck when they found out that the school was interested in helping their children in more ways than just by the lessons from their books. Their great complaint was poverty, no money to buy clothes, no way to keep those they already had whole and no time to mend or clean up the children before sending them to school in the morning. When I learned more about them I found the home was very scantily supplied with anything. They had no needles or sewing cotton, nor anything with which to mend old clothes. All the little bundles of cloth, sewing cotton, needles etc., that could be spared from our sewing room were given to the mothers for home use. Thus with a little encouragement in the way of learning for the children's sake, these mothers are trying hard, and the children who come now present a much better appearance. The mothers soon learnt how to send the children to bed early in order to wash out and dry by the fire the one set of clothes, so that the little boy with one jacket could keep clean every day. These meetings became a source of information and help. We discussed practical subjects bearing on the home life: such as the care of the children, and of the girl of sixteen; the care of the kitchen and the necessity of keeping it clean, when to wash the dishes, etc. I cannot say that a community of women was changed in one day, but they have tried and many have succeeded in making their homes much better. So many of the homes had no kitchen at all, so the women went to work, cut down the trees, rived the boards and built a queer looking room, but it held a stove and all the cooking things the family owned. On the road from Mt. Meigs to the city of Montgomery are two or three of these home-made kitchens, six by six feet. I know they are kitchens because there is a small stove pipe in the middle of each roof, from which the smoke is pouring out.

My friends, I have watched these women for nine years, and my conclusions in regard to the changes that must come about to better, in any effectual way, their condition, make me feel much discouraged.

The school, with its teachers, brought to the doors of the people of Mt. Meigs village is helping to bring about better things. The church, with its good upright pastor, is doing what it can, but back and beneath all these things is the home. First, in order to have any sort of a home for these mothers and their children, the work system for women must be changed. No woman can be a home-keeper that spends twelve hours of the day in the field. An appeal has been made for a girls' home in connection with our work, where we hope to take twenty-five girls from their homes and train them in the way of house and home-keeping. The only hope for these women and our community lies in the boys and girls who, after being trained, will return to their homes and change things. Right along with the girls the boys must be trained also, since they will be a powerful actor in changing the work system for the women. A few of the young men and women have been sent from Mt. Meigs to Hampton and Tuskegee. We hope to have them back after finishing school, to work at some trade that is needed in our community. We need Tuskegee's and Hampton's idea of work deep rooted in the hearts and minds of these young people in order that when sent back to the South, they may change the old ways of farming, gardening, raising chickens and caring for stock, so that where there is now all desert land, oases may be formed. Then, and not till then, will a real change take place in the condition of our women of the rural districts of Alabama.

Introduction to Fannie Barrier Williams's
"The Problem Of Employment For Negro Women"

"The Problem of Employment For Negro Women" emphasizes the possibilities for employment in domestic service. Williams explores realistically the social consequences of women who opted for domestic work, these consequences taking the form of ridicule and social ostracism. The speaker's challenge is that domestic service be elevated to a profession so that women of color could engage in this occupation with competence and pride. She enumerates the benefits that would redound to African American women if they would take domestic work seriously, among them the paucity of competition and the opportunity to establish an enviable reputation. Williams concludes the speech with a nine-point summary of the major emphases in her address.

Fannie Barrier Williams was born to a middle class family in Brockport, New York. She was a graduate of the New England Conservatory of music and the first woman to be appointed to Chicago's Library Board and one of the few Black members of the Chicago Women's Club. Paula Giddings quotes a statement by Fannie Barrier Williams that dramatizes Williams's perception of the strength and centrality of women in the affairs of the times: "At the very time when race interest seems at such a low ebb, when our race leaders seem tongue-tied and stupidly inactive in the presence of unchecked lawlessness and violent resistance to Negro advancement, it is especially fortunate and reassuring to see and feel the rallying spirit of our women" (Neverdon-Morton 1989, 95).

Williams delivered this address at the Hampton Negro Conference of 1903. These annual conferences, initiated in 1897, traditionally invited Hampton graduates and other prominent Americans of African descent to discuss important

191

problems confronting the race. Many of the conferences addressed the employment needs of the race as employment opportunities for African Americans were systematically limited. Cynthia Neverdon-Morton characterizes the perception of African American women at the time as "vocal, industrious, and innovative educators and social workers" (113).

The Problem of Employment for Negro Women
Fannie Barrier Williams
1903

It can be broadly said that colored women know how to
work, and have done their full share of the paid and unpaid
service rendered to the American people by the Negro race.
This is a busy world; the world's work is large, complicated,
and increasing. The demand for the competent in all kinds of
work is never fully supplied. Woman is constantly receiving
a larger share of the work to be done. The field for her skill,
her endurance, her finer instincts and faithfulness is ever
enlarging; and she has become impatient of limitations,
except those imposed by her own physical condition. In this
generalization, colored women, of course, are largely
excepted. For reasons too well understood here to be
repeated, ours is a narrow sphere. While the kinds and grades
of occupation open to all women of white complexion are
almost beyond enumeration, those open to our women are
few in number and mostly menial in quality. The girl who is
white and capable is in demand in a thousand places. The
capable Negro girl is usually not in demand. This is one of
the stubborn facts of today. Shall we waste our energy and
soul in fretting over it, or shall we bravely say "Well, what
I would do, I cannot, so I will do that which I can in the best
way I can." Thoreau said that "if people would spend half as
much effort in trying to be happy with what they have, as
they spend in wishing for what they haven't got, the world
would be far happier." It seems to me that this bit of
philosophy aptly applies to our case in this matter of
employment.

In the face of this condition, then, what can we do? To
answer this question there is required large-heartedness and
much wisdom. This answer must be worked out, not by our

women alone, but by the cooperation of the best minds and best hearts of all the people. In considering the present day opportunities and lack of opportunities for colored women I shall not consider the teachers nor the few women here and there who are in the professions. We need have no anxiety about the superior woman. She will make her way in the world in spite of restrictions. But it is with the average colored women that we must reckon. We find her engaged in some one of the following occupations—domestic service, laundering, dressmaking, hair dressing, manicuring, and nursing. Here and there is a typewriter and stenographer, a bookkeeper, or a government employee. In Northern communities colored women as a rule are not employed in factories, nor do they form part of the great army of clerks of all kinds and grades.

In the city of Chicago domestic service is the one occupation in which the demand for colored women exceeds the supply. In one employment office during the past year there were 1,500 applications for colored women and only 1,000 of this number were supplied. Girls of other nationalities do not seem to compete with colored women as domestics. It is probably safe to say that every colored woman who is in any way competent can find good employment. Her wages, for general housework, range from four to seven dollars per week, while a good cook receives from seven to ten dollars. Now what is the condition of this service? The two most important things are that the wages paid are higher than those given for the same grade of intelligence in any other calling, and that colored women can command almost a monopoly of this employment.

It might be safe to presume that since our women are so much in demand for this service they give perfect satisfaction in it. In considering this it is important to bear in mind that there are two kinds of colored women who perform domestic service:—First, there are those who take to the work naturally and whose training and habits make them perfectly satisfied with it; and second, those who have had more or less education and who are ambitious to do something in the line of "polite occupations." The women of the latter class do not take to domestic service very kindly. They do not enter the service with any pride. They feel compelled to do this work because they can find nothing else to do. They are always sensitive as to how they may be regarded by their associates and friends, and shrink from the term servant as something degrading "per se." There is a general complaint among housekeepers that the younger and more intelligent colored women are unreliable as domestics. They say that as soon as a young woman has earned enough money to buy a fine dress she leaves her place; that she demands a holiday every time there is a picnic or a funeral and wears herself out in social dissipations of all kinds. These are some of the complaints that may be heard concerning the present generation of young women who "work out." I am sorry to say that there is a great deal of truth in them. Women who take up any kind of work with a fixed dislike and shame for it, are not apt to win the good will of their employers.

But of course there is another side to this story. It must be remembered that the ordinary mistress of a house is far from being an angel. Although I am a woman and a housekeeper, I must admit that the average housewife is apt to be a petty tyrant, and while she has smiles, graciousness, and gentleness for the parlor, to show all kinds of meanness and harshness in the kitchen. She seldom assumes that there is a higher nature in her helpers that might sometimes be appealed to. Many mistresses cannot rid themselves of the idea that the woman whom she employs to do housework is inferior and servile by nature, and must receive the treatment accorded to inferiors. The woman who understands this haughtiness of spirit and exaggerated superiority is always resentful and on the defensive. If it were possible to change the disposition and heart of the average American housewife, and so to elevate the service that the cook or housemaid would not be looked down upon because she is a servant and as such not supposed to possess womanly instincts and aspirations, a better grade of helpers would gladly enter this field of employment.

It is of course an easy thing to condemn our young women who have been fairly educated and have had good home training, because they prefer idleness to domestic service, but I am rather inclined to think that we must share in that condemnation. If our girls work for wages in a nice home, rather than in a factory or over a counter, they are ruthlessly scorned by their friends and acquaintances. Our young men, whose own occupations by the way, will not always bear scrutiny, will also give her the cut direct, so that between the scorn of her associates and the petty tyranny of the housewife, the colored girl who enters domestic service is compelled to have more than ordinary strength of character.

But after all is said, I believe that it is largely in the power of the young woman herself to change and elevate the character of domestic service. She certainly cannot improve it by taking into it ignorance, contempt, and inefficiency. There is no reason why a woman of character, graciousness, and skill should not make her work as a domestic as respectable and as highly regarded as the work of the girl behind the department-store counter. For example; if, by special training in domestic service, a girl can cook so well and do everything about a house so deftly and thoroughly that she will be called a real home helper and an invaluable assistant, it is in her power, with her intelligent grasp upon the possibilities of her position, to change the whole current of public opinion in its estimate of domestic service. These young women, as a general thing, belong to families that are too poor to keep them well dressed if they are idle, yet colored girls on the streets of Chicago and other cities are often better dressed than the girls of any other race in like circumstances. There is a strong suspicion prevalent that this fine dressing is at a cost that demoralizes the social life of the colored people. This is the most serious consequence of our restricted employment. The girl who is barred from the occupation she would like to follow, and has no taste, talent, or desire for what she must do, is apt to become discouraged and indifferent. If she finds that society on all sides is hostile to her ambitions, she will become in turn hostile to society and contemptuous of its ethics and code of morals.

What, then, shall we do for the young colored woman with refined instincts and fair education? She is ambitious to choose and follow the occupation for which she is best fitted by talents and inclination, but she is shut out from most of the employments open to other women, and does not realize that her refinement and training are as much needed and as well paid for in domestic service as in other occupations. We are afraid of the word "servant." In England the terms master and servant are not hateful to the thousands of self-respecting Englishmen who bear them. If we could in some way create a sentiment that the girl who can carry as much intelligence and graciousness of manner into the kitchen will be as much respected and will get married just as soon as her sisters in other occupations, much of the present-day false notions about domestic service would be changed. A young woman of character and intelligence who is competent to do domestic work, can never be a servant in an offensive sense and will not be so regarded. To bring about this change so as to enable our girls to enter upon this occupation without loss of self-respect and without the danger of ostracism by so-called society, is a problem worthy of the best thought and devotion of our men and women.

What is called the servant-girl problem is one of the most vexatious of the many social questions of the hour. The work of housekeeping is neither a trade nor a profession; it is governed by no code of social ethics; it is without discipline or organization and is largely irresponsible and uncertain. It is usually a case of a good mistress and a bad servant or a bad mistress and a good servant. Thousands of housekeepers attempt to manage their help who have never learned to manage themselves. The housekeeper's manner to the butcher, the baker, the milkman, the shoemaker, the dressmaker, and the milliner and to every other person upon whom she is more or less dependent, is often more respectful than it is to the woman upon whom she is dependent every hour of the day for ease and comfort, health and happiness. Many of the leading women of the country have begun to study this problem for the purpose of elevating the service. The first thing to be done is to bring it strongly to our consciousness that domestic service is not necessarily degrading. In the city of Chicago, schools of domestic science are as eagerly patronized as schools in which book-keeping and typewriting are taught. They are slowly teaching the all-important fact that the thing we call domestic service has in it the elements of high art and much science. It is an occupation that intelligence elevates, that character adorns and ennobles, and that even now brings a higher salary to women than almost any other kind of employment.

When domestic service becomes a profession, as it surely will, by the proper training of those who shall follow it, what will be the condition of colored girls who would participate in its benefits? It is now time to prepare ourselves to answer this question. In my opinion, the training for this new profession should be elevated to the dignity and importance of the training in mathematics and grammar and other academic studies. Our girls must be made to feel that there is no stepping down when they become professional housekeepers. The relative dignity, respectability, and honor of this profession should first be taught in our schools. As it is now, the young woman in school or college knows that if she enters domestic service, she loses the relationships that she has formed. But schools of domestic science cannot do it all. The every-day man and woman who make society must change their foolish notions as to what is the polite thing for a young woman to do. The kind of stupidity that calls industrial education drudgery is the same kind of stupidity that looks upon the kitchen as a place for drudges. We must learn that the girl who cooks our meals and keeps our houses sweet and beautiful deserves just as high a place in our social economy as the girl who makes our gowns and hats, or the one who teaches our children. In what I have said on this particular phase of our industrial life, I do not wish to be understood as advocating the restriction of colored girls to house service, even when that service is elevated to the rank of a profession. My only plea is that we shall protect and respect our girls who honestly and intelligently enter this service, either from preference or necessity.

It seems to me that we lose a great opportunity if we fail to take hold of this problem in a thoroughly broad and philosophic way and work out its solution. If we wish to contribute something substantial to the social betterment of American living, we have the opportunity in helping to solve this servant-girl problem. Vexation of spirit, waste, indigestion, and general demoralization cry out from the American home for relief from its domestic miseries. We have it in our power to assist in answering this Macedonian cry. It would help to give our race a standing if we could count several of our men and women as the best thinkers and most effective workers in the solution of this problem. Shall we lead or shall we follow in this movement? Shall we, in this as in many other things, beg for an opportunity further on instead of helping to create opportunities now?

There is still another consideration which suggests the importance to the colored people of taking the lead in helping to improve and elevate this service. Race prejudice is kept up and increased in thousands of instances by the incompetent and characterless women who are engaged in this work. While there are thousands of worthy and really noble women in domestic service who enjoy the confidence and affection of their employers, there is a large percentage of colored women who, by their general unworthiness, help to give the Negro race a bad name, for white people North and South are very apt to estimate the entire race from the standpoint of their own servant girls. When intelligence takes the place of ignorance, and good manners, efficiency, and self-respect take the place of shiftlessness, and irresponsibility in American homes, one of the chief causes of race prejudice will be removed.

It should also be borne in mind that the colored girl who is trained in the arts of housekeeping is better qualified for the high duties of wifehood and motherhood.

Let me say by way of summary that I have dwelt mostly upon the opportunities of domestic service for the following reasons:—

1. It is the one field in which colored women meet with almost no opposition. It is ours almost by birthright.

2. The compensation for this service, in Northern communities at least, is higher than that paid for average clerkships in stores and offices.

3. The service is susceptible of almost unlimited improvement and elevation.

4. The nature of the work is largely what we make it.

5. White women of courage and large intelligence are lifting domestic service to a point where it will have the dignity of a profession; and colored women are in danger, through lack of foresight, of being relegated to the positions of scrub women and dishwashers.

6. The colored girl who has no taste or talent for school teaching, dress making, or manicuring is in danger of being wasted in idleness, unless we can make domestic service worthy of her ambition and pride.

7. There can be no feature of our race problem more important than the saving of our young women; we can, perhaps, excuse their vanities, but idleness is the mildew on the garment of character.

8. Education has no value to human society, unless it can add importance and respectability to the things we find to do.

9. Though all the factories and offices close their doors at our approach, this will be no calamity if we are strong enough to so transform the work that we must do, that it shall become an object of envy and emulation to those who now deny us their industrial fellowship.

Introduction to Mary Church Terrell's "The Progress of Colored Women"

"The Progress of Colored Women" is an optimistic account of the triumph of African American women over numerous obstacles and difficulties. The address summarizes the achievements of women in several dimensions: moral integrity, intellectual development, benevolent activism, and political and social participation. Terrell challenges unfavorable stereotypes of African American women and articulates the legacy of service and achievement characterizing this disadvantaged group, noting the duality of the discrimination suffered. She argued that "not only are colored women with ambition and aspiration handicapped on account of their sex, but they are almost everywhere baffled and mocked because of their race" (Par. 1). The speech applauds the progress made by the group and their enduring faith in the efficacy of perseverance and commitment.

The speaker, Mary Church Terrell, was born in Memphis, Tennessee, on 23 September 1863, to newly emancipated parents. A graduate of Oberlin College, Terrell was an accomplished lecturer who addressed numerous women's groups and directed the organization of black voters in Republican campaigns. She was the first president of the National Association of Colored Women and an activist in the women's suffrage movement. Lynchings and other racial atrocities motivated Terrell's shift from a moderate to a more militant philosophical stance on the race issue.

The Progress Of Colored Women
Mary Church Terrell
1904

When one considers the obstacles encountered by colored women in their effort to educate and cultivate themselves, since they became free, the work they have accomplished and the progress they have made will bear favorable comparison, at least with that of their more fortunate sisters, from whom the opportunity of acquiring knowledge and the means of self-culture have never been entirely withheld. Not only are colored women with ambition and aspiration handicapped on account of their sex, but they are almost everywhere baffled and mocked because of their race. Not only because they are women, but because they are colored women are discouragement and disappointment meeting them at every turn. But in spite of the obstacles encountered, the progress made by colored women along many lines appears like a veritable miracle of modern times. Forty years ago for the great masses of colored women there was no such thing as home. Today in each and every section of the country there are hundreds of homes among colored people, the mental and moral tone of which is as high and as pure as can be found among the best people of any land.

To the women of the race may be attributed in large measure the refinement and purity of the colored home. The immorality of colored women is a theme upon which those who know little about them or those who maliciously misrepresent them love to descant. Foul aspersions upon the character of colored women are assiduously circulated by the press of certain sections and especially by the direct descendants of those who in years past were responsible for the moral degradation of their female slaves. And yet, in spite of the fateful heritage of slavery, even though the safeguards usually thrown around maidenly youth and innocence are in some sections entirely withheld from colored girls, statistics compiled by men not inclined to falsify in favor of my race show that immorality among the colored women of the United States is not so great as among women with similar environment and temptations in Italy, Germany, Sweden and France.

Scandals in the best colored society are exceedingly rare, while the progressive game of divorce and remarriage is practically unknown.

The intellectual progress of colored women has been marvelous. So great has been their thirst for knowledge and so Herculean their efforts to acquire it that there are few colleges, universities, high and normal schools in the North, East and West from which colored girls have not graduated with honor. In Wellesley, Vassar, Ann Arbor, Cornell and in Oberlin, my dear alma mater, whose name will always be loved and whose praise will always be sung as the first college in the country broad, just and generous enough to extend a cordial welcome to the Negro and to open its doors to women on an equal footing with the men, colored girls by their splendid records have forever settled the question of their capacity and worth. The instructors in these and other institutions cheerfully bear testimony to their intelligence, their diligence and their success.

As the brains of colored women expanded, their hearts began to grow. No sooner had the heads of a favored few been filled with knowledge than their hearts yearned to dispense blessings to the less fortunate of their race. With tireless energy and eager zeal, colored women have worked in every conceivable way to elevate their race. Of the colored teachers engaged in instructing our youth it is probably no exaggeration to say that fully eighty percent are women. In the backwoods, remote from the civilization and comforts of the city and town colored women may be found courageously battling with those evils which such conditions always entail. Many a heroine of whom the world will never hear has thus sacrificed her life to her race amid surroundings and in the face of privations which only martyrs can bear.

Through the medium of their societies in the church, beneficial organizations out of it and clubs of various kinds, colored women are doing a vast amount of good. It is almost impossible to ascertain exactly what the Negro is doing in any field, for the records are so poorly kept. This is particularly true in the case of the women of the race. During the past forty years there is no doubt that colored women in their poverty have contributed large sums of money to charitable and educational institutions as well as to the foreign and home missionary work. Within the twenty-five years in which the educational work of the African Methodist Episcopal Church has been systematized, the women of that organization have contributed at least five hundred thousand dollars to the cause of education. Dotted all over the country are charitable institutions for the aged, orphaned and poor which have been established by colored women. Just how many it is difficult to state, owing to the lack of statistics bearing on the progress, possessions and prowess of colored women.

Among the charitable institutions either founded, conducted or supported by colored women, may be mentioned the Hale Infirmary of Montgomery, Alabama, the Carrie Steel Orphanage of Atlanta, the Reed Orphan Home of Covington, and the Haines Industrial school of Augusta, all three in the state of Georgia; a home for the aged of both races in New Bedford, and St. Monica's Home of Boston, in Massachusetts, Old Folks Home of Memphis, Tennessee, and the colored Orphan's Home of Lexington, Kentucky, together with others which lack of space forbids me to mention. Mt.

Meigs Institute is an excellent example of a work originated and carried into successful execution by a colored woman. The school was established for the benefit of colored people on the plantations in the black belt of Alabama. In the township of Mt. Meigs the population is practically all colored. Instruction given in this school is of the kind best suited to the needs of the people for whom it was established. Along with some scholastic training, girls are taught everything pertaining to the management of the home, while boys are taught practical farming, wheelwrighting, blacksmithing, and have some military training. Having started with almost nothing, at the end of eight years the trustees of the school owned nine acres of land and five buildings in which several thousand pupils had received instructions, all through the energy, the courage and the sacrifice of one little woman.

Up to date, politics have been religiously eschewed by colored women, although questions affecting our legal status as a race is sometimes agitated by the most progressive class. In Louisiana and Tennessee colored women have several times petitioned the legislatures of their respective states to repel the obnoxious Jim-Crow-car laws. Against the convict-lease system, whose atrocities have been so frequently exposed of late, colored women here and there in the South are waging a ceaseless war. So long as hundreds of their brothers and sisters, many of whom have committed no crime or misdemeanor whatever, are thrown into cells whose cubic contents are less than those of a good size grave, to be overworked, underfed and only partially covered with vermin-infested rags, and so long as children are born to the women in these camps who breathe the polluted atmosphere of these dens of horror and vice from the time they utter their first cry in the world till they are released from their suffering by death, colored women who are working for the emancipation and elevation of their race know where their duty lies. By constant agitation of this painful and hideous subject they hope to touch the conscience of the country, so that this stain upon its escutcheon shall be forever wiped away. Alarmed at the rapidity with which the Negro is losing ground in the world of trade, some of the farsighted women are trying to solve the labor question, so far as it concerns the women at least, by urging the establishment of schools of domestic science wherever means therefor can be secured. Those who are interested in this particular work hope and believe that if colored women and girls are thoroughly trained in domestic service, the boycott which has undoubtedly been placed upon them in many sections of the country will be removed. With so few vocations open to the Negro and with the labor organizations increasingly hostile to him, the future of the boys and girls of the race appears to some of our women very foreboding and dark.

The cause of temperance has been eloquently espoused by two women, each of whom has been appointed national superintendent of work among colored people by the Woman's Christian Temperance Union. In business, colored women have had signal success. There is in Alabama a large milling and cotton business belonging to and controlled by a colored woman, who has sometimes as many as seventy-five men in her employ. Until a few years ago the principal ice plant of Nova Scotia was owned and managed by a colored woman, who sold it for a large amount. In the professions there are dentists and doctors whose practice is lucrative and large. Ever since a book was published in 1773 entitled "Poems on Various Subjects, Religious and Moral by Phillis Wheatley, Negro Servant of Mr. John Wheatley," of Boston, colored women have given abundant evidence of literary ability. In sculpture we were represented by a woman upon whose chisel Italy has set her seal of approval; in painting by one of Bouguereau's pupils and in music by young women holding diplomas from the best conservatories in the land.

In short, to use a thought of the illustrious Frederick Douglass, if judged by the depths from which they have come, rather than by the heights to which those blessed with centuries of opportunities have attained, colored women need not hang their heads in shame. They are slowly but surely making their way up to the heights, wherever they can be scaled. In spite of handicaps and discouragements they are not losing heart. In a variety of ways they are rendering valiant service to their race. Lifting as they climb, onward and upward they go struggling and striving and hoping that the buds and blossoms of their desires may burst into glorious fruition ere long. Seeking no favors because of their color nor charity because of their needs they knock at the door of Justice and ask for an equal chance.

Introduction to Mary McLeod Bethune's "A Century of Progress of Negro Women"

"A Century of Progress of Negro Women" notes the accomplishments of women that demonstrate a marked contrast to the previous status as "a thing" a hundred years earlier. Mary McLeod Bethune claims considerable elevation of women of color and enumerates the productivity and success of women in various fields of endeavor. She discusses the contributions of women in the arts, business, social organizations, the Red Cross, private enterprise, and religion. According to her perception, "the Negro woman embodies one of the modern miracles of the New World." Listed among the noteworthy achievements is the miracle of the Negro woman's ability to maintain the stability of the home. Bethune argues that women's achievements are comparable to those of men and, in consequence, women deserve a share of the recognition accorded the race for its progress across time. She uses concrete, specific examples to dramatize the impressive role of African American women in "making history."

Mary McLeod Bethune, the fifteenth of seventeen children, was born in Mayesville, South Carolina, on 10 July 1875. Born and reared in poverty on land purchased by her parents, Bethune emerged as one of the race's most influential and eloquent women. She was the founder of what is now known as Bethune Cookman College in Daytona Beach, Florida, having started the school on the site of a garbage dump. Bethune served for several terms as the President of the National Council of Negro Women. Giddings describes Bethune's influence in elaborate praise: "Every aspect of Bethune's philosophy of leadership came into play when she acted as advocate for Black women. She articulated her faith in them with a passion that no other Black woman leader has

211

expressed since. She was adamant about the unheralded achievements of women, always encouraging them to "go to the front and take our rightful place; fight our battles and claim our victories" (Giddings 1984, 228). Bethune made laudatory contributions in the Franklin Roosevelt era, serving as advisor in several capacities and establishing a profitable friendship with Eleanor Roosevelt.

"A Century of Progress of Negro Women" was delivered on 30 June 1933, before the Chicago Women's Federation Clubs. Women's clubs during this period were vocal and industrious, often endorsing what was then perceived as radical courses of action. Some were, of course, more conservative than others, but the general characteristic embodied in Bethune was boldness, one of the qualities that led to her appointment as director of the division of Negro affairs of the National Youth Administration under the tenure of President Franklin D. Roosevelt.

A Century of Progress of Negro Women
Mary McLeod Bethune
1933

To Frederick Douglass is credited the plea that, "The Negro be not judged by the heights to which he is risen, but by the depths from which has climbed. Judged on that basis, the Negro woman embodies one of the modern miracles of the New World.

One hundred years ago she was the most pathetic figure on the American continent. She was not a person, in the opinion of many, but a thing—a thing whose personality had no claim to the respect of mankind. She was a household drudge, —a means for getting distasteful work done; she was an animated agricultural implement to augment the service of mules and plows in cultivating and harvesting the cotton crop. Then she was an automatic incubator, a producer of human live stock, beneath whose heart and lungs more potential laborers could be bred and nurtured and brought to the light of day.

Today she stands side by side with the finest manhood the race has been able to produce. Whatever the achievements of the Negro man in letters, business, art, pulpit, civic progress and moral reform, he cannot but share them with his sister of darker hue. Whatever glory belongs to the race for a development unprecedented in history for the given length of time, a full share belongs to the womanhood of the race.

By the very force of circumstances, the part she has played in the progress has been of necessity, to a certain extent, subtle and indirect. She has not always been permitted a place in the front ranks where she could show her face and make her voice heard with effect. But she has been quick to seize every opportunity which presented itself to come more and more into the open and strive directly for the uplift of the race and nation. In that direction, her achievements have been amazing.

Negro women have made outstanding contributions in the arts. Meta V. W. Fuller and May Howard Jackson are significant figures in fine arts development. Angelina Grimke, Georgia Douglass Johnson and Alice Dunbar Nelson are poets of note. Jessie Fausett has become famous as a novelist. In the field of Music Anita Patti Brown, Lillian Evanti, Elizabeth Greenfield, Florence Cole-Talbert, Marion Anderson and Marie Selika stand out pre-enimently.

Very early in the post-emancipation period women began to show signs of ability to contribute to the business progress of the Race. Maggie L. Walker, who is outstanding as the guiding spirit of the Order of Saint Luke, in 1902 went before her Grand Council with a plan for a Saint Luke Penny Savings Bank. This organization started with a deposit of about eight thousand dollars and twenty-five thousand in paid-up capital, with Maggie L. Walker as the first woman bank President in America. For twenty-seven years she has held this place. Her bank has paid dividends to its stockholders; has served as a depository for gas and water accounts of the city of Richmond and has given employment to hundreds of Negro clerks, bookkeepers and office workers.

With America's great emphasis on the physical appearance, a Negro woman left her washtub and ventured into the field of facial beautification. From a humble beginning Madame C. J. Walker built a substantial institution that is a credit to American business in every way.

Mrs. Annie M. Malone is another pioneer in this field of successful business. The C. J. Walker Manufacturing Company and the Poro College do not confine their activities in the field of beautification to race. They serve both races and give employment to both.

When the ballot was made available to the Womanhood of America, the sister of darker hue was not slow to seize the advantage. In sections where the Negro could gain access to the voting booth, the intelligent, forward-looking element of the Race's women have taken hold of political issues with an enthusiasm and mental acumen that might well set worthy examples for other groups. Ofttimes she has led the struggle toward moral improvement and political record, and has compelled her reluctant brother to follow her determined lead.

In time of war as in time of peace, the Negro woman has ever been ready to serve for the people's and the nation's good. During the recent world War she pleaded to go in the uniform of the Red Cross nurse and was denied the opportunity only on the basis of racial distinction.

Addie W. Hunton and Kathryn M. Johnson gave yeoman service with the American Expeditionary Forces with the Y.M.C.A. group.

Negro women have thrown themselves whole-heartedly into the organization of groups to direct the social uplift of their fellowmen, one of the greatest achievements of the race.

Perhaps the most outstanding individual social worker of our group today is Jane E. Hunter, founder and executive secretary of the Phillis Wheatley Association, Cleveland, Ohio.

In November, 1911, Miss Hunter, who had been a nurse in Cleveland for only a short time, recognizing the need for a Working Girls' Home, organized the Association and prepared to establish the work. Today the Association is housed in a magnificent structure of nine stories, containing one hundred thirty-five rooms, offices, parlours, a cafeteria and beauty parlour. It is not only a home for working girls but a recreational center and ideal hospice for the young Negro woman who is living away from home. It maintains an employment department and a fine, up-to-date camp.

Branches of the activities of the main Phillis Wheatley Association are located in other sections of Cleveland, special emphasis being given to the recreational facilities for children and young women of the vicinities in which the branches are located.

In no field of modern social relationship has the hand of service and the influence of the Negro woman been felt more distinctly than in the Negro orthodox church. It may be safely said that the chief sustaining force in support of the pulpit and the various phases of missionary enterprise has been the feminine element of the membership. The development of the Negro church since the Civil War has been another of the modern miracles. Throughout its growth the untiring effort, the unflagging enthusiasm, the sacrificial contribution of time, effort and cash earnings of the black woman have been the most significant factors, without which the modern Negro church would have no history worth the writing.

Both before and since emancipation, by some rare gift, she has been able to hold onto the fibres of family unity and keep the home one unimpaired whole. In recent years it has become increasingly the case where in many instances, the mother is the sole dependence of the home, and single-handed, fights the wolf from the door, while the father submits unwillingly to enforced idleness and unavoidable unemployment. Yet in myriads of instances she controls home discipline with a tight rein and exerts a unifying influence that is the miracle of the century.

The true worth of a race must be measured by the character of its womanhood. As the years have gone on the Negro woman has touched the most vital fields in the civilization of today. Wherever she had contributed she has left the mark of a strong character. The educational institutions she has established and directed have met the needs of her young people; her cultural development has concentrated itself into artistic presentation accepted and acclaimed by meritorious critics; she is successful as a poet and a novelist; she is shrewd in business and capable in politics; she recognizes the importance of uplifting her people through social, civic and religious activities; starting at the time when as a "mammy" she nursed the infants of the other race and taught him her meagre store of truth, she has been a contributing factor of note to interracial relations. Finally, through the past century she has made and kept her home intact—humble though it may have been in many instances. She has made and is making history.

Introduction to Shirley Anita St. Hill Chisholm's "For The Equal Rights Amendment"

"For the Equal Rights Amendment" delivered before the 91st Congress is an analysis of the nature and demands of the controversial amendment. In this address, Chisholm explicates the prevalence of gender bias and refutes arguments against legislation that would mitigate the bias, characterizing the counter arguments as unacceptable protests that would be categorically dismissed were they invoked for any other kind of bias. She outlines the adjustments that implementation of the proposed legislation would require and explores the full implications of the eradication of gender bias, a bias accorded more respectability in this society than any other bias. She discusses the limited commitment on the part of the nation and the administration to equality for women and challenges the Congress to remedy what the Founding Fathers left undone: "The Constitution they wrote was designed to protect the rights of white, male citizens. As there were no Black Founding Fathers, there were no founding mothers—a great pity, on both counts. It is not too late to complete the work they left undone. Today, here, we should start to do so" (Par. 2).

Shirley Anita St. Hill Chisholm was born on 30 November 1924, to parents of Barbadian descent. Her father, Charles St. Hill, was born in British Guyana but grew up in Cuba and Barbados. And her mother, the former Ruby Seale, grew up in Barbados. Chisholm herself grew up in Brooklyn and attended Brooklyn College where she learned many of the realities of race and culture from which her family had protected her. After completing her undergraduate studies at Brooklyn College, she went on to earn a masters degree from Columbia University. In 1968, she became the first African American woman to be elected to the United States Congress.

219

Chisholm herself pointed out the implications of this phenomenon: "That I am a national figure because I was the first person in 192 years to be at once a congressman, black, and a woman proves, I would think, that our society is not yet either just or free" (Chisholm 1970).

For The Equal Rights Amendment
Shirley Anita St. Hill Chisholm
1970

Mr. Speaker, House Joint Resolution 264, before us today, which provides for equality under the law for both men and women, represents one of the most clear-cut opportunities we are likely to have to declare our faith in the principles that shaped our Constitution. It provides a legal basis for attack on the most subtle, most pervasive and most institutionalized form of prejudice that exists. Discrimination against women, solely on the basis of their sex, is so widespread that it seems to many persons normal, natural and right. Legal expression of prejudice on the grounds of religious or political belief has become a minor problem in our society. Prejudice on the basis of race is, at least, under systematic attack. There is reason for optimism that it will start to die with the present older generation. It is time we act to assure full equality of opportunity to those citizens who, although in a majority, suffer the restrictions that are commonly imposed on minorities, to women.

The argument that this amendment will not solve the problem of sex discrimination is not relevant. If the argument were used against a civil rights bill—as it has been used in the past—the prejudice that lies behind it would be embarrassing. Of course laws will not eliminate prejudice from the hearts of human beings. But that is no reason to allow prejudice to continue to be enshrined in our laws—to perpetuate injustice through inaction.

The amendment is necessary to clarify countless ambiguities and inconsistencies in our legal system. For instance, the Constitution guarantees due process of law, in the fifth and Fourteenth amendments. But the applicability of due process of sex distinctions is not clear: Women are

221

excluded from some state colleges and universities. In some states, restrictions are placed on a married woman who engages in an independent business. Women may not be chosen for some juries. Women even receive heavier criminal penalties than men who commit the same crime.

What would the legal effects of the equal rights amendment really be? The equal rights amendment would govern only the relationship between the State and its citizens—not relationships between private citizens.

The amendment would be largely self-executing, that is, any Federal or State laws in conflict would be ineffective one year after date of ratification without further action by the Congress or State legislatures.

Opponents of the amendment claim its ratification would throw the law into a state of confusion and would result in much litigation to establish its meaning. This objection overlooks the influence of legislative history in determining intent and the recent activities of many groups preparing for legislative changes in this direction.

State labor laws applying only to women, such as those limiting hours of work and weights to be lifted would become inoperative unless the legislature amended them to apply to men. As of early 1970 most States would have some laws that would be affected. However, changes are being made so rapidly as a result of Title VII of the Civil Rights Act of 1964, it is likely that by the time the equal rights amendment would become effective, no conflicting State laws would remain.

In any event, there has for years been great controversy as to the usefulness to women of these State labor laws. There has never been any doubt that they worked a hardship on women who need or want to work overtime and on women who need or want better paying jobs, and there has been no persuasive evidence as to how many women benefit from the archaic policy of the laws. After the Delaware hours law was repealed in 1966, there were no complaints from women to any of the State agencies that might have been approached.

Jury service laws not making women equally liable for jury service would have to be revised.

The selective service law would have to include women, but women would not be required to serve in the Armed Forces where they are not fitted any more than men are required to serve. Military service, while a great responsibility, is not without benefits, particularly for young men with limited education or training. Since October 1966, 246,000 young men who did not meet the normal mental or physical requirements have been given opportunities for training and correcting physical problems. This opportunity is not open to their sisters. Only girls who have completed high school and meet high standards on the educational test can volunteer. Ratification of the amendment would not permit application of higher standards to women.

Survivorship benefits would be available to husbands of female workers on the same basis as to wives of male workers. The Social Security Act and the civil service and military service retirement acts are in conflict.

Public schools and universities could not be limited to one sex and could not apply different admission standards to men and women. Laws requiring longer prison sentences for women than men would be invalid, and equal opportunities for rehabilitation and vocational training would have to be provided in public correctional institutions.

Different ages of majority based on sex would have to be harmonized.

Federal, State, and other governmental bodies would be obligated to follow nondiscriminatory practices in all aspects of employment, including public school teachers and State university and college faculties.

What would be the economic effects of the equal rights amendment? Direct economic effects would be minor. If any labor laws applying only to women still remained, their amendment or appeal would provide opportunity for women in better-paying jobs in manufacturing. More opportunities in public vocational and graduate schools for women would also tend to open up opportunities in better jobs for women.

Indirect effects could be much greater. The focusing of public attention on the gross legal, economic, and social discrimination against women by hearings and debates in the Federal and State legislatures would result in changes in attitude of parents, educators, and employers that would bring about substantial economic changes in the long run.

Sex prejudice cuts both ways. Men are oppressed by the requirements of the Selective Service Act, by enforced legal guardianship of minors, and by alimony laws. Each sex, I believe, should be liable when necessary to serve and defend this country.

Each has a responsibility for the support of children.

There are objections raised to wiping out laws protecting women workers. No one would condone exploitation. But what does sex have to do with it? Working conditions and hours that are harmful to women are harmful to men; wages that are unfair for women are unfair for men. Laws setting employment limitations on the basis of sex are irrational, and the proof of this is their inconsistency from State to State. The physical characteristics of men and women are not fixed, but cover two wide spans that have a great deal of overlap. It is obvious, I think, that a robust woman could be more fit for physical labor than a weak man. The choice of occupation would be determined by individual capabilities, and the rewards for equal work should be equal.

This is what it comes down to: artificial distinctions between persons must be wiped out of the law. Legal discrimination between the sexes is, in almost every instance, founded on outmoded views of society and the prescientific beliefs about psychology and physiology. It is time to sweep away these relics of the past and set future generations free of them.

Federal agencies and institutions responsible for the enforcement of equal opportunity laws need the authority of a Constitutional amendment. The 1964 Civil Rights Act and the 1963 Equal Pay Act are not enough; they are limited in their coverage—for instance, one excludes teachers, and the other leaves out administrative and professional women. The Equal Employment Opportunity Commission has not proven to be an adequate device, with its powers limited to investigation, conciliation and recommendation to the Justice Department. In its cases involving sexual discrimination, it has failed in more than one-half. The Justice Department has been even less effective. It has intervened in only one case involving discrimination on the basis of sex, and this was on a procedural point. In a second case, in which both sexual and racial discrimination were alleged, the racial bias charge was given far greater weight.

Evidence of discrimination on the basis of sex should hardly have to be cited here. It is in the Labor Department's employment and salary figures for anyone who is still in doubt. Its elimination will involve so many changes in our State and Federal laws that, without the authority and impetus of this proposed amendment, it will perhaps take another 194 years. We cannot be parties to continuing a delay. The time is clearly now to put this House on record for the fullest expression of that equality of opportunity which our founding fathers professed.

They professed it, but they did not assure it to their daughters, as they tried to do for their sons.

The Constitution they wrote was designed to protect the rights of white, male citizens. As there were no black Founding Fathers, there were no founding mothers—a great pity, on both counts. It is not too late to complete the work they left undone. Today, here, we should start to do so.

In closing I would like to make one point. Social and psychological effects will be initially more important than legal or economic results. As Leo Kanowitz has pointed out:

Rules of law that treat of the sexes per se inevitably produce far-reaching effects upon social, psychological and economic aspects of male-female relations beyond the limited confines of legislative chambers and courtrooms. As long as organized legal systems, at once the most respected and most feared of social institutions, continue to differentiate sharply, in treatment or in words, between men and women on the basis of irrelevant and artificially created distinctions, the likelihood of men and women coming to regard one another primarily as fellow human beings and only secondarily as representatives of another sex will continue to be remote. When men and women are prevented from recognizing one another's essential humanity by sexual prejudices, nourished by legal as well as social institutions, society as a whole remains less than it could otherwise become.

Introduction to Angela Davis's
"Let Us All Rise Together:
Radical Perspectives On Empowerment
For Afro-American Women"

"Let Us All Rise Together" recounts the legacy of women's struggle for economic and political power and explores the factors militating against the advancement of women. Davis seeks to correct the alienation of affected groups in the struggle, noting the differences in experiences contributing to the breach between white and Afro-American women but insisting on the need for multiracial unity. She analyzes the relationship between the treatment of women and the treatment of African Americans. What she observes is a striking degree of similarity. The speaker explains that the preparation for and scope of the movement must involve both sexes and both races, or all will be defrauded. She recognizes the numerous obstacles that will confront the movement and is cognizant of the fact that all the problems will not magically disappear. Yet she concludes her speech with the hope that the social order which she envisions "should provide us with the real opportunity to further extend our struggles, with the assurance that one day we will be able to redefine the basic elements of our oppression as useless refuse of the past."

The biographical sketch in *Women, Culture, And Politics*, a collection of Angela Davis's speeches and writings, includes the following information: "Angela Davis was born and raised in Birmingham, Alabama. She graduated magna cum laude from Brandeis University and pursued graduate studies at the Goethe Institute in Frankfurt, Germany and the University of California, San Diego." Other information included in the sketch at the end of the work is her membership in the Communist Party, her 1980 and 1984 candidacies for Vice President of the United States, and her acquittal on conspiracy charges in 1970. The characterization of Davis included in the sketch is that she "has emerged as an internationally regarded writer, scholar, lecturer, and fighter for human rights." "Let Us All Rise Together" was presented at Spelman College in Atlanta, Georgia, on 25 June 1987, before the National Women's Studies Association.

Let Us All Rise Together:
Radical Perspectives On Empowerment
For Afro-American Women
Angela Davis
1987

The concept of empowerment is hardly new to Afro-American women. For almost a century, we have been organized in bodies that have sought collectively to develop strategies illuminating the way to economic and political power for ourselves and our communities. During the last decade of the nineteenth century, after having been repeatedly shunned by the racially homogeneous women's rights movement, Black women organized their own Club Movement. In 1895—five years after the founding of the General Federation of Women's Clubs, which consolidated a club movement reflecting concerns of middle-class White women—one hundred Black women from ten states met in the city of Boston, under the leadership of Josephine St. Pierre Ruffin, to discuss the creation of a national organization of Black women's clubs. As compared to their White counterparts, the Afro-American women issuing the call for this national club movement articulated principles that were more openly political in nature. They defined the primary function of their clubs as an ideological as well as an activist defense of Black women—and men—from the ravages of racism. When the meeting was convened, its participants emphatically declared that, unlike their White sisters, whose organizational policies were seriously tainted by racism, they envisioned their movement as one open to all women:

Our woman's movement is woman's movement in that it is led and directed by women for the good of women and men, for the benefit of all humanity, which is more than any one branch or section of it. We want, we ask

229

the active interest of our men, and, too, we are not drawing the color line; we are women, American women, as intensely interested in all that pertains to us as such as all other American women; we are not alienating or withdrawing, we are only coming to the front, willing to join any others in the same work and cordially inviting and welcoming any others to join us (Lerner 1972, 443).

The following year, the formation of the National Association of Colored Women's Clubs was announced. The motto chosen by the Association was "Lifting As We Climb."

The nineteenth-century women's movement was also plagued by classism. Susan B. Anthony wondered why her outreach to working-class women on the issue of the ballot was so frequently met with indifference. She wondered why these women seemed to be much more concerned with improving their economic situation than with achieving the right to vote (Schneir 1972, 138-42). As essential as political equality may have been to the larger campaign for women's rights, in the eyes of Afro-American and White working-class women it was not synonymous with emancipation. That the conceptualization of strategies for struggle was based on the peculiar condition of White women of the privileged classes rendered those strategies discordant with working-class women's perceptions of empowerment. It is not surprising that many of them told Ms. Anthony, "Women want bread, not the ballot" (Schneir 1972, 138-42). Eventually, of course, working-class White women, and Afro-American women as well, reconceptualized this struggle, defining the vote not as an end in itself—not as the panacea that would cure all the ills related to gender-based discrimination—but rather as an important weapon in the continuing fight for higher wages, better working conditions, and an end to the omnipresent menace of the lynch mob.

Today, as we reflect on the process of empowering Afro-American women, our most efficacious strategies remain those that are guided by the principle used by Black women in the club movement. We must strive to "lift as we climb." In other words, we must climb in such a way as to guarantee that all of our sisters, regardless of social class, and indeed all of our brothers, climb with us. This must be the essential dynamic of our quest for power—a principle that must not only determine our struggles as Afro-American women, but also govern all authentic struggles of dispossessed people. Indeed, the overall battle for equality can be profoundly enhanced by embracing this principle.

Afro-American women bring to the women's movement a strong tradition of struggle around issues that politically link women to the most crucial progressive causes. This is the meaning of the motto, "Lifting As We Climb." This approach reflects the often unarticulated interests and aspirations of masses of women of all racial backgrounds. Millions of women today are concerned about jobs, working conditions, higher wages, and racist violence. They are concerned about plant closures, homelessness, and repressive immigration legislation. Women are concerned about homophobia, ageism, and discrimination against the physically challenged. We are concerned about Nicaragua and South Africa. And we share our children's dream that tomorrow's world will be delivered from the threat of nuclear omnicide. These are some of the issues that should be integrated into the overall struggle for women's rights if there is to be a serious commitment to the empowerment of women who have been rendered historically invisible. These are some of the issues we should consider if we wish to lift as we climb.

During this decade we have witnessed an exciting resurgence of the women's movement. If the first wave of the women's movement began in the 1840's, and the second wave in the 1960's, then we are approaching the crest of a third wave in the final days of the 1980's. When the feminist historians of the twenty-first century attempt to recapitulate the third wave, will they ignore the momentous contributions of Afro-American women, who have been leaders and activists in movements often confined to women of color, but whose accomplishments have invariably advanced the cause of white women as well? Will the exclusionary policies of the mainstream women's movement—from its inception to the present—which have often compelled Afro-American women to conduct their struggle for equality outside the ranks of that movement, continue to result in the systematic omission of our names from the roster of prominent leaders and activists of the women's movement? Will there continue to be two distinct continuums of the women's movement, one visible and another invisible, one publicly acknowledged and another ignored except by the conscious progeny of the working-class women—Black, Latina, Native American, Asian, and white—who forged that hidden continuum? If this question is answered in the affirmative, it will mean that women's quest for equality will continue to be gravely deficient. The revolutionary potential of the women's movement still will not have been realized. The racist-inspired flaws of the first and second waves of the women's movement will have become the inherited flaws of the third wave.

How can we guarantee that this historical pattern is broken? As advocates and activists of women's rights in our time, we must begin to merge that double legacy in order to create a single continuum, one that solidly represents the aspirations of all women in our society. We must begin to create a revolutionary, multiracial women's movement that seriously addresses the main issues affecting poor and working-class women. In order to tap the potential for such a movement, we must further develop those sectors of the movement that are addressing seriously issues affecting poor and working-class women, such as jobs, pay equity, paid maternity leave, federally subsidized child care, protection from sterilization abuse, and subsidized abortions. Women of all racial and class backgrounds will greatly benefit from such an approach.

For decades, white women activists have repeated the complaint that women of color frequently fail to respond to their appeals. "We invited them to our meetings, but they didn't come." "We asked them to participate in our demonstration, but they didn't show." "They just don't seem to be interested in women's studies."

This process cannot be initiated merely by intensified efforts to attract Latina women or Afro-American women or Asian or Native American women into the existing organizational forms dominated by white women of the more privileged economic strata. The particular concerns of women of color must be included in the agenda.

An issue of special concern to Afro-American women is unemployment. Indeed, the most fundamental prerequisite for empowerment is the ability to earn an adequate living. At the height of its audacity, the Reagan government boasted that unemployment had leveled off, leaving only (!) 7.5 million people unemployed. These claims came during a period in which Black people in general were twice as likely to be unemployed as white people, and Black teenagers almost three times as likely to be unemployed as white teenagers. We must remember that these figures do not include the millions who hold part-time jobs, although they want and need full-time employment. A disproportionate number of these underemployed individuals are women. Neither do the figures reflect those who, out of utter frustration, have ceased to search for employment, nor those whose unemployment insurance has run out, nor those who have never had a job.

Women on welfare are also among those who are not counted as unemployed.

At the same time that the Reagan administration attempted to convey the impression that it had successfully slowed the rise of unemployment, the AFL-CIO estimated that 18 million people of working age were without jobs. These still-critical levels of unemployment, distorted and misrepresented by the Reagan administration, are fundamentally responsible for the impoverished status of Afro-American women, the most glaring evidence of which resides in the fact that women, together with their dependent children, constitute the fastest-growing sector of the 4 million homeless people in the United States. There can be no serious discussion of empowerment today if we do not embrace the plight of the homeless with an enthusiasm as passionate as that with which we embrace issues more immediately related to our own lives.

The United Nations declared 1987 to be the Year of Shelter for the Homeless. Although only the developing countries were the initial focus of this resolution, eventually it became clear that the United States is an "undeveloping country." Two-thirds of the four million homeless in this country are families, and forty percent of them are Afro-American. In some urban areas, as many as seventy percent of the homeless are Black. In New York City, for example, sixty percent of the homeless population are Black, twenty percent Latino, and twenty percent white. Presently, under New York's Work Incentive Program, homeless women and men are employed to clean toilets, wash graffiti from subway trains, and clean parks at wages of sixty-two cents an hour, a mere fraction of the minimum wage. In other words, the homeless are being compelled to provide slave labor for the government if they wish to receive assistance.

Black women scholars and professionals cannot afford to ignore the straits of our sisters who are acquainted with the immediacy of oppression in a way many of us are not. The process of empowerment cannot be simplistically defined in accordance with our own particular class interests. We must learn to lift as we climb.

If we are to elevate the status of our entire community as we scale the heights of empowerment, we must be willing to offer organized resistance to the proliferating manifestations of racist violence across the country. A virtual "race riot" took place on the campus of one of the most liberal educational institutions in this country not long ago. In the aftermath of the World Series, white students at the University of Massachusetts, Amherst, who were purportedly fans of the Boston Red Sox, vented their wrath on Black students, whom they perceived as a surrogate for the winning team, the New York Mets, because of the predominance of Black players on the Mets. When individuals in the crowd yelled "Black bitch" at a Black woman student, a Black man who hastened to defend her was seriously wounded and rushed unconscious to the hospital. Another one of the many dramatic instances of racist harassment to occur on college campuses during this period was the burning of a cross in front of the Black Students' Cultural Center at Purdue University. In December 1986, Michael Griffith, a young Black man, lost his life in what amounted to a virtual lynching by a mob of White youths in the New York suburb of Howard Beach. Not far from Atlanta, civil rights marchers were attacked on Dr. Martin Luther King's birthday by a mob led by the Ku Klux Klan. An especially outrageous instance in which racist violence was officially condoned was the acquittal of Bernhard Goetz, who, on his own admission, attempted to kill four Black youths because he *felt* threatened by them on a New York subway.

Black women have organized before to oppose racist violence. In the nineteenth century the Black Women's Club

Movement was born largely in response to the epidemic of lynching during that era. Leaders like Ida B. Wells and Mary Church Terrell recognized that Black women could not move toward empowerment if they did not radically challenge the reign of lynch law in the land. Today, Afro-American women must actively take the lead in the movement against racist violence, as did our sister-ancestors almost a century ago. We must lift as we climb. As our ancestors organized for the passage of a federal anti-lynch law—and indeed involved themselves in the woman suffrage movement for the purpose of securing that legislation—we must today become activists in the effort to secure legislation declaring racism and anti-Semitism as crimes. Extensively as some instances of racist violence may be publicized at this time, many more racist-inspired crimes go unnoticed as a consequence of the failure of law enforcement to specifically classify them as such. A person scrawling swastikas or "KKK" on an apartment building may simply be charged—if criminal charges are brought at all—with defacing property or malicious mischief. Recently, a Ku Klux Klanner who burned a cross in front of a Black family's home was charged with "burning without a permit." We need federal and local laws against acts of racist and anti-Semitic violence. We must organize, lobby, march, and demonstrate in order to guarantee their passage.

As we organize, lobby, march, and demonstrate against racist violence, we who are women of color must be willing to appeal for multiracial unity in the spirit of our sister-ancestors. Like them, we must proclaim: We do not draw the color line. The only line we draw is one based on our political principles. We know that empowerment for the masses of women in our country will never be achieved as long as we do not succeed in pushing back the tide of racism. It is not a coincidence that sexist-inspired violence—in particular, terrorist attacks on abortion clinics—has reached a peak during the same period in which racist violence has proliferated dramatically. Violent attacks on women's reproductive rights are nourished by these explosions of racism. The vicious antilesbian and antigay attacks are a part of the same menacing process. The roots of sexism and homophobia are found in the same economic and political institutions that serve as the foundation of racism in this country and, more often than not, the same extremist circles that inflict violence on people of color are responsible for the eruptions of violence inspired by sexist and homophobic biases. Our political activism must clearly manifest our understanding of these connections.

We must always attempt to lift as we climb. Another urgent point on our political agenda—for Afro-American and for all progressive women—must be the repeal of the Simpson-Rodino Law. The Simpson-Rodino Law is a racist law that spells repression for vast numbers of women and men who are undocumented immigrants in this country. Camouflaged as an amnesty program, its eligibility restrictions are so numerous that hundreds of thousands of people stand to be prosecuted and deported under its provisions. Amnesty is provided in a restricted way only for those who came to this country before 1982. Thus, the vast numbers of Mexicans who have recently crossed the border in an attempt to flee intensified impoverishment bred by the unrestricted immigration of U.S. corporations into their countries are not eligible. Salvadorans and other Central Americans who have escaped political persecution in their respective countries over the last few years will not be offered amnesty. We must organize, lobby, march, and demonstrate for a repeal of the Simpson-Rodino Law. We must lift as we climb.

When we as Afro-American women, when we as women of color, proceed to ascend toward empowerment, we lift up with us our brothers of color, our white sisters and brothers in the working class, and, indeed, all women who experience the effects of sexist oppression. Our activist agenda must encompass a wide range of demands. We must call for jobs and for the unionization of unorganized women workers, and, indeed, unions must be compelled to take on such issues as affirmative action, pay equity, sexual harassment on the job, and paid maternity leave for women. Because Black and Latina women are AIDS victims in disproportionately large numbers, we have a special interest in demanding emergency funding for AIDS research. We must oppose all instances of repressive mandatory AIDS testing and quarantining, as well as homophobic manipulations of the AIDS crisis. Effective strategies for the reduction of teenage pregnancy are needed, but we must beware of succumbing to propagandistic attempts to relegate to young single mothers the responsibility for our community's impoverishment.

In the aftermath of the Reagan era, it should be clear that there are forces in our society that reap enormous benefits from the persistent, deepening oppression of women. Members of the Reagan administration include advocates for the most racist, antiworking class, and sexist circles of contemporary monopoly capitalism. These corporations continue to prop up apartheid in South Africa and to profit from the spiraling arms race while they propose the most vulgar and irrational forms of anti-Sovietism—invoking, for example the "evil empire" image popularized by Ronald Reagan—as justifications for their omnicidal ventures. If we are not afraid to adopt a revolutionary stance—if, indeed, we wish to be radical in our quest for change—then we must get to the root of our oppression. After all, *radical* simply means "grasping things at the root." Our agenda for women's empowerment must thus be unequivocal in our challenge to monopoly capitalism as a major obstacle to the achievement of equality.

I want to suggest, as I conclude, that we link our grassroots organizing, our essential involvement in electoral politics, and our involvement as activists in mass struggles to the long-range goal of fundamentally transforming the socioeconomic conditions that generate and persistently nourish the various forms of oppression we suffer. Let us learn from the strategies of our sisters in South Africa and Nicaragua. As Afro-American women, as women of color in general, as progressive women of all racial backgrounds, let us join our sisters—and brothers—across the globe who are attempting to forge a new socialist order—an order which will reestablish socioeconomic priorities so that the quest for monetary profit will never be permitted to take precedence over the real interests of human beings. This is not to say that our problems will magically dissipate with the advent of socialism. Rather, such a social order should provide us with the real opportunity to further extend our struggles, with the assurance that one day we will be able to redefine the basic elements of our oppression as useless refuse of the past.

The Right To Life:
What Can The White Man Say To The Black Woman?
Alice Walker
1989

What can the white man say to the black woman?

For four hundred years he ruled over the black woman's womb.

Let us be clear. In the barracoons and along the slave shipping coasts of Africa, for more than twenty generations, it was he who dashed our babies' brains out against the rocks.

What can the white man say to the black woman?

For four hundred years he determined which black women's children would live or die.

Let it be remembered. It was he who placed our children on the auction block in cities all across the Eastern half of what is now the United States, and listened to and watched them beg for their mothers' arms, before being sold to the highest bidder and dragged away.

What can the white man say to the black woman?

We remember that Fannie Lou Hamer, a poor sharecropper on a Mississippi plantation, was one of twenty-one children; and that on plantations across the South black women often had twelve, fifteen, twenty children. Like their enslaved mothers and grandmothers before them, these black women were sacrificed to the profit the white man could make from harnessing their bodies and their children's bodies to the cotton gin.

What can the white man say to the black woman?

We see him lined up, on Saturday nights, century after century, to make the black mother, who must sell her body to feed her children, go down on her knees to him.

Let us take note:

He has not cared for a single one of the dark children in his midst, over hundreds of years.

Where are the children of the Cherokee, my great-grandmother's people?

Gone.

Where are the children of the Blackfoot?

Gone.

Where are the children of the Lakota?

Gone.

Of the Cheyenne?

Of the Chippewa?

Of the Iroquois?

Of the Sioux?

Of the Akan?

Of the Ibo?

Of the Ashanti?

Of the Maori and the Aborigine?

Where are the children of "the slave coast" and Wounded Knee?

We do not forget the forced sterilizations and forced starvations on the reservations, here as in South Africa. Nor do we forget the small-pox infested blankets Indian children were given by the Great White Fathers of the United States Government.

What has the white man to say to the black woman?

When we have children you do everything in your power to make them feel unwanted from the moment they are born. You send them to fight and kill other dark mothers' children around the world. You shove them onto public highways into the path of oncoming cars. You shove their heads through plate glass windows. You string them up and you string them out.

What has the white man to say to the black woman?

From the beginning, you have treated all dark children with absolute hatred.

30,000,000 African children died on the way to the Americas, where nothing awaited them but endless toil and the crack of a bullwhip. They died of a lack of food, or lack of movement in the holds of ships. Of lack of friends and relatives. They died of depression, bewilderment and fear.

What has the white man to say to the black woman?

Let us look around us: Let us look at the world the White man has made for the black woman and her children.

It is a world in which the black woman is still forced to provide cheap labor, in the form of children, for the factory farms and on the assembly lines of the white man.

It is a world into which the white man dumps every foul, person-annulling drug he smuggles into Creation.

It is a world where many of our babies die at birth, or later of malnutrition, and where many more grow up to live lives of such misery they are forced to choose death by their own hands.

What has the white man to say to the black woman, and to all women and children everywhere?

Let us consider the depletion of the ozone; let us consider homelessness and the nuclear peril; let us consider the destruction of the rain forests—in the name of the almighty hamburger. Let us consider the poisoned apples and the poisoned water and the poisoned air, and the poisoned earth.

And that all of our children, because of the white man's assault on the planet, have a possibility of death by cancer in their almost immediate future.

What has the white male law giver to say to any of us? Those of us who love life too much to willingly bring more children into a world saturated with death.

Abortion, for many women, is more than an experience of suffering beyond anything most men will ever know, it is an act of mercy, and an act of self-defense.

To make abortion illegal again, is to sentence millions of women and children to miserable lives and even more miserable deaths.

Given his history, in relation to us, I think the white man should be ashamed to attempt to speak for the unborn children of the black woman. To force us to have children for him to ridicule, drug, turn into killers and homeless wanderers is a testament to his hypocrisy.

What can the white man say to the black woman?

Only one thing that the black woman might hear.

Yes, indeed, the white man can say, your children have the right to life. Therefore I will call back from the dead those 30,000,000 who were tossed overboard during the centuries of the slave trade. And the other millions who died in my cotton fields and hanging from my trees.

I will recall all those who died of broken hearts and broken spirits, under the insult of segregation.

I will raise up all the mothers who died exhausted after birthing twenty-one children to work sunup to sundown on my plantation. I will restore to full health all those who perished for lack of food, shelter, sunlight, and love; and from my inability to recognize them as human beings.

But I will go even further:

I will tell you, black woman, that I wish to be forgiven the sins I commit daily against you and your children. For I know that until I treat your children with love, I can never be trusted by my own. Nor can I respect myself.

And I will free your children from insultingly high infant mortality rates, short life spans, horrible housing, lack of food, rampant ill health. I will liberate them from the ghetto. I will open wide the doors of all the schools and hospitals and businesses of society to your children. I will look at your children and see, not a threat, but a joy.

I will remove myself as an obstacle in the path that your children, against all odds, are making toward the light. I will not assassinate them for dreaming dreams and offering new visions of how to live. I will cease trying to lead your children, for I can see I have never understood where I was going. I will agree to sit quietly for a century or so, and meditate on this.

This is what the white man can say to the black woman.
We are listening.

PART THREE

LAYING CLAIM TO THE PROMISE:
THE STRUGGLE FOR EMPOWERMENT

Chronology and Publication History of Speeches

Mary McLeod Bethune, "Breaking The Bars To Brotherhood." 1935. Delivered before the twenty-first annual conference of the National Association for the Advancement of Colored People in St. Louis, Missouri on 28 June 1935 in acceptance of the Spingarn Medal; Speech text in Mary McLeod Bethune Papers, Amistad Research Center at Tulane University at New Orleans, Louisiana.

Sadie T. M. Alexander, "Founders Day Address." 1963. Delivered before the Founders Day Convocation at Spelman College in Atlanta, Georgia; published in *The Negro Speaks* (1970) edited by Jamye and McDonald Williams.

Lorraine Hansberry, "A Challenge To Artists." 1963. Delivered at a rally to abolish the House Un-American Activities Committee on 27 October 1962; published in *Freedomways* (Winter 1963).

Patricia Roberts Harris, "The Law And Moral Issues." 1963. Delivered at the 1963 Convocation of the Howard University School of Religion at Washington, D. C.; published in *The Journal Of Religious Thought*, Volume XXI, Number 1, 1964-65.

Edith S. Sampson, "Choose One Of Five." 1963. Delivered at the Centennial Commencement at North Central College in Illinois on 30 May 1965; published in *The Negro Speaks* (1970) edited by Jamye Williams and McDonald Williams.

Margaret Walker Alexander, "Religion, Poetry, and History: Foundations For A New Educational System." 1988; Delivered before the National Urban League Conference, New Orleans, Louisiana, 29 July 1968; published in *Vital Speeches Of The Day* (15 October 1968).

Shirley Chisholm, "It Is Time For A Change." 1969. Delivered before the House of Representatives, 26 March 1969; published in the *Congressional Record* (91st Congress, 1st Session).

Coretta Scott King, "We Need To Be United." 1970. Delivered before the twenty-second Automobile Workers' Constitutional Convention in Atlantic City; published in transcript of *What If I Am A Woman?* by Folkways Records (1977).

Alice Walker, "The Unglamorous But Worth While Duties Of The Black Revolutionary Artist, Or Of The Black Writer Who Simply Works and Writes." 1970. Delivered at Sarah Lawrence College; published in *In Search Of Our Mothers Gardens* by Alice Walker (1983).

Coretta Scott King, "The Right To A Decent Life And Human Dignity." 1970. Delivered before farm workers of the Mexican-American Agricultural workers;

published in *El Malcriado*, publication of the United Farm Workers' organizing committee (15 January 1971).

Barbara Jordan, "Democratic Convention Keynote Address." 1976. Delivered before the Democratic National Convention in New York City on 12 July 1976; published in *Vital Speeches Of The Day* (15 August, 1976).

Mary McLeod Bethune, "Last Will And Testament." Written for *Ebony* magazine shortly before her death on 18 May 1955; published as a special feature thirty years later in *Ebony* (November 1985).**

**The last entry is not a speech, yet the "Will" has been frequently quoted in public addresses across the years and indeed speaks to the spirit of other African American orators actively involved in laying claim to the promises.

Introduction to Part Three

The subordinate status characterizing the lives of African Americans has dictated that much of the struggle would be reactive, as it were. For a people physically and psychologically enslaved, the predominant interest obviously resided in obtaining the basic needs of physical freedom and survival and combatting the forces that contained them, seeking what many would categorize as minimal rights. Perhaps no legitimate claim can be made that these conditions have been completely overcome, but there is a psychological need for even a disadvantaged people to look beyond the "basics" and to consider expanding possibilities and envision a more abundant existence in keeping with the intrinsic or innate yearning for dignity and respectability.

In this division of the work, the speeches address issues that encompass, but go beyond, basic human rights. They suggest an expansiveness communicating that physical freedom, mere survival, and basic rights are inadequate goals for a striving group that has contributed so significantly to the larger community of which it is a part. The women orators represented in this section attempted to lay claim to the opportunities and advantages this country purports to extend to its citizens. They looked beyond the mere attainment of physical freedom, while remaining fully cognizant of deficiencies in the distribution of justice. Yet they rejected the traditional limitations and dared to dream of becoming true heirs to the participatory governance implied in America's codified claims.

When Mary McLeod Bethune accepted the Spingarn medal from the National Association for the Advancement of Colored people in 1935, much remained undone in securing firmly the basic rights of African Americans. Yet in "Breaking the Bars to Brotherhood," perhaps the most influential American woman of African descent spoke boldly of an expanded vision. The positive tone of her address communicated confidence that the race would prosper, although she noted objectively the barriers threatening the full realization of the possibilities. In similar fashion, Sadie T.M. Alexander in her "Founders Day Address" at Spelman College in 1963, spoke to the possibilities of the race and enumerated strategies with the potential of yielding an elevated status for women of color. Alexander linked the impressive legacy of African Americans, impressive because of the unfavorable circumstances under which it had evolved, with the future progress of the race.

Lorraine Hansberry and Alice Walker, creative artists, provided an enhancing dimension to prospects of African Americans. In "A Challenge To Artists" in 1963, Hansberry recognized the responsibility of creative artists to articulate and guard zealously the aspirations of the race. Lamenting the reality of forces conspiring to maintain the silence of artists, she declared her own commitment not only to communicate her perception of the conscience of her people but to participate actively in effectuating social change. Alice Walker in "The Unglamorous But Worthwhile Duties Of The Black Revolutionary Artist" delivered in 1970, enumerated the multiplicity of issues that should engage the energies of artists. She argued for the subordination of fame and glory to the often mundane tasks that would ultimately enrich the quality of life for African Americans.

Assuming responsibility for the moral climate of the nation is Patricia Robert Harris' primary appeal in "The Law And Moral Issues." In this speech, delivered in 1963, Harris explicated the inappropriate transference of moral arbitration from the community and the clergy to members of the legal profession. Harris's address challenged auditors to moral initiative, a posture that could significantly enhance the quality of life and promote self-determination. The theme of self-determination also permeates Edith S. Sampson's address "Choose One Of Five." Sampson's charge, delivered in 1965, suggested individual empowerment. This empowerment derives from making appropriate choices and requires the willingness to sacrifice ease and simplicity for the more exacting, but ultimately more rewarding, challenges of perseverance, dedication, and moral courage.

Margaret Walker Alexander's "Religion, Poetry, And History: Foundations For A New Educational System" (1968) is at once a corrective and an exhortation. In the address, Walker analyzes distorted perspectives that have clouded the vision and perception of the youth of both races. Clarification of these distortions, she argued eloquently, would obtain only in an altered educational system that corrected the "miseducation" militating against understanding and good will. She urged collaboration among groups toward the end of expanding our world view and, thereby, our possibilities for growth and progress.

In 1969, Shirley Chisholm delivered her first address before the House of Representatives. "It Is Time For A Change" went beyond the immediate realities of poverty and suffering to a rendering of national priorities that would justify the reputation of America as a land of opportunity. Although the specific issue before the House at the time was that of financial expenditures, Chisholm's vision was far more expansive in that it suggested a new and progressive mentality that would inform the future conduct of the republic. This transformed perspective would go beyond basic freedom and render possible expanded horizons for those traditionally trapped by subordination and oppression.

Coretta Scott King's "We Need To Be United" expanded the concerns of the race to global issues. In this expansion, however, she in no way minimized the reality of continuing prejudices and biases dictated by racial identification. She urged the abandonment of myths and prejudices dividing potentially powerful coalitions and a vision extending beyond mere survival. Battles won in the past under more unfavorable circumstances, she suggested, should serve as incentives for the rapidly expanding concerns that must be considered by any aspiring group. Barbara Jordan's "Keynote Address" before the Democratic National Convention in 1976 also spoke to the possibilities of expanded horizons and empowerment. The spirit of inclusion demonstrated by her place of prestige on this occasion held, in her view, the seeds for a national community wherein the aspirations of the race could be more fully realized.

One speech presented in this section without analysis that represents the spirit of empowerment is Coretta Scott King's "The Right To A Decent Life And Human Dignity" delivered in 1970. In this address, King recognizes the power of the masses in effecting social change. Such a conviction underscores the centrality of self-determination. King's primary emphasis in this speech is the strength deriving from unity that renders more accessible the empowerment so continuously sought by the disadvantaged. The closing selection in the work is not a speech *per se*, yet it represents a resounding exhortation to women of color and is frequently invoked for inspiration. Mary McLeod Bethune's "Last Will And Testament" encompasses the numerous considerations that should comprise the continuing agenda of women of color. Editors of *Ebony* magazine, refer to Bethune's work as "one of the great historical documents of our times."

Speeches in this section range, chronologically, from 1833 to 1976. As the status of the race and the gender shifted in more positive directions during this time span, a considerable transformation of attitudes and behavior on the part of oppressor and oppressed was indicated. The crucial attribute of speeches in this section is an attitude of hope tempered by an awareness of the realities. This attitude encompasses a spirit that has refused to yield to the crushing forces of prejudice and injustice, one that recognizes transcendence as a reasonable eventuality in the lives of African American women. From Maria Stewart to Barbara Jordan, woman orators have imbued their expression with a vigor worthy of transcendence and ultimate empowerment. Through their expanded vision, they were laying claim to the promises espoused by a nation whose codes of justice implied empowerment for all its citizens.

Introduction to Mary McLeod Bethune's
"Breaking the Bars to Brotherhood"

Mary McLeod Bethune's "Breaking the Bars to Brotherhood" encompasses features of both ceremonial and deliberative discourse. Bethune commends the philosophy and efforts of the National Association for the Advancement of Colored People and appropriately expresses her gratitude for their endorsement of her own efforts, as demonstrated by the presentation of the Spingarn medal awarded annually by the NAACP in honor of "the highest or noblest achievement by an American Negro during the preceding year or years" (Peare 1951, 158). Peare describes the Spingarn Medal as "a gold medal on which was embossed a figure holding the scales of justice in one hand and the sword of courage in the other" (Peare 1951, 15). Much of the speech is an appeal for brotherhood and a challenge to embrace the full implications of that concept. The speaker presents a compelling analysis of brotherhood, noting as well impediments to its attainment. Her constructive argument, though, consists of a series of challenges and possibilities with the potential of removing or minimizing the obstacles threatening the struggle. Using the metaphor of dead branches to symbolize the obstacles, she offers cogent arguments suggesting strategies for clearing the dead branches so that the journey toward freedom can proceed more efficiently.

Born on 10 July 1875, Mary McLeod Bethune was the fifteenth of seventeen children born to slave parents in Mayesville, South Carolina. Educated at Scotia Seminary and Moody Bible Institute, Bethune was possessed with an intense desire to do missionary work in Africa. With that dream thwarted by circumstances, she turned her mind to an equally important domestic project—the education of African American girls. Starting with the property on which stood the

257

dump where she once salvaged discarded items, she established the Daytona School for Girls. That school grew and later merged with Cookman Seminary to become the school now known as Bethune Cookman College in Daytona Beach, Florida. Bethune went on to become President of the National Association of Colored Women, advisor to four Presidents, and one of history's most highly esteemed African American women. A statue erected to commemorate her extraordinary accomplishments and prominence in American affairs now stands in the District of Columbia's Lincoln Park. According to an article in the *Montgomery Advertiser* (2 June 1974), this statue is the "first memorial to a black American woman to be erected on public land in the nation's capital."

Bethune's appearance as the Spingarn medalist winner in 1935 placed her in an impressive legacy. The National Association for The Advancement of Colored People (NAACP) was founded in 1909. Noted historian John Hope Franklin places the organization of the NAACP within a legacy of several other efforts of African Americans to demonstrate their pride in the race and its possibilities: Negro Health Week initiated by Booker T. Washington, and Negro History Week by Carter G. Woodson. The awarding of the Spingarn medal was initiated in 1914 (Franklin 1980, 429). Earlier recipients of the award include George Washington Carver, W.E.B. DuBois, James Weldon Johnson, Walter White, Marian Anderson, Roland Hayes, A. Phillip Randolph, William F. Hastie, Dr. Percy Julian, and Ralph J. Bunche.

Mary McLeod Bethune's ascent from a life of poverty in Mayesville, South Carolina to this achievement remains one of this country's most phenomenal success stories. Her biographer recounts Bethune's response to the announcement of the organization's decision to bestow this significant honor upon her, the announcement in the form of a letter from Walter E. White, Executive Secretary of the NAACP and himself a prominent writer and politician of considerable prominence. Peare writes that Mrs. Bethune carefully put the letter from Walter White aside. "Deep within her still lurked the barefoot cotton picker who so desperately wanted to learn to read and who wept so profusely when she was told there would be a school for her. That little girl still went wild with joy when fortune smiled at her, still fell on her knees and thanked the sky" (Peare 1951, 157).

Breaking The Bars to Brotherhood
Mary McLeod Bethune
1935

Mr. Chairman, My Fellow Citizens, Members and Officers of the National Association for the Advancement of Colored People: There is a great happiness in my heart tonight—not a selfish, personal happiness, but a happiness and satisfaction that come to one who has labored in the heat of the day for the common good, and now as the shadows of life begin to lengthen comes to receive a "Well Done," a signal of recognition of one's life work. And with this happiness comes a humble gratitude for the distinguished approval of this organization dedicated to the cause of social justice and human welfare. To be worthy of being included in the illustrious group of Spingarn medalists, who by their intelligence, courage, devotion, faith and work have helped to shape and build a better world, one must respond to the stimulus of this occasion with a spirit of rededication to service, of reconsecration to the needs of the people. This spirit of rededication and reconsecration permeates me now as I stand before you.

The National Association for the Advancement of Colored People has for the past twenty-six years accepted the challenge of the times and has ventured forth upon its task, high endeavor for human understanding, and the world has responded to this endeavor. I seem to hear this call, coming from the pioneers of this great movement:

> Come, Clear the way; then, clear the way.
> Blind kings and creeds have had their day.
> Break the dead branches from the path.
> Our hope is in the aftermath.
> Our hope is in heroic man,

Star-led to build the world again.
To this event all ages ran;
Make way for brotherhood;
Make way for man.

This dauntless organization has spent its efforts almost wholly in clearing the way for a race, in breaking dead branches from the paths of liberty and the pursuit of happiness. The success of the early clearers of the way is but an indication of what is yet to be done by those who follow in their train. The dead branches hewn away by those stalwart pioneers left plain and straight the highway which the youths are travelling. That way brought us hope. That is the song which the past has taught us. Now we keep faith with that hope to sing the song which the present challenges.

If I have merited the honor of receiving the Spingarn medal, it is because my life has been dedicated to the task of breaking the bars to brotherhood. Brotherhood is not an ideal. It is but a state or a condition attendant upon achievement of an ideal. It is one of the components of an ideal. I believe that brotherhood depends upon and follows achievement. In the light of this belief, I wish to indicate and develop briefly those fundamental principles and issues involved in bringing about a state of brotherhood.

The law of life is the law of cooperation, and unless we learn thoroughly this fundamental tenet of social organization I fear that the historian of the future, when he attempts to record the history of the black man in America, will write "a people possessed of tremendous possibilities, potentialities and resources, mental and physical, but a people unable to capitalize [on] them because of their racial non-cohesiveness." If we would make way for social and political justice and a larger brotherhood, we must cooperate. Racial cohesion means making a road of all of the achievements of those who have educational advantages until we reach the lowest man, the lowest strata of the masses; that mass that is standing so helplessly waiting for you and for me to administer the human touch.

Unless the people have vision, they perish. What can we see; and, having seen, are we willing to venture? Do we see our large opportunity for the race to produce? Do we see an intellectual interpretation of our religious thought unhampered by superstitious belief, or limited by too great a satisfaction? Do we see the brotherhood of the peoples of the world working out an abundant life in their activities, of duty, of art, of business, of every day living?

The National Association for the Advancement of Colored People has always sought men of vision to lead the way. Today we pray for the expansion of that vision from a few to an ever increasing group of prepared men and women and of youths of all races to guide and direct the mass. The veil of ignorance and superstition is not yet lifted. Broad vision, zeal and preparedness will do much to lift it. Social group understanding and appreciation are necessary to brotherhood. The dead branches of misunderstanding and lack of appreciation have kept our existence clouded with prejudice. Human understanding is the key to brotherhood. The march of racial advancement is continually hindered by misunderstanding. Misunderstandings clutter up the highways of life which make for true harmonious relations.

But right must triumph and prejudice must be done away with. In this staunch belief, men and women of this organization continue to struggle toward the goal of social justice and to strive for worthy and proper consideration for every man in his right to live, to be, to do, to possess, and to pursue happiness. Now is the time for thinking men and women, for thinking youths of every race, to stand up with those who have labored for years and be counted, in their participation in this great forward marcn of the National Association for the Advancement of Colored People. No greater crime can there be than that one in which a man should be unfair to his neighbor and interferes with his right to develop harmonious relationships and realize the highest attainment of his abilities. The great unrest in the world today, the great doubts which assail men, the enormous amount of mistrust entangles our lives and makes us look askance at our brothers, all are the products of injustice, wrought by one man upon another.

Equality of opportunity is necessary to brotherhood. We stand in adoration of those who, regardless of the section of the country in which they live, have been big enough, courageous enough, to stand for social justice and equality of opportunity, even at the risk of their lives. The National Association for the Advancement of Colored People has proven the necessity for breaking the bars to brotherhood through their advocacy of the destruction of blind kings and creeds which have been rulers in the lives of humanity. The creeds of selfishness, self-centered ideas, have led to narrow leadership. The creed of over-ambition and self domination has led to unfair publicity. Let us cease to give allegiance to such unmoral kinship in our lives. Above all, let us cease now to render allegiance to the creed of belief in the inherent superiority of white and the inherent inferiority of black. Let us rest with confidence on the creed of larger development in our narrow selves; greater scope of opportunity to work out our ambitions; sure and certain belief in all convictions which are ours; and towering over all, our belief in becoming free men.

The creed of freedom has not yet been written. Humanity is yet a slave to her desires, her fears, her intelligence, her social standing, her craving for power. Let us as workers under this banner make free men spread truth about economic adjustment; truth about moral obligation; truth about segregation; truth about citizenship; truth about home building; yes, truth wherever truth is needed. Then our lives may be lived with freedom and we shall be what ourselves demand us to be.

Who shall disseminate this truth? I would call tonight upon those who are star-led, who have clearly in mind a purpose in life; who do not fear the struggle and the work which must needs be the lot of those who dare to live above the cloud of popular thought and limited desires.

My fellow citizens, in the light of this dream, in the light of this firm hope, in the belief that brotherhood is the desired end in life, in accordance with God's plan, and with a rededication to share in the responsibility of rebuilding and inspiring vision, to keep faith with the ideals and purposes of the National Association for the Advancement of Colored People, I, in the name of the womanhood of America, accept this medal. I accept it with gratitude for the opportunity for God-given service. I accept it as a badge which will mark me before all men as an advocate of respect and justice for all mankind. The brightness which we saw so many years ago has become a light, a star. May we challenge ourselves anew and follow in its radiance, ever thoughtful, ever courageous, ever enduring, in molding lives with highest principles. And may those who follow after us gain inspiration because we dare to stand at a time like this.

Mr. Chairman, my fellow citizens, I am grateful.

Introduction to Sadie T. M. Alexander's "Founders' Day Address"

Sadie Alexander's "Founders' Day Address" confirms the assertion made by Williams in *The Negro Speaks* that when an African American "mounts the platform to speak for a university convocation or commencement, to keynote a conference or convention, to inspire a mammoth civil rights rally or a march on Washington, his speech reflects a concern for both the general problems of our democracy and the specific problems of the race" (Williams and Williams 1970, XI-XII). The speech is indeed a Founders' Day address and accords to Spelman College its rightful place in the legacy of colleges contributing to national progress, but the emphasis is on what the students and alumnae can do to enhance the status of the race. Alexander links the multi-level legacy of African Americans in general, noted leaders of the race, and Negro colleges to the destiny and commission of those to whom she speaks. The address also enumerates strategies that auditors can employ to contribute to the goals of the race.

Sadie T. Mossell was born in Philadelphia in 1898. Her educational achievements were outstanding, and her influence continued for decades. Reviewing her accomplishments is a long recital of "firsts." She was the first woman to earn a law degree from the University of Pennsylvania and the first African American woman to gain admittance to the Pennsylvania bar. And she was the first African American woman to earn a Ph.D. in the United States as well as the first Black woman solicitor in the state of Pennsylvania. Alexander was an early proponent of women's participation in the work force, claiming that "the satisfaction which comes to the woman in realizing that she is a producer makes for peace and happiness, the chief requisites in any home" (Giddings 1984, 197).

267

The speech considered here was the Founders' Day Address delivered at Spelman College in 1963. Spelman College opened on April 11, 1881, in the basement of Friendship Baptist Church in Atlanta, Georgia. Grants from the Rockefeller Foundation and other agencies ensured the survival of the school as an independent institution, averting a recommended merger with the Atlanta Seminary for Men, later Morehouse College. The school was officially named Spelman Seminary after the mother of Laura Spelman Rockefeller. Beginning with an industrial emphasis, Spelman College emerged as one of the nation's most prestigious colleges for African American women. Sophia B. Packard and Harriet Giles, white northerners, "chose Atlanta as the site of the industrial school for women because its healthful climate, railroad connections, and spirit of enterprise, have made it largely the political, commercial and educational center of the state" (Neverdon-Morton 1989, 41).

Founders' Day Address
Sadie T. M. Alexander
1963

Dr. Manley, Members of the Board of Trustees, Members of the Faculty, Students, and Friends of Spelman College:

I consider it a privilege and honor to have been invited to deliver the Founders' Day Address at your renowned institution. The high academic standing of Spelman is recognized not only by your membership in the Southern Association of Colleges and Schools, and the appearance of your College on the approved list of the Association of American Universities, as well as the American Association of University Women, but more important, by the distinction attained in the life of our country by too many of your graduates for time to permit me to enumerate.

When Spelman College was established on April 11, 1881, only sixteen years after the Civil War, both Negroes and concerned whites, such as your founders, Sophia B. Packard and Harriet E. Giles, realized that the Negro had only been freed from physical shackles, and that if the mind of the Negro was to be freed so that he could develop the ability and will to secure for himself and posterity the rights guaranteed under the Constitution or the Bill of Rights, emphasis must be placed upon education. At the beginning, as evidenced by the training provided the eleven students of the first class of your college, who were "eager to learn to read the Bible and write well enough to send letters to their children," the courses of study involved only the most rudimentary elements, such as learning to read, write, and count. From this meager start developed classes in sewing, cooking, millinery, and nurse training, but as public education began to fulfill these needs, Spelman, along with similar Negro institutions, began to train for leadership.

269

From your College and other Negro colleges and universities came most of the professional men and women who have assumed leadership at the local and national level. There is indeed little racial strategy today which was not to some degree developed by them, including the pickets and sit-ins. In 1913, my uncle, Doctor Nathan F. Mossell (a graduate of Lincoln University, class of 1879, and of the University of Pennsylvania Medical School, class of 1882, from which latter institution he was the first Negro to receive a degree from any department), having protested in vain to the Mayor of Philadelphia against the showing of *The Birth of a Nation*, led more than one thousand Negroes in a march from the heart of the Negro population to the center of the city, where the theater was located. This tumultuous demonstration broke up the show. Moreover, the relatively small number of colored men and women who were trained at the eastern and western colleges and universities made notable contributions; among these were Doctor W. E. B. Du Bois, the first historian to study sympathetically and scientifically Negro communities and institutions; Carter G. Woodson, who dedicated his life to recording and preserving Negro history; Abram Harris in economics; E. Franklin Frazier in sociology; Ralph Bunche in political science; and Charles Houston, who brought the first successful civil rights action, taught and gave the inspiration which produced Thurgood Marshall and his volunteer staff of consultants.

It is my confirmed opinion that had it not been for the continuous, never-ending efforts and demands of the American Negro to "secure these rights" guaranteed by the fundamental laws of this nation, the United States might have forgotten and lost its claim to being a democracy. Not until the Hitler holocaust did the Jews in America join our fight for equality. Not until the Japanese-Americans were placed in concentration camps did they even form an organization of their own people. The Negro ministers, whose church doors have always been open to us; the pioneer political and social workers of the stature of Walter White and Eugene Kinckle Jones; educators, such as Mary McLeod Bethune and John Hope; and Negro lawyers, such as Charles Houston, Austin Walden, Raymond Pace Alexander have carried on a relentless battle to keep alive and give meaning to the rights guaranteed American citizens.

In the Far East, Asia, Western Europe, Central and South America, college students have over the years taken the lead in effecting social change. Two years ago in Japan, I witnessed the demonstrations of students against rearmament. I also saw students in Chile marching in protest against an increase in bus fares. I have seen unnumbered hordes of students in India stopping all traffic as they filled the streets of New Delhi protesting the delay of the United States in shipping wheat. Where there has been hunger, imperialism, dictatorship, exploitation, college students have in many countries often demonstrated against what they believe to be unjust. In the United States and England, the usual protest has been, until recently, by debate rather than by positive action. In this country, it was the southern Negro student who first undertook sustained direct action. First he started the sit-ins and later was joined by freedom riders. These activities reflect a growing sense of security of an increasing middle class and the effect of world pressure on the United States to root out and destroy discrimination. The rise of twenty-one independent African states has had tremendous influence on Negroes in the United States and has caused them to be determined to secure freedom for the oppressed peoples of their native country.

You students of Spelman College, and your counterparts in other colleges and universities of the United States, will live after your graduation in communities of a nation where there is constant agitation and action for the eradication of the situations which cause us to be called Negroes rather than Americans. Your problem will be one of strategy and techniques. You must realize the calculated risk inherent in any leadership efforts, and be prepared to face criticism if your approach proves not to be generally acceptable to the community or if you refuse to join a movement which, after careful consideration, you do not believe is sound morally and technically. What is the best approach?

I am by no means wise enough, nor foolish enough, to offer you the answer . . . However, based upon long years of experience in the vineyard, I should like to suggest some guiding principles and point out a few of the problems you and I will face in the next decade:

1. There is an expression used by some colored people when referring to others of their racial background, that is, "She is colored just like I am." The mentally enslaved Negro who makes such a remark well knows that you college students, your professors, your president, and other leaders are subject to the same disrespect and indignities by the ignorant, poor, socially unaccepted white man, that he is. Only by achieving equality of opportunity for the lowest man on the totem pole, do we secure the rights of all of our people—white and colored alike.

2. Only by making democracy work in the United States, not tinkling cymbal and sounding brass, do we make secure our way of life. The people of the world have the choice between democracy and communism or possibly annihilation. There is no question that all of us, regardless of the inequities, privation, and suffering we have so long endured in the United States, would choose first to live and next to live the democratic way of life . . . In our struggle to secure equality of opportunity, personal security, respect for individual dignity, and rights of full citizenship we are

making a heroic struggle not only for ourselves but, of greater importance, a struggle for the survival of the United States. America cannot hope that the uncommitted nations of the world, or those controlled by dictatorship, will choose the democratic way if our failures to put into practice our pronounced belief in freedom continue to be heralded around the world. By destroying every vestige of discrimination at home, we make democracy secure at home and, in so doing, are the hope of the people of the world. Yes, the freedom riders and the sit-ins work not only to free themselves but also to make America free.

3. The capacity for peaceful, orderly change in America has kept this nation vigorous and alive. It is the hope for change which must motivate the masses of American Negroes. But despite all that has been accomplished, we are still suffering from racial and religious discrimination. It exists in education, employment, housing, and public accommodations—North, South, East, and West. Here and there individuals have been able to break through the barriers in the communities in which they reside. But, as you and I know, they are exceptions to the rule . . . The great mass of colored people in the United States have had no such advantage. As a result we have been slow in developing even a small middle class. According to the census of 1960, only 13,056 nonwhites in Philadelphia and 1644 in Atlanta made over $6,000 in 1959.

The great mass of our people, discouraged by years of closed doors, have not accepted middle-class goals and values. For the past ten years, I have been a member of the Philadelphia Commission on Human Rights. We have a staff of twenty-nine persons, including eleven highly trained professionals, and a budget of close to $300,000. We do not receive in one year thirty complaints in discrimination in employment. Filing a complaint is meaningless to a man who has worn thin the soles of his shoes filing applications for work and then watched less skilled white applicants being employed. Our Commission has to send inspectors into the industries to count the number of colored employees, skilled and unskilled, and examine employment applications in order to ferret out the discrimination. We must subpoena the records when the employer is uncooperative and hold expensive, prolonged public hearings to throw the light of public opinion on the employment problem.

When the masses of Negroes upon whom lack of opportunity had imposed low horizons, limited aspirations and motivation, reflect consciously or unconsciously on these matters, they conclude it is not worthwhile to try to emerge into the middle class. The chance of succeeding is too slim to be worth the terrific effort. This attitude will not change by the masses' seeing, reading, or hearing about the limited number of Negroes who have emerged into the stream of American life. It will change only as the unceasing number of educated youths dedicate their lives not exclusively to making money but to convincing the Negro masses that the rewards of the American way of life are available to all who are willing to make sacrifices and to arousing the people in the communities in which they live to the acceptance of the Negro, the Puerto Rican, the Mexican, all the people of this heterogeneous nation into the mainstream of American life—into the churches, industries, and places of public accommodation, amusement, and culture.

4. The opportunities for unskilled labor, filled by mass migration in World War I and the employment of a million Negro workers in World War II in civilian jobs within four years, gave us an opportunity to prove ability to perform basic factory operations in a variety of businesses, in semiskilled and skilled capacities. Today, however, the demand is no longer for the unskilled or semiskilled workers;

in the present industrial expansion in electronics, television, air-conditioning, spacecraft, and plastics, a worker is required to be highly skilled. Thus, the man or woman without skills today is destined to excessive or continuous periods of unemployment. Are you college students and alumnae prepared with the high degree of skill that employment requires today? In my profession, we call the secretaries "the prima donnas." A competent legal secretary demands and receives better pay than the average public school teacher. The shortage is so great that white law offices are seeking capable colored secretaries who know how to spell, can comprehend what they read, and understand the meaning of material dictated to them.

The freedom rides, sit-ins, boycotts are performing a service which history alone can fully evaluate. These activities have proven their effectiveness by the results you have seen in Georgia—where the University of Georgia has its first colored students; where the legislature adopted a local option law which permits localities to determine whether or not schools are to be desegregated; where by edict of the United States Supreme Court, the unit voting system has been broken, and as a result, for the first time in ninety-two years a Negro Senator has been elected to the Georgia State Legislature. Certainly much remains to be done in Georgia as well as all over the United States. But the momentum has opened the dike, and the hole, pouring out the forces of opposing desegregation, is constantly widening.

My concern is that you and I be prepared to live in the highly competitive world in which we will find ourselves as the walls of segregation come tumbling down. Will the few who secure the first top jobs remember the many who are still at the bottom of the ladder and continue to bring them to the top? Will we remember that our apparent security is dependent upon the degree of security enjoyed by all citizens of this country and the world, and thus concern ourselves with foreign affairs, world disarmament, or the plight of the deprived at home, in South America, Asia, and the world? Will we be determined to prepare ourselves with such excellence in skills needed in this atomic age that our talents will be sought after with more zeal than we can seek the opportunity to use them? In what degree we answer these questions will depend not only the freedom of Negroes in the United States but also the securing of freedom to all the people of this nation and the world.

Introduction to Lorraine Hansberry's
"A Challenge To Artists"

"A Challenge To Artists" addresses a theme explored by creative minds across time, the responsibility of artists to the bigger world outside their own creative realms. Lorraine Hansberry concedes experiencing a degree of inadequacy in her contemplation of the issues of "real life" and examines some of the forces contributing to the isolation traditionally experienced by artists. She acknowledges, however, the responsibility of artists to participate in the protection of their own well being and then proceeds to criticize directly the political actions of President John F. Kennedy in the Carribeans. Her final appeal is a continuing courageous response to the issues that influence not only their lives but the lives of those around them. She adds a cosmic dimension to the address as she acknowledges the common links in the destiny of all humankind.

Lorraine Vivian Hansberry, widely acclaimed author of *A Raisin in the Sun* (1959), was born in 1930 in Chicago, Illinois, the youngest of four children. Hansberry was the author of at least seven books and a political activist according to her own convictions. She grew up among parents and relatives who exhibited social consciousness and the courage to be advocates of the causes in which they believed. Steven Carter describes the scope of Hansberry's political concerns in addition to her work in drama and her commitment to scholarship. Hansberry, according to Steven R. Carter, received another education: "Another part of her education came through her involvement in peace and freedom movements which led her to marching on picket lines, speaking on Harlem street corners, and taking part in delegations to try to save persons whom she considered to be unjustly convicted of crimes" (Carter 1985, 38). Although she reserved time for her creative work, she "devoted considerable time to interviews, lectures, speeches at demonstrations, and essays on issues that she felt must be addressed to move her country toward its vitally needed transformation" (Carter 1985, 38).

A Challenge To Artists
Lorraine Hansberry
1963

I am afraid that I haven't made a speech for a very long time, and there is a significance in that fact, which is part of what I should like to talk about this evening.

A week or so ago I was at my typewriter working on a scene in a play of mine in which one character, a German novelist, is trying to explain to another character, an American intellectual, something about what led the greater portion of the German intelligentsia to acquiesce to Nazism. He says this: "They (the Nazis) permitted us to feel, in return for our silence, that we were nonparticipants—merely irrelevant if inwardly agonized observers who had nothing whatsoever to do with that which was being committed in our names."

Just as I put the period after that sentence, my own telephone rang and I was confronted with the voice of Dr. Otto Nathan, asking this particular American writer if she would be of this decade and this nation and appear at this rally this evening and join a very necessary denunciation of a lingering *American* kind of travesty.

It is the sort of moment of truth that dramatists dearly love to put on the stage but find as uncomfortable as everyone else in life. To make it short, however, I am here.

I mean to say that one can become detached in this world of ours; we can get to a place where we read only the theater or photography or music pages of our newspapers. And then we wake up one day and find that the better people of our nation are still where they were when we last noted them: in the courts defending *our* Constitutional rights for us.

279

This makes me feel that it might be interesting to talk about where are our artists in the contemporary struggles. Some of them, of course, are being heard and felt. Some of the more serious actresses such as Shelley Winters and Julie Harris and a very thoughtful comedian such as Steve Allen have associated themselves with some aspect of the peace movement and Sidney Poitier and Harry Belafonte have made significant contributions to the Negro struggle. But the vast majority—where are they?

Well, I am afraid that they are primarily where the ruling powers have always wished the artist to be and to stay: in their studios. They are consumed, in the main, with what they consider to be larger issues—such as "the meaning of life," etcetera. I personally consider that part of this detachment is the direct and indirect result of many years of things like the House Committee and concurrent years of McCarthyism in all its forms. I mean to suggest that the climate of fear, which we were once told, as I was coming along, by wise men, would bear a bitter harvest in the culture of our civilization, has in fact come to pass. In the contemporary arts, the rejection of this particular world is no longer a mere grotesque threat, but a fact.

Among my contemporaries and colleagues in the arts the search for the roots of war, the exploitation of man, of poverty and of despair itself, is sought in any arena other than the one which has shaped these artists. Having discovered that the world is incoherent, they have—some of them—also come to the conclusion that it is also unreal and, in any case, beyond the corrective powers of human energy. Having determined that life is in fact an absurdity, they have not yet decided that the task of the thoughtful is to try and help impose purposefulness on that absurdity. They don't yet agree, by and large, that simply being against life as it is is not enough; that simply *not* being a "rhinoceros" is not enough. That, moreover, replacing phony utopianism of one kind with vulgar and cheap little philosophies of accommodation is also not enough. In a word, they do not yet agree that it is perhaps the task, I should think certainly the joy, of the artist to chisel out some expression of what life can conceivably be.

The fact is that this unwitting capitulation really does aim to be a revolt; really does aim to indict—*something*. Really does aim to be partisan in saying no to a world which it generally characterizes as a "brothel." I am thinking now, mainly, of course, of writers of my generation. It is they, upon whom we must depend so heavily for the refinement and articulation of the aspiration of man, who do not yet agree that if the world is a brothel, then someone has built the edifice; and that if it was the hand of man, then the hand of man can reconstruct it—that whatever man renders, creates, imagines, he can render afresh, re-create and even more gloriously re-imagine. But, I must repeat, that anyone who can even think so these days is held to be an example of unparalleled simple-mindedness.

Why? For this is what is cogent to our meeting tonight; the writers that I am presently thinking of come mainly from my generation. That is to say that they come from a generation which was betrayed in the late forties and fifties by the domination of McCarthyism. We were ceaselessly told, after all, to be everything which mutilates youth: to be silent, to be ignorant, to be without unsanctioned opinions, to be compliant and, above all else, obedient to all the ideas which are in fact the dregs of an age. We were taught that agitational activity in behalf of changing this world was nothing but an expression, among other things, of our "neurotic compulsions" about our own self-dissatisfactions because our mothers dominated our fathers or some such as that. We were told in an age of celebrated liberations of repressions that the repression of the urge to protest against war was surely the only respectable repression left in the universe.

As for those who went directly into science or industry it was all even less oblique than any of that. If you went to the wrong debates on campus, signed the wrong petitions, you simply didn't get the job you wanted and you were forewarned of this early in your college career.

And, of course, things are a little different that in my parents' times—I mean, with regard to the candor with which young people have been made to think in terms of money. It is the only single purpose which has been put before them. That which Shakespeare offered as a curse, "Put money in thy purse," is now a boast. What makes me think of that in connection with what we are speaking of tonight? Well, I hope that I am wise enough to determine the nature of a circle. If, after all, the ambition in life is merely to be rich, then all which might threaten that possibility is much to be avoided, is it not? This means, therefore, not incurring the disfavor of employers. It means that one will not protest war if one expects to draw one's livelihood from, say, the aircraft industry if one is an engineer. Or, in the arts, how can one write plays which have either implicit or explicit in them a quality of the detestation of commerciality, if in fact one is beholden to the commerciality of the professional theatre? How can one protest the criminal persecution of political dissenters if one has already discovered at nineteen that to do so is to risk a profession? If all one's morality is wedded to the opportunistic, the expedient in life, how can one have the deepest, most profound moral outrage about the fact of the condition of the Negro people in the United States? Particularly, thinking of expediency, when one has it dinned into one's ears day after day that the only reason why, perhaps, that troublesome and provocative group of people must some day be permitted to buy a cup of coffee or rent an apartment or get a job—is *not* because of the recognition of the universal humanity of the human race, but because it happens to be extremely expedient international politics to now *think* of granting these things!

As I stand here I know perfectly well that such institutions as the House Committee, and all the other little committees, have dragged on their particular obscene theatrics for all these years not to expose "Communists" or do anything really in connection with the "security" of the United States, but merely to create an atmosphere where, in the first place, I should be afraid to come here tonight at all and, secondly, to absolutely guarantee that I will not say what I am going to say, which is this:

I think that my government is wrong. I would like to see them turn back our ships from the Caribbean. The Cuban people, to my mind, and I speak only for myself, have chosen their destiny and I cannot believe that it is the place of the descendants of those who did not ask the monarchists of the eighteenth century for permission to make the United States a republic, to interfere with the twentieth-century choice of another sovereign people.

I will go further, speaking as a Negro in America, and impose a little of what Negroes say all the time to each other on what I am saying to you. And that is that it would be a great thing if they would not only turn back the ships from the Caribbean but turn to the affairs of our country that need righting. For one thing, empty the legislative and judicial chambers of the victims of political persecution so we know why that lamp is burning out there in the Brooklyn waters. And, while they are at it, go on and help fulfill the American dream and empty the Southern jails of the genuine heroes, practically the last vestige of dignity that we have to boast about at this moment in our history; those students whose imprisonment for trying to insure what is already on the book is our national disgrace at this moment.

And I would go so far—perhaps with an over sense of drama, but I don't think so—to say that maybe without waiting for another two men to die, that we send those troops to finish the Reconstruction in Alabama, Georgia, Mississippi, and every place else where the fact of our federal flag flying creates the false notion that what happened at the end of the Civil War was the defeat of the slavocracy at the political as well as the military level. And I say this not merely in behalf of the black and oppressed but, for a change—and more and more thoughtful Negroes must begin to make this point—also for the white and disinherited of the South, those poor whites who, by the millions, have been made the tragic and befuddled instruments of their own oppression at the hand of the most sinister political apparatus in our country. I think perhaps that if our government would do that it would not have to compete in any wishful way for the respect of the new black and brown nations of the world.

Finally, I think that all of us who are thinking such things, who wish to exercise these rights that we are here defending tonight, must really exercise them. Speaking to my fellow artists in particular, I think that we must paint them, sing them, write about them. All these matters which are not currently fashionable. Otherwise, I think, as I have put into the mouth of my German novelist, we are indulging in a luxurious complicity—and no other thing.

I personally agree with those who say that from here on in, if we are to survive, we, the people—still an excellent phrase—we the people of the world must oblige the heads of all governments to become responsible to us. I personally do not feel that it matters if it be the government of China presently engaging in incomprehensible and insane antics at the border of India or my President, John F. Kennedy, dismissing what he knows to be in the hearts of the American people and engaging in overt provocation with our sister people to the South. I think that it is imperative to say "No" to all of it—"No" to war of any kind, anywhere. And I think, therefore, and it is my reason for being here tonight, that it is imperative to remove from the American fabric any and all such institutions or agencies as the House Committee on Un-American Activities which are designed expressly to keep us from saying "No!"

Introduction to Patricia Roberts Harris's
"The Law and Moral Issues"

"The Law and Moral Issues" explores traditional perceptions of the custodians of morality and the relationship obtaining between morality and law. The discourse analyzes the evolutionary, but informal, transference of moral responsibility from the clergy to the members of the legal profession. Lamented in the address is the absence of sustained national debate on current issues that the speaker perceives to be appropriately designated as moral issues ideally requiring the considered judgment of communities, such judgments deriving from the leadership of the clergy. The speaker emphasizes the importance of public debate on issues that define and limit acceptable codes of conduct. Noting that lawyers had spearheaded many of the current moral initiatives, the speaker clarifies the moral and legal dimensions of several pivotal issues and underscores the appropriate considerations in each domain.

Patricia Roberts Harris delivered this address at Howard University's Fall Convocation of the School of Religion in 1963, returning to her undergraduate alma mater from which she graduated in 1945. Born in Mattoon, Illinois, on 31 May 1924, Patricia Roberts Harris attended the public schools in Illinois, graduated from Howard University and George Washington University Law School. President John Kennedy appointed her co-chairman of the National Women's Committee for Civil Rights in 1963. In 1964, she received an appointment to the Commission on the Status of Puerto Rico by President Johnson and later alternative representative to the twenty-second General Assembly of the United Nations. She returned to Howard University in 1967, being named at that time Dean of the law school.

Volume twenty-nine of the *Howard Law Journal* (1969) was a memorial to Patricia Roberts Harris. Vernon E. Jordan, President of the National Urban League, characterized Harris as follows: "As an advocate for equality and as a worker in the vineyards of justice, Patricia Roberts Harris joins ranks with Harriet Tubman, Sojourner Truth, Mary Church Terrell, Mary McLeod Bethune, and countless other heroic black women who have illuminated our days and eased the pain of our passage from darkness unto light" (Jordan 1969, 419).

The Law And Moral Issues
Patricia Roberts Harris
1963

Law and morality frequently meet as the powers of government are sought to enforce and reinforce private notions of morality.

As a matter of fact, the early history of this country is a history of a surprisingly successful effort to mold the law to conform to the notions of morality of the majority community. The Puritans, in rejecting the theory of the law as the reflection of the will of the sovereign, sought instead to make it a manifestation of the Puritan ethic (an ethic which figured only recently in a debate, with the Puritan ethic affirmed as a great American principle which could not successfully be opposed). Frequently, however, these most excellent men, the Puritans, confused the ethics of individuals, the leaders of the community, such as Governor Winthrop, with the preferences of the majority, with the result not unlike the Gilbert and Sullivan quotation from *Iolanthe*:

> The Law is the true embodiment
> Of everything that's excellent.
> It has no kind of fault or flaw,
> And I, my Lords, embody the Law.

The wish carried by these lines that the law be "the true embodiment/ Of everything that's excellent" subsists today and results in attempts either to retain or to secure an enunciation of law which conforms to individual or group conviction with respect to what is excellent in the sense of what is morally sound.

And if it is the purpose of law to so order society that it may achieve the goals it has set for itself, the adoption of that part of the moral code deemed to constitute the imperative for the living of the good life would seem essential.

Any discussion of law and morality may be brought to naught if, at the outset, it is not admitted that neither the term law nor the term morality has clear and inherent meaning on which even reasonable lawyers, philosophers, or theologians will agree. I will the word *will*, rather than *can*, because the inherently disputatious nature of the three disciplines suggested, law, philosophy, and theology, accord high value to the identification and maintenance of differences and distinctions; and even though the objective experience of students of the disciplines might well lead to substantial agreement with respect to the meaning of the terms (and surprisingly often has), in order to avoid catering to our mutual disposition to disputation and argumentation, I shall define, admittedly roughly, the meaning assigned to the words in this discussion.

By law, I mean that body of rules and regulations established by official governmental units to control public and private behavior, the observance of which is secured by the threat of the imposition of penalties in the nature of fine, imprisonment, or withdrawal of a government granted benefit.

By morality, I mean that body of concepts of right behavior accepted by substantial segments of our society as standards for the evaluation of the conduct of individuals.

I am not concerned with whether or not the law is enforced; it is, for present purposes, denominated law if there exists, either under statute or subsisting precedent, the power to give effect to the law. With respect to morality, for purpose of discussion it is deemed to subsist if the concept of right behavior is applied in making judgments about the character of individuals or if the position asserted to be moral is articulated consistently as a value to be adopted by society in general and individuals in particular.

Thus, so far as my definition is concerned, the law is that men may not commit adultery. This is the law, according to S22-301 of the District of Columbia Code, despite the fact that prosecution for adultery is rare.

Also, adultery is considered immoral—is contrary to the Ten Commandments—and even among my somewhat radical friends, there is no disposition to consider such behavior desirable, even though records of divorces, and our general knowledge of modern behavior, suggest that significantly large numbers of persons engage in adulterous activity.

In illustrating that which is for present purposes denoted as law and that which is denoted as morality, I have also suggested the most apparent relationship between the two.

But as suggested in the citation of the criminal code of the District of Columbia, both laws and the articulation of moral codes live beyond the period when either can be deemed to be imperative for the appropriate ordering of society. For while I would join all who would condemn adultery, our sophisticated society now admits that its existence does not necessarily end, or even imperil, the marital or family relationship; and when it does, requirements of our domestic relations law for support of the injured spouse and children make it wiser to apply funds which might be used for a fine to that support and to permit freedom, rather than incarceration, in order to encourage the earning of sufficient money.

Nevertheless, the Damoclean Sword of possible criminal penalty hangs over the head of the wrongdoer, never really to fall, and seldom even to deter, but present to reassure us that law is the "true embodiment/ Of everything that is excellent," for it supports our morality!

But if honesty is a value—if we, as I believe we do, purport to judge behavior on the basis of its honesty—we must find immorality in the continued existence of laws that derive from notions of morality which are in process of reevaluation. It is here, it seems to me, that each person concerned with the effectuation of both law and morality must come to grips with the questions of the appropriate merging of special and general moral concepts with legal pronouncement.

Lawyers and clergymen play special roles as the interpreters and enforcers of law and morality and, through such roles, occupy positions of trust in evaluating law and morality in the context of the community's responsibility in the enforcement of each. The identification of moral imperative has been the special responsibility of the philosopher and his kinsman, the theologian. But the interpretation of these insights has been a role that communities have expected the clergy to assume, while relegating the lawyer to the role of contender for the special interests of special individuals and groups known as clients. We have historically expected the clergy to identify for the laity and to lead the laity in discussion of the nature of morality and its practical consequences for the religious communicant.

I question if today this is the role played by significant numbers of the clergy. But a short time ago a great (great in the sense of large) religious body in a nearby southern state congratulated its clergy for remaining in communication with the laity on the moral issue of racial adjustment—for not getting too far ahead of the membership on the moral issue. The custodians and articulators of moral values were complimented for not having articulated these values so clearly that they could be understood, and possibly rejected, by their parishioners.

Again, in a southern city, where a Negro church was desecrated and lives lost, four days after the tragedy the report was that not a single white minister and not a single white church had been in communication with the desecrated house of worship.

But in that city, on the day of the desecration, one voice spoke to the city and to the world of the immorality of the event, and that voice was not the voice of a minister. It was the voice of a lawyer.

This fact serves to highlight a surprising phenomenon in our present-day society. That phenomenon is that the debate about the ethical content of the law, and the moral and societal imperatives it represents, is today most likely to start with the legal profession.

With due regard to the magnificent contribution made by the clergy and others in the civil rights movement, the impetus for the present activity was the adoption of concepts riven from the rigors of legal combat, the 1954 school desegregation cases.

The debate about the appropriate role of religious observances in the publicly supported institutions of this nation had no real force until the enunciation of lawyers as advocates and of lawyers as judges required an examination of the moral imperatives of our pluralistic society. Only recently, three members of the Supreme Court opened what I hope will be a national debate about the morality of the death penalty for rape where the life of the victim was not placed in jeopardy, asking if life should be taken to preserve any value other than another life.

Thus, lawyers, rather than seeing law as the "true embodiment/Of everything that's excellent," subject it to a continuing critical scrutiny, seeking to ascertain if the law does in truth support the highest ethical and moral values of the society as it is expected to do, or if, instead, it perverts them. It is true that, in our legal system, this scrutiny is often possible for the lawyer only as he contends for the interest of his clients or as he sits in judgment of the competing contentions of disputants. Herein, of course, lies a significant limitation upon the effectiveness of the lawyer as lawyer in this area. (Of course, the lawyer as citizen or as legislator can and does make a contribution, but the chief contribution made by the lawyer to the confrontation of law and moral assertion has been in his formal activities as advocate.)

But no such limitation exists in fact or in practice upon the rest of society, and there is no reason why the aforementioned issues or any others should await the fortuitous appearance of a client whose interests permit the articulation of a demand for a reexamination of the moral base of the law.

For example, it is appalling that there has not been general national debate, of sustained duration and significant strength, on the imposition of the death penalty for rape. But the social fear of dealing with a sex crime in our eminently respectable churches and elsewhere, is, no doubt, the explanation for lack of concern about this serious issue.

But then, how do we explain the failure of our community's moral leadership to examine critically and honestly the implications of the imposition of the death penalty for any crime? Why must we await a Chessman Case to consider the moral issue involved in capital punishment?

The quick answer is, of course, that these are legal questions which only the expertise of the lawyer can deal with. But clearly they are not. Whether or not we are permitted to pray in public schools is a legal issue, but whether or not we ought to pray in school is a question with which we are all competent to deal. Whether rape or murder carries with it a death penalty or not is a legal question, but if either should, morally, or ideally, carry the death penalty is a question requiring the reconciliation of competing social values—a moral issue, which must be decided by the community. Whether or not the Fourteenth Amendment prohibits distinctions based on race is a legal question, but whether or not a democratic society can be democratic in the presence of public or private racial distinction is an issue involving judgments about the worth of the human spirit and the dignity of men—a moral question.

Thus, the decision with respect to the morality that ought to be reflected in our law is a decision to be made as a result of the enlightening activity of public debate focused upon the identification of moral values and the societal imperatives which flow from these values in the form of law. But such debate must have leadership which is sustained and itself enlightened. The strictures of present debate in these suggested areas and others is due largely to the fact that those to whom the society has delegated the task of providing moral leadership have all too frequently interpreted morality in its most narrow and parochial terms.

There is a fear of identifying broad value areas and of testing specific acts against competingly broad value assertions. Today, de Tocqueville could not say of Americans, as he did in 1835:

They have all a lively faith in the *perfectibility* of men . . . They all consider society as a body in a state of improvement, humanity as a changing scene, in which nothing is or ought to be permanent; and they admit that what appears to them today to be good may be superseded by something better tomorrow (Tocqueville 1835).

Instead, there is a general wish not to rock the boat; not to change the imperfections of today's world, because the world of tomorrow, if we change things, may be worse. But another observation of de Tocqueville's, "a republic could not exist . . . if the influence of lawyers in public business did not increase in proportion the power of the people," has meaning today.

For, as has been suggested, the most frequent initiators of significant national dialogue are these custodians of the law and not the would-be custodians of morality. . . .

Introduction to Edith S. Sampson's
"Choose One Of Five"

"Choose One Of Five" is an address that would be characterized as ceremonial or epideictic in the traditional canon. In this address, Judge Edith S. Sampson challenges members of a graduating class to one of five courses of action as they contemplate the direction of their future efforts. She delineates the choices and challenges of different courses of action and levels of commitment available to college graduates. Escalating demands accompany each option, the illustrations revelatory of the dynamics of reciprocity in relation to energy invested and rewards received.

In *The Negro Speaks* (1970) Williams and Williams present a biographical sketch of Judge Edith S. Sampson that highlights the major events of her life. And John Hope Franklin in *From Slavery To Freedom* lists her among the prestigious group serving as alternate delegates to the General Assembly of the United Nations, the group also including Archibald Carey, Charles H. Mahoney, Marian Anderson, and Jewell Lafontant. Born on 13 October 1901, the daughter of Louis and Elizabeth McGruder Spurlock, Edith Spurlock was one of eight children. She attended night school in her pursuit of higher education and earned a law degree from Loyola University in 1935 and one from the University of Chicago in 1927. Pursuing a noteworthy legal career, Judge Sampson was the second black woman elected to the bench in the United States, fulfilling the unexpired term of an Illinois judge and subsequently elected to that office. Judge Sampson received an honorary LL.D from North Central College in Illinois on May 30, 1965. The speech text presented here is her acceptance of that honor and the commencement address at this centennial commencement of North Central.

Choose One Of Five
Edith S. Sampson
1965

This degree that you have bestowed upon me out of your magnificent kindness is not just an honor. It's outright flattery —and I love it.

Recognizing that it's impossible adequately to express my gratitude, I shall take the coward's way out and not even try.

Let me, instead, talk briefly to these graduates who have won their degrees the hard way instead of by the simple expedient of traveling from Chicago to Naperville.

You graduates have every right to expect penetrating words of profound wisdom from an LL.D. even when the doctorate is honorary.

You look for too much, of course, if you ask that I settle all affairs, both international and domestic, in anything under an hour. But I surely ought to be able to handle either one or the other of the side-by-side package without imposing too great a strain on your patience and your posteriors.

I should be able to untangle the enigma of Vietnam for you in ten minutes and solve the Dominican problem in another five. This would still give me, within a twenty-minute limit, ample time to pronounce with authority on the assorted crises in the UN, NATO, the Organization of American States, the Congo, Laos, Cambodia, Malaysia, Indonesia, India, and Pakistan.

Or, if I were to talk about the domestic scene, I should be able to sum up for you my definitive solutions to the problems of interracial relations, poverty, urban renewal, mass transportation, education—both higher and lower—organized crime, juvenile delinquency, the balance of payments, the labor-management controversy, and what's to become of those dreadful people in Peyton Place.

299

If you wanted an analysis of the current state of art, literature, music, drama, and philosophy, you would naturally have to give me another ten minutes.

Unfortunately, though, I am going to have to disappoint you, and I can only hope that you survive the sharp shock of disillusion. The degree that I've been given, precious as it is to me, did not endow me with instant wisdom.

As a result, I've been forced to fall back on a substitute for the all-revealing address that is your due today.

It's worse than that, really. Compounding what is already an offense, I'm going to present to you a multiple-choice test—the last of your college career.

The only consolations that I can offer in presenting the test are that it involves no bluebooks, you may consult texts freely, the test is self-scoring, and you have a lifetime at your disposal now to complete it.

This exam will be proctored, though. The proctors will be two—the community in which you live and, hardest taskmaster of all, your inner self.

The question: What do you do with your college education now that you have it—and now that it is beginning to become obsolete even as you sit here?

Choose One of Five Possible Answers:

Choice One: Put your diploma in a convenient drawer and close the drawer. Put whatever textbooks you've accumulated in a bookcase and close the bookcase. Put your mind to the dailiness of earning a satisfactory livelihood and close your mind.

I should warn you that it will take a bit of doing to follow this course with the rigor that it deserves.

You will have to take care not to read anything except, in the case of men, the sports pages or, in the case of women, columns of household hints.

You'll have to choose your friends with extreme care to make sure that you don't rub up against any stimulating personalities.

You'll have to build your own defenses against a world of complex realities that will insist on trying to intrude on you at the most inconvenient times.

But it can be done. I've known college graduates who have achieved it. They've wrapped themselves in an apathy so thick that they're in a position to say in all truth, "No opinion," to any Gallup or Roper pollster who might question them on any subject.

It's a choice that is available to you—choice one.

Choice Two: Go forth into that waiting world, carefully assess the prevailing opinions, and then conform.

Forget this theoretical nonsense they've been feeding you here at North Central. What do professors and assistants and associates and instructors know about the real world anyway? Academics, all of them.

You'll have your degree. That certifies you're educated. Let it go at that.

This choice gives you more latitude than choice one.

You can scan the whole of the daily newspaper, as long as you make certain it's a newspaper that agrees with you and all other right-thinking citizens on all critical issues.

You can keep *Time* or *Newsweek*, *Life* or *Look* on the coffee table.

You can subscribe to the *Reader's Digest* and had better read at least some of it for conversational purposes.

You are even permitted, if you take this choice, to buy two books a year as long as you make sure they're best-sellers. Reading the books is optional.

You don't have to be nearly so selective in making friends if you go this route instead of the first one. Just avoid the kooks—although that's easier said than done when that prevailing opinion recognizes as unmistakable kooks come in bewildering variety. But with a little caution you can easily manage.

After all, about 80, perhaps 85, percent of the people with whom you'll come in contact fit nicely in this choice-two category. It isn't that they're particularly talented at blending into the background. They are the background.

You, too, can be a pillar-of-society conformist. No strain, no pain.

Well, almost no pain. The anguish of those moments in your middle age when you lie sleepless at 2 a.m. or 3 and wonder whatever happened to all your bright ambitions of college days—that anguish and those moments don't count too much.

Most of the time you can be comfortable with choice two, and who could ask for more than that?

One footnote at this point: Don't worry that your college degree will set you apart and make it impossible for you to be a really thoroughgoing conformist.

That was a slight danger in my day, but it's none at all now.

Ever since people have come to recognize the dollars-and-cents value of a college diploma as a passport to employment, more and more people have been going to college. Only the bigoted, narrow-minded people hold a degree against a person today, and the ranks of the conformists are filled with those who have had campus and even classroom exposure. B.A.s, B.S.s, masters, doctors-they can all live in the ticky-tacky houses.

Choice Three: Refuse to relax into the commoner forms of conformity. Find yourself, instead, a clique of the elite, an "in" group, and conform yourself to it.

You might imagine, from that bare description of this choice, that this would be a difficult thing to do. It isn't at all.

There are just two requisites.

First, you must have a specialty of your own, some one field—or, better, part of a field—in which you're expert. It might be something in the arts—music before Vivaldi, for instance, or the epic poetry of Afghanistan. On the whole, though, it's better if your specialty is a little more practical —intellectual but moneymaking.

Then to the specialty, whatever it is, you add a dedication to everything that is avant-garde and an amused contempt for everything else that isn't.

One thing you can't have if you go the third-choice way—at least not today—and that's a conviction that human beings and the history they have made and are making are important. Nothing is important really—nothing, that is, except your one staked-out small field of specialization.

A James Reeb is beaten to death for daring to assert in action the dignity of man. A Mrs. Luizzo is shot, killed after the Selma to Montgomery march. Too bad.

But someone suggests that *The Cabinet of Dr. Caligari* isn't really such great shakes as a movie. This is monumental heresy. Tie him to the stake and put a torch to the faggots.

You must preserve the proper hierarchy of values, you see.

If you join the sort of "in" group I have in mind, your reading becomes constricted again, I'm afraid.

You mustn't read the daily papers, or at a minimum, you mustn't admit it if you do. The Sunday *New York Times*, on occasion, can be tolerated, but no more than tolerated.

You may not read *Life, Look, Time, Newsweek*, or the *Reader's Digest*, not to mention such unmentionables as

Better Homes and Gardens or *Family Circle*. Nothing more popular than *Scientific American*.

No best-sellers, of course—that goes without saying. It's much better to criticize Saul Bellow without having read *Herzog* all the way through, although you should read enough to be able to say it nauseated you so much you couldn't finish it.

This constriction of your reading is rather unfortunate in one way, really. You can't read things like the *New Republic*, or the *National Review*, or *Commentary*, or *Foreign Affairs*, or the *Bulletin of the Atomic Scientists*, or the *Reporter*, or anything of the sort. Those all deal with political and social and economic matters, you see, and an "in" conformist who attached importance to such matters would be drummed out of the corps. Serves him right.

Choice Four: Choice four, though, offers an alternative for those who cannot erase their political-social economic consciousness.

Join an extremist group.

There is real effort involved in this at the very beginning. You have to study the various groups that present themselves and make your initial commitment.

The beauty of this choice, though, is that, once you've made it, you can turn off your thinking and let yourself be carried by the forward surge of what is obviously a significant movement.

Say you link yourself to the far right.

Your enemies are immediately identified for you—Negroes, Jews, and communists. Communists are easy to recognize—they're all the people who don't agree with you.

You know immediately what to oppose—fluorine in the water supply, income taxes, aid to foreign nations, the Supreme Court, movements for mental health, and any squeamishness about dropping nuclear bombs at will or whim.

You know immediately what to support—anything that the leaders of your group find good and pleasing, although unfortunately they find little that's either.

Say you link yourself to the far left.

Your enemies are immediately identified for you—capitalists, the poor misled sheep of the middle class, and Fascists. Fascists are easy to recognize—they're all the people who don't agree with you.

You know immediately what to oppose—all business corporations with no exceptions, all Trotskyites, all deviationists, all revisionists, all efforts to help established governments resist communist revolt.

You know immediately what to support—anything that the leaders of your group find good and pleasing, which is whatever the men in Moscow have smiled upon for the day.

What is so attractive about choice four is that it requires no mental effort of you beyond the initial effort of making your selection. Yet it provides a wide-open emotional release that isn't possible with any of the first three choices.

With choice four you can convince yourself that every action you perform has world-molding significance. In sharp contrast to the choice-three people, choice-four people are convinced that everything is important because everything links somehow to the cause.

Choice Five: And then, finally, there's CHOICE FIVE. It's hard to state this one. About as close as I can come to it is this: Hang loose, but stay vibrantly alive.

This one's strenuous. This one's demanding.

Choice five would demand of you that you consider today's graduation no more than a pause to catch your breath before continuing the lifelong job of education.

It would demand of you that you be your own unique best self. And there is no higher demand than that.

Choice five entails wide-ranging reading and deep-probing thought.

It calls for a contradictory thing—a mind that is constantly open to new facts that dictate change but at the same time is resolutely committed to what seems best at any given point of time.

It calls for human involvement, a compassionate concern for everyone on this fast shrinking little planet of ours and for the generations to come.

It calls for the resolute rejection of all stereotypes and insists on the thoughtful examination of even the most widely held assumptions that are too easily taken for granted.

If only choice five involved only one thing or the other—thought or action—it would be ever so much easier. It doesn't, though. It involves both.

And as if that weren't bad enough, this choice usually brings with it a certain amount of inner ache, because this way is a lonely way.

Those who make choice four are caught up on a wave of fervent enthusiasm that is all the more compelling because there's so little of the rational in it. They have the company of their Birchite brothers or their communist comrades.

Those who make choice three clump together with others of their kind to exchange small coins of comment about existentialism and Zen, the hilarious glories of Busby Berkeley movies, and the charm of Tiffany lampshades.

Those who make choice two are protected by the great crowd of which they've so willingly, gladly made themselves an anonymous part, no different from every other anonymous part.

Those who make choice one deliberately dull their sensitivities. They are cud-chewing, content to join the boys at the bar on a Saturday night or the girls at the bridge table Wednesday afternoon. They vegetate.

But those who make choice five are never fully comfortable.

They are nagged by their realization that they could be wrong.

They're prodded by their recognition that they've still so much more to learn and even more than that to understand.

They're made restless by their knowledge that no matter how much they do, there's still ever so much more left to be done.

Choice-five people have to live constantly with an acceptance of the fact that there are no simple answers in this world because there are no simple questions.

This makes life exciting for them, challenging, at least intermittently rewarding. But comfortable? No.

I would not urge choice five on any of you graduates. It asks so much of you.

Any of the other four will see you through to age sixty or sixty-five, retirement, and a modest pension. They might easily do better than that and make you rich. In dollars, that is.

Five is there, though, one of the multiple choices on the test.

If any of you in this class of '65 makes the fifth choice, I wish you'd let me know about it. You I'd like to know better than I possibly can just by having made a speech here.

You I would treasure even above the LL.D. with which North Central College has so graciously honored me—and that, you can believe me, is saying a great deal.

Introduction to Margaret Walker Alexander's "Religion, Poetry, And History: Foundations For A New Educational System"

"Religion, Poetry, and History: Foundations For A New Educational System" examines the multifaceted components that form a culture and perpetuate its essence. Margaret Walker Alexander systematically analyzes societal realities that render imperative a different system of education, more accurately a reeducation that clarifies distorted perceptions currently limiting society's possibilities. She describes the miseducation that informs the conduct and consciousness of black and white children and the need for new definitions. She explores as well the centrality of our religious inclinations and how these inclinations define, limiting or expanding our world view. She posits for consideration the actions and concerns that have the potential of releasing our creative selves and the resulting experience. The speech overall examines the need for a new education and suggests strategies for establishing the educational, creative, religious, and social foundations that the current world situation requires.

Margaret Abigail Walker was born in Birmingham, Alabama in 1915, the daughter of a minister. The attitude toward cultural heritage she discusses in her speech seems to have been a part of her own experiences as she derived from her family an appreciation for her heritage, a feeling of self worth, and a desire for an education. Walker received advanced degrees from Northwestern University and the University of Iowa. The acclaimed author of *Jubilee* and *For My People* has published two books, poetry, essays, and critical articles and is currently Emerita Professor of English at Jackson State University in Jackson, Mississippi.

Walker presented the speech considered here before the National Urban League Conference in New Orleans, Louisiana on 29 July 1968. The National League was formed to address dimensions of African American life that seemed outside the agenda of the National Association for the Advancement of Colored People. Three organizations merged in 1911 to form the National League on Urban Conditions Among Negroes. The scope of the new organization was more expansive than that of the NAACP, adding social, economic, and educational emphases to other racial concerns.

Religion, Poetry, And History
Foundations For A New Educational System
Margaret Walker Alexander
1968

Members of the Council of Guilds and friends of the National Urban League: I have chosen a subject which I believe vital to our people in this year of extreme crisis: Our Religion, Poetry, and History: Foundations for a New Educational System. Such a subject immediately poses questions and demands a definition of terms. Why do we need a new Educational system? How are the values of a Society formed? What is the role of Religion in a Society? What is the meaning of Poetry? And what is the essential worth of a People's heritage in developing their social consciousness? The answers to these questions should then automatically lead to a set of basic assumptions: one, that the philosophy and aesthetic values of a society are fundamental to the development of certain basic institutions and the social phenomena of that society; two, when these social phenomena and institutions erupt in chaos the basic philosophy must be re-examined and ultimately changed; three, when the society thereby undergoes such violent change the people are morally responsible to create a new set of values on which they can build better institutions for a better society.

Why do we need a new Educational System? We stand today in the throes of cataclysmic social change. We are caught in a world-wide societal revolution that breeds ideological and military conflict between nations. We are impaled on a cross of constant economic problems such as automation and cybernation have brought us with the electronic revolution. We are deeply distressed by the conditions of our inner cities. We are equally concerned with the confusing drama on our college campuses which reflects the search of our young people for values different from our own.

Our young people seem to be seething in a boiling caldron of discontent. Like the youth of every generation they want to know and they demand to be heard. Like youth in every age they are the vanguard of our revolutionary age. They are the natural leaders of revolution whether that revolution be of race, class, or caste; whether it is sexual or academic; whether it is political or intellectual. Today the revolutions we are witnessing encompass all of these, for the violence of revolution not only threatens but definitely promises to sweep out every corner of our outmoded existence. Violence today is more than the tool of tyranny, as it has always been, it is also the tool of revolution.

We are not only shedding the old ways of the past. We are over-whelmed by the problems of a new universe. Here in this decade of the 1960's we stand under the watershed of the twentieth century totally unprepared for the innovations of the twenty-first century already rushing headlong among us. The historical process, of which we are a part, does not necessarily mark off the cycles of man's progress with the man-made dates or hours we have set for change. The life of the twenty-first century has already begun while the debris of the structures in a dying twentieth century crashes all around us.

Our basic institutions of the home, the school, and the church are threatened by the same violent destruction undermining our socio-economic and political system, for they are part and parcel of the whole. Three hundred and fifty years ago, when the American colonies were not yet a nation, a set of built in values were super-imposed upon the American continent and people by European powers. These values were composed of three basic philosophies: (1) a religious body of belief containing the Protestant work ethic with duty and work as a moral imperative, with the puritanical and Calvinistic aversion to pleasure of secular play, song, and dance, coupled with (2) the economic theories of a Commonwealth only groping for the rising industrialism and capitalism that did not fully emerge until a century later, but which were hidden under (3) the American political dream of Democracy. This democracy was based on the idealism of Christianity which declared all men are brothers and the children of God. Except for the facts of chattel slavery and inhuman segregation the ideal dream might have become a reality. Slavery and Segregation as Institutions contradicted the ideal dream and America developed instead a defensive philosophy or rationale of Racism, the fruits of which we are reaping today.

Black people in America have so long borne the stigma of slavery and segregation that every community, black and white, has been warped by this wanton subjugation. For a very long time after Slavery, almost a century in time, the Federal Government gave tacit consent to Jim Crow and Segregation was supported boldly by law which of course became custom. Now it has been outlawed, but the mark of Cain is still on the land. White America has educated black and white children with a set of monstrous lies—half truths and twisted facts—about Race. Both black and white children, as a result, have been stunted in their mental growth and poisoned in their world outlook. The American white child in the north and south is just as distorted in his thinking as the black child although the expressed manifestations are not the same. The white child has been taught to value Race more than humanity. He has been taught to over-estimate his intelligence and human worth because of race, and at the same time to under-estimate the human worth and intelligence of anyone who is not of his race. The white American is therefore basically ignorant of the cultures of other people, and has no appreciation for any other language, art, religion, history, or ethical system save his own. He is in no way prepared to live in a multi-racial society without hostility, bigotry and intolerance. He believes that he must convert all people to his way of thinking because he cannot possibly conceive that his way of thinking may not always be right for everyone else. Everyone must dress, think, pray, and amuse himself as he does. Every socio-economic and political system must emphasize or epitomize the values of his mechanistic and materialistic society. He falsely assumes that his values are idealistic and altruistic, that he is democratic and Christian while all others are totalitarian and pagan, yet in all his actions he contradicts his preaching. His every waking hour is spent getting and spending for himself, while denying his brother any and all of the same rights he claims for himself. Self-righteous and self-centered he thanks God daily that he is not as other men (meaning other races) are.

On the other hand, our black children have been taught to hate themselves, to imitate people whom they have been taught to believe are superior. Every day they read in the schoolbooks, the newspapers, the movies, and the television the monstrous lies that deny their existence and denigrate their world. They have been led to believe that we have no black history, no black culture, no black beauty, nor anything black that has value or worth or meaning that is good. They have been told that our world is white and western with a cultural heritage that is Graeco-Roman, Christian in Religion, Protestant in Ethic, and Democratic in politics; that all these things are right and of necessity good and civilized while all the opposites of these are wrong and of necessity evil and savage. The non-western or Oriental world which is colored is therefore primitive in culture, heathen in religion, pagan in ethics, communistic in economics, and totalitarian in politics.

This of necessity is evil, anti-Christian, and anti-white, and therefore anti-American. Ancient civilizations and empires of Egypt, Babylonia, and Persia, ancient cultures and empires of Ethiopia, Karnak, Ghana, Mali, and Songhai, to say nothing of that famous city of Carthage which the Roman orator, Cato, constantly declared must be destroyed, these ancient names are not recited in our history books nor is the fact that both Asians and Africans and all the Arab world enjoyed their great renaissance eras before the Europeans and the Christians. Thus our world has been divided into East and West, into black and white, and given the separate connotations of good and evil. For the most part our people have been gullible and believed the half-lies and the half-truths denying our blackness and wishfully affirming their whiteness by seeking to become carbon copies of white people. But the fact remains that we are living in a multi-racial world in which there are varying cultures, religious beliefs, and socio-economic or political systems and whether we like or dislike it our children must be educated to live in such a world. They must learn to live in a world that is four-fifths colored, nine-tenths poor, and in most cases neither Christian in religion nor democratic in ideals.

The struggle of black people in America in this decade of societal revolution must therefore re-emphasize the battle for intellectual emancipation. A new self-concept must be instilled in the black child and a new perspective must be developed in the white child. Moreover, it becomes the awesome task of every well meaning, clear-thinking American, black and white alike to rectify the wrongs caused by Racism, to change the basic attitudes and twisted facts still erroneously held by Segregationist America, by racists who are white and black. All America must move toward a new humanism with a preoccupation of providing a full measure of human dignity for everyone. We must create a new ethic that is neither Protestant, Catholic, Jewish, Moslem, Buddhist nor any other ethic narrowed by creed but liberated into respect for the human rights of all men. Our ethic will then become a universal blessing of mutual respect and concern for every living spirit. We need a new educational philosophy in order to achieve this. A knowledge of world religions, world cultures, and all the racial and nationalistic strains that make up the human family will make such an ethic possible. The appreciation of other people and their cultures is predicated upon an understanding of them and understanding is predicated purely upon genuine knowledge. We need a new Educational System. The recent revolution in teaching has been largely electronic, an intellectual revolution is of necessity a revolution in basic ideas.

Our present day system of Education began in the nineteenth century when the scientific revolutions of the eighteenth and nineteenth centuries were charting a new Universe with Newtonian physics. The Einsteinian revolution has outmoded such thinking. We no longer live in the nineteenth century. Even the twentieth century is largely behind us. Yet our religion is still that of the Middle Ages and the Protestant Reformation. What should a creative and spiritually vital Religion do for our Society? Why is the Christian Church in America today derelict in its duty and slow to move its feet toward full integration of all Americans into the mainstream of American life? All America knows that institutionalized Religion has lost its basic meaning because it has too long been in the employ of Racism that has viciously used the Church and the Christian Religion for selfish ends and vested interests. Segregationists such as the Ku Klux Klan and the Americans for the Preservation of the White Race have so long declared themselves as the true representatives of Christianity, the true American Patriots, and the standard bearers of such nonsense as racial purity and integrity that they have whipped the truth of Christianity—the truth of brotherhood of man and the fatherhood of God, whipped it senseless beyond recognition. Their lynchropes, their high explosives, boxes of dynamite, long range rifles, and burning crosses are all used in the name of Christ and the Christian Religion. Our burned churches are quite symbolic of racial hatred and spiritual decay. Our people deserve something better than a begging ministry in the employ of a powerful and wealthy hierarchy. The pages of history that tell the true story of Slavery and Segregation are stained with the blood of black men who were crucified by white Christians. No hypocritical white-washing of moribund congregations that are stinking with moral decay will deliver us today. Perhaps it is time for a new Avatar. Violently shaken by class, caste, and racial disturbance the Church in America craves a new awakening in which spiritual meaning is reborn and revitalized. Religion in a Society should be the underlying philosophy of the People. It is their way of life, of thought, and of action. It is part of the aesthetic or cultural heritage of the people which undergirds the basic institutions of that society and gives dynamic impetus to all the group action and subsequent phenomena of that society. When the Religion of the People is dead, then they are without vision, without moral imperatives, and without all their aesthetic or cultural values. Anything false that is used in the name of Religion is then the opiate or drug by which men lull themselves into a false consciousness, into deadly apathy, and supine complacency. A vital and dynamic Religion is necessary to the cultural advancement of all people. Religious faith is personal, but Religious Institutions are of necessity Social. As such they must serve all the people or they have no value.

Black men, before they came to America, had a religion and ethic that was tribal or communal and that was based on their group participation in rites and ceremonies that gave impetus to their living and moral order to their community. White Puritan Americans at home and abroad as missionaries frowned on this as superstitious nonsense. In America black people lost their ties with Mother Africa but they have neither lost religious faith nor mystical charisma. We are still a people of spirit and soul. We are still fighting in the midst of white American Racism for the overwhelming truth of the primacy of human personality and the spiritual destiny of all mankind. We fight for freedom and peace because we know these are spiritual entities and have nothing to do with guns and money and houses and land. Contrary to the prevailing belief of Racist society all black men do not necessarily believe that a guaranteed employment of all the people is the highest essence and accomplishment of a society. Artists and the Religious of all nations know this is not so. Wise men are not all bankers and soldiers. Some are philosophers and poets and they too make their religious contribution to society. Some men therefore serve their society with the creative gifts of themselves, neither for money nor fame but for the cause of righteousness and with human integrity for the advancement of all mankind. Whether we remain the test of democracy, the soul of the Nation, the conscience of America, the redemptive suffering people of the world, or the tragic black heroes of a dying society, we know that the essence of life is in Spirit, not in cars, whiskey, houses, money, and all the trappings of an affluent society. Call it soul if you wish, but it is our great gift and a part of our black heritage. We declare it worthy to offer on the altars of the world toward the enduring philosophy of a new and necessary humanism.

Our music, and Art, our literature born out of our folkways and folk-beliefs are also part and parcel of this cultural gift and heritage. Like Religion, the Poetry of a People, their Art,

Songs, and Literature, come from the deep recesses of the unconscious, the irrational, and the collective body of our ancestral memories. They are indeed the truth of our living, the meaning and the beauty of our lives, and the knowledge of this heritage is not only fundamental to complete understanding of us as a People, it is a fundamental ingredient in the development of our world consciousness. Black people today in America are more than ever before socially conscious, aware of the damage that racism has done to our psyche, the traumatic injury to our children's moral and mental growth. We know the effects of the brutalizing, stigmatizing, dehumanizing systems of Slavery and Segregation under which we have existed in America for three hundred and fifty years.

A new awareness of this black history has taken hold of us in the wake of the riot commission's report that white racism is the creeping sickness destroying America. How, then, shall we diagnose this racism and prescribe for its cure? Will more jobs, better housing, more ballots, and less guns cure racism? Hardly. This is a battle for the minds of men. In the words of one of our greatest thinkers who predicted that the problem of the color line would be the problem of the twentieth century, in the words of that classic, *The Souls of Black Folk*, let us remember that we have three great gifts, a gift of song, a gift of labor or brawn with which we have helped to build a nation, and a gift of Spirit or Soul. Let us stir up the gift of God that is within us and let us create a new world for all Americans. Let us use our heritage of religion, poetry, and history as foundations for a new Educational system. Let us teach our children that we are a great people, that they have a great heritage, and that their destiny is even greater.

It must come as a shock to many of our people living in the inner cities of America when they read about the deplorable conditions in the ghettoes, to discover that all this abuse directed against criminals, against dope addicts, against looters and conspirators, all this abuse and condemnation directed against those of us who live in sub-human conditions of black colonies of the white power structure, all of this is a blanket condemnation of us as a Race and as a People. What, then, is a ghetto and how did it come into existence? Must we be blamed for this too, on top of all the other Racist hatred and injustice vented upon us? Who owns all this property and where do the owners live? Do they value their property more than they value our lives? Is this why they send the police to protect their property while only God protects our lives? Is it not true that the ghetto is a black colony of the white power structure in which we are exploited with no representation in the political and economic system? Do the people in the ghettoes control their economic and political lives? Is the money spent in the ghetto returned to the ghetto? Do the people living in the inner cities run the governments of those municipalities? Somewhere we must truly place the blame where it belongs. Poor black people can no longer be the scapegoats who bear the blame for everything in our society. We not only must build economic and political power in the ghettoes; we must change the thinking in the ghettoes as we must change the thinking of all America. We must create a new mental climate.

Fortunately for many of our people all of us have not been blighted by ignorance of our heritage. Some of us have come from homes where all our lives this positive healing process has existed. While we were simultaneously reading the lies in the history books at school we were learning our true history at home from our parents. We have neither the Segregationists' views of the South nor the racist views of the North about slavery, the Civil War, and Reconstruction. Some of us grew up reading *Opportunity* and *Crisis* magazines, reading the *Louisiana Weekly*, the *Chicago*

Defender, and the *Pittsburgh Courier* or whatever our local newspaper was. We heard the poetry of DuBois and James Weldon Johnson and Langston Hughes, and the music of Roland Hayes, Paul Robeson, and Marian Anderson. We learned the names of our leaders such as Harriet Tubman, Sojurner Truth, and Mary McCleod Bethune. We knew our great Blues singers and Broadway stars and prizefighters and Olympic winners. I was delighted to hear Dr. Sam Proctor say at Commencement that he did not need Stokely to tell him he was beautiful, his mother told him that. That is what mothers are supposed to do. But all our children do not know how beautiful they are for all of them have not been so fortunate. All of them do not know that physical beauty is relative according to man-made standards and that what we believe in our minds and hearts is what we are; that we need not become what our enemies wish us to become. We can be what we want to be and most of all we want to be ourselves, and not an imitation of other people.

Contrary to what some of our black brothers believe, this new Educational System must not be one of racial exclusion or this will become another face for racism. This learning must be all inclusive. Any notions that a wider cleavage in the American people based on race, class, caste, sex, or age —any such notion is unrealistic, naive, negative, and detrimental. Whether black and white Americans are divided by yellow men, red men, or the little green men of Mars, the result can mean nothing but chaos. Shall we divide and conquer? Who will conquer, and who stands to benefit from such cleavage? If any foreign nation can divide us by indoctrination it can also completely destroy us. Some of our black brothers seem confused by the conflict, and the tactics of the struggle seem to cloud the issues. When we were subjected to Segregation by law we sought to become assimilated into the mainstream of American life. We regarded this as a worthy and positive goal. Now some of us seem to have some extreme thinking in the opposite direction. These seem to be appalled with the apparent failure of integration, and disappointed with the slow business of desegregation. Shocked and stung by the ugly face of white racism, they now declare that the sickness of America makes Segregation and Apartheid more to be desired than either desegregation or integration. This is not a clear incentive toward building power in the ghettoes nor rebuilding the moral fibre of America. Whatever we have learned from our struggles in the past, at least a few facts should be clear: We fight with faith in the goodness of the future. No matter how troubled we have been, we have not lost our perspective. Our sense of history tells us that our human personality is potentially divine, hence our destiny must be spiritual. These may not seem much but they are enough, if in terms of these truths we teach our children the worth of their human personality, a pride in their heritage, a love for all people in the recognition of our common humanity, and a sense of dignity and purpose in living. They help us realize that freedom like peace is spiritual. It is with such tools that we must build our houses for tomorrow.

Just as we minister to the physical needs that are human we must minister to our mental needs that are also human. We must recognize the worth of every living person. All America is crying for this new humanism, for a new educational system, for a new and creative ministry from a new and spiritually vital religion, meaningful and with a genuine moral imperative. A new Space Age of the twenty-first century craves a vital and new religion to usher in the millennium. A new century promises to erase the color line. A new humanism must prevail. We must find the strength and the courage to build this new and better world for our children. Many of us will die trying in these last years of a dying century but in the twenty-first century our progeny will raise their eyes to more than a vision of a brave new world. They will occupy the citadel. Their truth will be honored and freedom understood and enjoyed by everyone. Racial justice and understanding will be a prelude to international peace and good will. But we must begin now to destroy the lies, to attack the half truths, to give our children something in which they can believe, to build faith in themselves, love for mankind, and hope for the future. Most of all we must teach them that righteousness is more to be desired than money; for the great possession of money without guiding principles, without judgment, without pride and integrity, such possession is nothing that cars and houses and whiskey and clothes and all the trappings of an affluent society do not dress up empty minds, and ugly hearts, and loveless lives; that meaningless living is without immortality and that it does not give us heroes to honor. Our martyred dead are great because they died for freedom. Our list of heroes is three centuries long, but they are deathless and forever with us. Wisdom and understanding cannot be bought in the Vanity Fairs of the world. Justice and freedom are prizes to be sought and our martyred men of goodwill have already proven they are well worth dying to obtain.

Teach then, our children, that their heritage is great and their destiny is greater. That we are a great people with a great faith who have always fought and died for freedom. Teach them that life and love are for sharing and above all they are never to forget that we are all a part of the mainland, involved with humanity. We are not alone in our beauty and our strength. We are part of all Mankind who throughout all recorded time have bravely fought and nobly died in order to be free.

Our Religion, Poetry, and History—they are our folk heritage; they are our challenge today to social commitment;

they are the foundations of a new education, a new moral imperative, a new humanism on which we base our cultural hope for a free world tomorrow morning in the twenty-first Century.

> These things shall be:
> A nobler race than e'er the world hath known shall rise
> With flame of freedom in their souls
> And light of knowledge in their eyes.
> They shall be gentle, brave, and strong
> To spill no drop of blood, but dare
> All that may plant man's lordship firm
> On earth and fire and sea and air.
> Nation with nation, land with land
> Unarmed shall live as comrades free
> In every heart and brain shall throb
> The pulse of one fraternity
> New arts shall bloom of loftier mold
> And mightier music thrill the skies
> And every life shall be a song
> When all the earth is paradise.

Introduction to Shirley Chisholm's
"It Is Time For A Change"

"It Is Time For A Change" is Shirley Chisholm's first speech before the House of Representatives and highly revelatory of her commitment to appropriate national priorities as she perceived them. The address illustrates how military expenditures were being given precedence over the more immediate realities of internal poverty and suffering and calls for a reordering of national priorities. Chisholm compares military spending with spending on education and the future of the nation's children, boldly contending for the importance of the latter and asserting her intentions to vote "No" on every spending bill brought before the House until the nation's priorities were once again set in order.

Shirley Chisholm was born in Brooklyn on 30 November 1924, the daughter of Charles St. Hill and Ruby Seale St. Hill. She completed her undergraduate studies at Brooklyn College and earned a masters degree from Columbia. She was the first African American woman elected to the United States Congress, this historic event occurring in 1968. Chisholm perceived something pathological in this phenomenon. In her autobiography *Unbought And Unbossed*, she remarked: "That I am a national figure because I was the first person in 192 years to be at once a congressman, black, and a woman proves, I would think, that our society is not yet either just or free." She had served in the New York Assembly before her election to Congress where she became known as Fighting Shirley Chisholm. The speech presented here was her first speech before the House of Representatives presented in March of 1969.

It Is Time For A Change
Shirley Chisholm
1969

Mr. Speaker, on the same day President Nixon announced
he had decided the United States will not be safe unless we
start to build a defense system against missiles, the Headstart
program in the District of Columbia was cut back for the lack
of money.

As a teacher, and as a woman, I do not think I will ever
understand what kind of values can be involved in spending
nine billion dollars—and more, I am sure—on elaborate,
unnecessary and impractical weapons when several thousand
disadvantaged children in the nation's capital get nothing.

When the new administration took office, I was one of the
many Americans who hoped it would mean that our country
would benefit from the fresh perspectives, the new ideas, the
different priorities of a leader who had no part in the
mistakes of the past. Mr. Nixon had said things like this:

"If our cities are to be livable for the next generation, we
can delay no longer in launching new approaches to the
problems that beset them and to the tensions that tear them
apart."

And he said, "When you cut expenditures for education,
what you are doing is shortchanging the American future."

But frankly, I have never cared too much what people say.
What I am interested in is what they do. We have waited to
see what the new administration is going to do. The pattern
now is becoming clear.

Apparently launching those new programs can be delayed
for a while, after all. It seems we have to get some missiles
launched first.

Recently the new Secretary of Commerce spelled it out. The Secretary, Mr. Stans, told a reporter that the new administration is "pretty well agreed it must take time out from major social objectives" until it can stop inflation.

The new Secretary of Health, Education and Welfare, Robert Finch, came to the Hill to tell the House Education and Labor Committee that he thinks we should spend more on education, particularly in city schools. But, he said unfortunately we cannot "afford" to, until we have reached some kind of honorable solution to the Vietnam war. I was glad to read that the distinguished Member from Oregon (Mrs. Green) asked Mr. Finch this:

"With the crisis we have in education, and the crisis in our cities, can we wait to settle the war? Shouldn't it be the other way around? Unless we can meet the crisis in education, we really can't afford the war."

Secretary of Defense Melvin Laird came to Capitol Hill, too. His mission was to sell the antiballistic-missile insanity to the Senate. He was asked what the new administration is doing about the war. To hear him, one would have thought it was 1968, that the former Secretary of State was defending the former policies, that nothing had ever happened—a President had never decided not to run because he knew the nation would reject him, in despair over this tragic war we have blundered into. Mr. Laird talked of being prepared to spend at least two more years in Vietnam.

Two more years, two more years of hunger for Americans, of death for our best young men, of children here at home suffering the lifelong handicap of not having a good education when they are young. Two more years of high taxes, collected to feed the cancerous growth of a Defense Department budget that now consumes two thirds of our federal income.

Two more years of too little being done to fight our
greatest enemies, poverty, prejudice and neglect, here in our
own country. Two more years of fantastic waste in the
Defense Department and of penny pinching on social
programs. Our country cannot survive two more years, or
four, of these kinds of policies. It must stop—this year—now.
Now, I am not a pacifist. I am deeply, unalterably opposed
to this war in Vietnam. Apart from all the other
considerations—and they are many—the main fact is that we
cannot squander there the lives, the money, the energy that
we need desperately here, in our cities, in our schools.

I wonder whether we cannot reverse our whole approach
to spending. For years, we have given the military, the
defense industry, a blank check. New weapons systems are
dreamed up, billions are spent, and many times they are
found to be impractical, inefficient, unsatisfactory, even
worthless. What do we do then? We spend more money on
them. But with social programs, what do we do? Take the
Job Corps. Its failure has been mercilessly exposed and
criticized. If it had been a military research and development
project, they would have been covered up or explained away,
and Congress would have been ready to pour more billions
after those that had been wasted on it.

The case of Pride, Inc., is interesting. This vigorous,
successful black organization, here in Washington, conceived
and built by young inner-city men, has been ruthlessly
attacked by its enemies in the government, in this Congress.
At least six auditors from the General Accounting Office
were put to work investigating Pride. They worked seven
months and spent more than $100,000. They uncovered a
fraud. It was something less than $2,100. Meanwhile, millions
of dollars—billions of dollars, in fact—were being spent by the
Department of Defense, and how many auditors and

investigators were checking into their negotiated contracts? Five.

We Americans have come to feel that it is our mission to make the world free. We believe that we are the good guys, everywhere—in Vietnam, in Latin America, wherever we go. We believe we are the good guys at home, too. When the Kerner Commission told white America what black America had always known, that prejudice and hatred built the nation's slums, maintain them and profit by them, white America would not believe it. But it is true. Unless we start to fight and defeat the enemies of poverty and racism in our own country and make our talk of equality and opportunity ring true, we are exposed as hypocrites in the eyes of the world when we talk about making other people free.

I am deeply disappointed at the clear evidence that the number-one priority of the new administration is to buy more and more weapons of war, to return to the era of the cold war, to ignore the war we must fight here—the war that is not optional. There is only one way, I believe, to turn these policies around. The Congress can respond to the mandate that the American people have clearly expressed. They have said, "End this war. Stop the waste. Stop the killing. Do something for your own people first." We must find the money to "launch the new approaches," as Mr. Nixon said. We must force the administration to rethink its distorted, unreal scale of priorities. Our children, our jobless men, our deprived, rejected and starving fellow citizens must come first.

For this reason, I intend to vote "No" on every money bill that comes to the floor of this House that provides any funds for the Department of Defense. Any bill whatsoever, until the time comes when our values and priorities have been turned right side up again, until the monstrous waste and the shocking profits in the defense budget have been eliminated and our country starts to use its strength, its tremendous resources, for people and peace, not for profits and war.

It was Calvin Coolidge, I believe, who made the comment that "the Business of America is Business." We are now spending eighty billion dollars a year on defense—that is two thirds of every tax dollar. At this time, gentlemen, the business of America is war, and it is time for a change.

Introduction to Coretta Scott King's
"We Need To Be United"

"We Need To Be United" articulates the potential strength of a coalition composed of labor union members, women, and African Americans. Coretta Scott King refers to her late husband's "affinity for the labor movement" and emphasizes the comprehensive feature of trade-union objectives. She chronicles the union's contribution to African Americans and urges a continuation of this propensity for inclusion. King submits that the problems of America are not limited to race relations and enumerates a plethora of social and environmental situations worthy of their attention and commitment. She cites the union's triumph "out of the depression thirties" and underscores the need for similar efforts in the current crisis. She appeals to them for sufficient vision to avoid the traps of myths and prejudices that divide potentially powerful coalitions and urges their elevation "to new heights of human dignity and equality . . ."

Coretta Scott King was born in Marion, Alabama, on 27 April 1927. She married Martin Luther King, Jr. in 1953 and currently serves as the president of the Martin Luther King, Jr. Center for Nonviolent Social Change located in Atlanta, Georgia. Speaking of her life with the civil rights leader, Coretta King noted, "I remember thinking one day in Montgomery, 'This is what I have been preparing for my entire life. This is the beginning of a journey. I don't know where it is going to take us, but we are involved in a worldwide struggle.' It was a good feeling to know that my life had purpose and meaning" (Lanker 1989, 80).

"We Need To Be United" was delivered before the twenty-second Automobile Worker's Constitutional Convention in Atlantic City on 22 April 1970. Coretta King's speech is an acceptance speech acknowledging the organizations's posthumous award to her late husband.

We Need To Be United
Mrs. Martin Luther King, Jr.
1970

It is a heart-warming privilege to accept this posthumous award to my husband from an organization that always made itself part of our struggle whether the scene of action was in Birmingham, Selma, Detroit or Washington.

Before moving on to my principal topic, because the men at this convention outnumber the women, I would like to call to their attention that this year, 1970, marks the fiftieth anniversary of woman's suffrage. This landmark amendment to the constitution was a vastly important step in the liberation of women, but unfortunately even now, half a century after its enactment, it is only partially effective. Not until the fifties and sixties did black women become voters in large numbers despite the mandates of the law. It is also noteworthy that the five states which rejected the Nineteenth Amendment were all Southern states, once again demonstrating where the roots of reaction are in the nation.

My husband in his lifetime, as many of you know, had a special affinity for the labor movement. His understanding of society was too profound to permit him to be caught up in superficial prejudices. Though part of the labor movement has joined in the oppression of black people, another part of it pioneered in welding a coalition of rights and opportunities. He knew both truths. My husband knew that in much of basic industry black people through unions have relatively more freedom than in other sectors of the economy.

His memorial thus could not be merely a shrine, though it had to be that. It developed from planning, necessarily complex as he was complex.

It is not an accident that my husband was assassinated while leading a strike, nor is it coincidental that the time of his assassination came when he was calling for a coalition of all the poor black and white, and urging that they create a union organization. He was arousing a sleeping giant when he was cut down.

The trade-union movement was never a movement merely to protect and advance living standards. It had noble objectives beyond these limitations. From its birth it sought to attain social justice in its broadest sense. A wage increase was important, but important too was its elevating effect on human dignity. It was under that banner that the U.A.W. made workers more than mere appendages to machines and attained for them the status of dignified, proud men. When the U.A.W. in the thirties made trade-unionism an instrument of social reform, it won the respect of a majority of the nation. In holding today to this larger vision of the trade-union movement, it is providing the base of leadership desperately needed in a divided and confused land.

It was your union and others of the C.I.O. that pioneered to admit black people to your ranks. By standing for equal justice you not only opened doors to blacks, but you defeated the employer's strategy to make black people a distinct group of strike-breakers. Thus you strengthen yourselves while you enlarge the democratic rights of others.

We would be less than candid, however, if we refused to recognize that the coalition of blacks and the trade-union movement faces tensions.

Some trade-unionists are hostile to the freedom movement, and some blacks are spreading the illusion that a separatist road exists in the journey to emancipation. Even worse, some blacks out of frustration and despair play with notions of terrorism, and some whites are no less drawn to solutions of violence.

It is not black workers or white workers who will profit if they fight each other. Only those will profit who wish to dominate all workers. Blacks are not looking for advancement at the expense of other working people. Industry and government have enough control of wealth to provide decent employment for every man, black and white. If we don't identify the right problems and isolate the right adversary, we will all play the role of fools. Our trade-unions torn by division can lose their independence, fighting strength and leadership.

More than ever in the past we need to be united, because in all the dimensions of our lives, not just in race relations, we are in serious jeopardy. It is an illusion to think routine or formal trade-unionism can solve the vast problems of society today. Indeed, today a union need not be broken to become ineffectual; your living standards are not solely in your wage envelope.

Taxes, swollen by an insane war in Vietnam, can shrink the envelope as you hold it in your hand. Inflation empties it further. Beyond these, the quality of life is diminished by the dying of our cities. Though our nation is the richest on the earth, and more opulent than any in world history, our slums are among the worst of any industrial nation. Our health services are primitive compared with European standards. We are choked by transportation, sickened by poisoned air and polluted rivers, lakes and seaways. The leisure time you fought for is nullified by narrowed opportunities for recreation and relaxation. Before long, the shortage of water and the diminished volume of breathable air will begin to threaten the lives of all.

We are now surrounded by dirt, congestion and impure air in all walks of our daily life, which you fought to eliminate in the factories because they were barbarous and inhuman.

Today, April 22, is an appropriate day to mention these things, because it is Earth Day, designed to remind all people that our planet can die.

Trade-unions will have to come out of the plants and move on to the state houses and centers of power if our nation is to survive. We are at a new crossroads of responsibility. You who make the wheels of society turn will have to apply your strength and dynamism to broader social problems, if a suicidal course is to be avoided.

The whole population cannot flee to the suburbs, or they too will become the inner city. In many suburbs unmanageable problems are catching up.

Thus, black communities and white communities will have to unite and write new laws of urban development. If they fail, America has to go into a decline no matter what wage scales it can afford, and many of the features of the nineteenth-century mill towns in all their bleakness and ugliness will overtake our cities. We will see again the dark, dismal municipalities where families cannot breathe, children cannot play or learn, order cannot be maintained because it is cheaper to let some live in squalor while others seek individual havens of retreat.

To fight the decomposition of the cities, to fight poisoned air, accumulating garbage, filthy rivers and dying schools constitutes the battle of the seventies. You fought out of the depression thirties for yourselves and everyone. You will have to repeat that victory, if an expanding industrial nation almost out of control is not to stagger into social catastrophe.

This social leadership is not special responsibility, first of all because it involves your own direct interests. More than this, you have the power, experience and a tradition of moral sense. This nation was in a more severe moral crisis in the thirties, when it was rescued by the vision and boldness of the young labor movement. The nation needs that quality of leadership today as it faces new perils. Black people in the majority are ready for a new crusade for radical reform; they will be a powerful force in a militant struggle for decent conditions of life, and they are ready for an honorable partnership in a progressive coalition. Divided, neither one of us can win, deluded by myths and prejudices, we will fail; but united we can put this nation together and restore social sanity, inspire hope and achieve the interracial harmony my husband always believed was possible.

I think such a crusade of decency and progress is also part of a memorial to Martin Luther King. He believed people would always fight for their rights against all prophets of doom and despair. As long as we lift ourselves to new heights of human dignity and equality the sacrifice will deepen in meaning and his life will be renewed in our own growth and development.

Introduction to Alice Walker's
"The Unglamorous But Worthwhile Duties
Of the Black Revolutionary Artist, or
Of The Black Writer Who Simply Works And Writes"

"The Unglamorous But Worthwhile Duties Of The Black Revolutionary Artist" summarizes the speaker's education at Sarah Lawrence College that, despite its quality and prestige, left numerous cultural gaps. Walker recounts the compensatory efforts undertaken in "the college of books" that expanded her knowledge and perspective. The speech also articulates the multifaceted duties of the revolutionary artist, many of which are often overlooked by those who consider only the prominence or public acclaim of the artist. Her characterization of these duties includes a realistic portrayal of the frequently mundane imperatives that attend the artist's responsibilities to herself and the society at large. Overall, the speech is an eloquent definition of art and its comprehensive requirements.

Alice Walker was born in 1944 in Eatonton, Georgia to sharecropper parents. She first attended Spelman College and later transferred to Sarah Lawrence; the text of the speech considered here gives some insight into her perceptions of those two experiences. Walker is a recognized poet and novelist and has published two volumes of essays. She was active in the civil rights movement of the 1960s and married Mel Levanthal, a civil rights lawyer. After graduating from Sarah Lawrence, she accepted a writing fellowship which she initially planned to spend in Africa. But the demands of the civil rights movement in the United States motivated her to opt instead for volunteer work in Mississippi. Walker explained her decision in the following way: "This decision came . . . out of the realization that I could never live happily

341

in Africa—or anywhere else—until I could live freely in Mississippi" (Norton 1989, 2318).

The Unglamorous But Worthwhile Duties Of The Black Revolutionary Artist, Or Of The Black Writer Who Simply Works and Writes
Alice Walker
1970

(This is a paper I presented to the Black Students' Association of Sarah Lawrence College on 12 February 1970. I began with "Greetings from the great sovereign state of Mississippi," which brought laughter.)

When I came to Sarah Lawrence in 1964, I was fleeing from Spelman College in Atlanta, a school that I considered opposed to change, to freedom, and to understanding that by the time most girls enter college they are already women and should be treated as women. At Sarah Lawrence I found all that I was looking for at the time—freedom to come and go, to read leisurely, to go my own way, dress my own way, and conduct my personal life as I saw fit. It was here that I wrote my first published short story and my first book, here that I learned to feel what I thought had some meaning, here that I felt no teacher or administrator breathing down my neck.

I thought I had found happiness and peace in my own time.

And for that time, perhaps, I had. It was not until after I had graduated and gone south to Mississippi that I began to realize that my lessons at Sarah Lawrence had left crucial areas empty, and had, in fact, contributed to a blind spot in my education that needed desperately to be cleared if I expected to be a whole woman, a full human being, a black woman full of self-awareness and pride. I realized, sometime after graduation, that when I had studied contemporary writers and the South at this college—taught by a warm, wonderful woman whom I much admired—the writings of Richard Wright had not been studied and that instead I had studied the South from Faulkner's point of view, from Feibleman's, from Flannery O'Connor's. It was only after trying to conduct the same kind of course myself—with black students—that I realized that such a course simply cannot be taught if *Black Boy* is not assigned and read, or if "The Ethics of Living Jim Crow" is absent from the reading list.

I realized further that when I had been yearning, while here, to do a paper on pan-Africanism in my modern world history class, my Harvard-trained teacher had made no mention of W. E. B. Du Bois (who attended Harvard too, in the nineteenth century), no doubt because he had never heard of him.

I also realized that I had wasted five of my hard-to-come-by dollars one semester when I bought a supposedly "comprehensive" anthology of English and American verse which had been edited by a Sarah Lawrence faculty member. A nice man, a handsome one even, who had not thought to include a single poem by a black poet. I believe this man, who was really very nice, did not know there were black poets, or, if he did, believed like Louis Simpson that "poetry that is identifiably Negro is not important." I've yet to figure out exactly what that means, but it sounds ugly and has effectively kept black poets out of "comprehensive" anthologies, where the reader would have the opportunity to decide whether their poems are "important" or not.

I began to feel that subtly and without intent or malice, I had been miseducated. For where my duty as a black poet, writer, and teacher would take me, people would have little need of Keats and Byron or even Robert Frost, but much need of Hughes, Bontemps, Gwendolyn Brooks, and Margaret Walker.

So for the past four years I've been in still another college. This time simply a college of books—musty old books that went out of print years ago—and of old people, the oldest old black men and women I could find, and a college of the young; students and dropouts who articulate in various bold and shy ways that they believe themselves to be without a valuable history, without a respectable music, without writing or poetry that speaks to them.

My enrollment in this newest college will never end, and for that I am glad. And each day I look about to see what can and should be done to make it a bigger college, a more inclusive one, one more vital and long living. There are things our people should know, books they should read, poems they should know by heart. I think now of *Black Reconstruction* by Du Bois, of *Cane* by Jean Toomer, of *Mules and Men* by Zora Neale Hurston. Ten years ago, the one copy of *Black Reconstruction* that could be found in Atlanta was so badly battered and had been pasted back together so many times that a student could check it out of the library for only thirty minutes, and was then not allowed to take it outside the reading room. *Cane* by Jean Toomer and *Mules and Men* by Zora Neale Hurston I found tucked away behind locked doors in the library of Lincoln University. Knowing both books were out of print at the time, I Xeroxed them and stole somebody's rights, but it was the least I could do if I wanted to read them over and over again, which I did.

Today it gives me pleasure to see a Black Students' Association at Sarah Lawrence. That must mean there are many black students to pay dues. When I was here there were six of us and none of us was entirely black. Much has clearly changed, here as in the rest of the country. But when I look about and see what work still remains I can only be mildly, though sincerely, impressed.

Much lip service has been given the role of the revolutionary black writer but now the words must be turned into work. For, as someone has said, "Work is love made visible." There are the old people, Toms, Janes, or just simply old people, who need us to put into words for them the courage and dignity of their lives. There are the students who need guidance and direction. Real guidance and real direction, and support that doesn't get out of town when the sun goes down.

I have not labeled myself yet. I would like to call myself revolutionary, for I am always changing, and growing, it is hoped for the good of more black people. I do call myself black when it seems necessary to call myself anything, especially since I believe one's work rather than one's appearance adequately labels one. I used to call myself a poet, but I've come to have doubts about that. The truest and most enduring impulse I have is simply to write. It seems necessary for me to forget all the titles, all the labels, and all the hours of talk and to concentrate on the mountains of work I find before me. My major advice to young black artists would be that they shut themselves up somewhere away from all debates about who they are and what color they are and just turn out paintings and poems and stories and novels. Of course the kind of artist we are required to be cannot do this. Our people are waiting. *But there must be an awareness of what is Bull and what is Truth*, what is practical and what is designed ultimately to paralyze our talents. For example, it is unfair to the people we expect to reach to give them a beautiful poem if they are unable to read it.

And so, what is the role of the black revolutionary artist? Sometimes it is the role of remedial reading teacher. I will never forget one of the girls in my black studies course last year at Jackson State. All year long she had been taught by one of the greatest black poets still living: Margaret Walker.

I took over the class when Miss Walker was away for the quarter. We were reading "For My People" and this girl came to the section that reads:

> Let a new earth rise. Let another world be born. Let a bloody peace be written in the sky. Let a second generation full of courage issue forth, let a people loving freedom come to growth, let a beauty full of healing and a strength of final clenching be the pulsing in our spirits and our blood. Let the martial songs be written, let the dirges disappear. Let a race of men now rise and take control!

"What do you think?" I asked the girl. (She had read the poem very well.) She shook her head. "What is the matter?" I asked. She said, "Oh, these older poets! They never write poems that tell us to fight!" Then I realized that she had read the poem, even read it passionately, and had not understood a word of what it was about. "What is a 'martial song'"? I asked. "What is a disappearing dirge?" The girl was completely thrown by the words.

I recall a young man (bearded, good-looking), a Muslim, he said, who absolutely refused to read Faulkner. "We in the revolution now," he said, "We don't have to read no more white folks." "Read thine enemy," I prodded, to no avail. And this same young man made no effort, either, to read Hughes or Ellison or McKay or Ernest Gaines, who is perhaps the most gifted young black writer working today. His problem was that the revolutionary rhetoric so popular today had convinced him of his own black perfection and of the imperfection of everybody and everything white, but it had not taught him how to read. The belief that he was already the complete man had stunted this young man's growth. And when he graduates from college, as he will, he will teach your children and mine, and still not know how to read, nor will he be inclined to learn.

The real revolution is always concerned with the least glamorous stuff. With raising a reading level from second grade to third. With simplifying history and writing it down (or reciting it) for the old folks. With helping illiterates fill out food-stamp forms—for they must eat, revolution or not. The dull, frustrating work with our people is the work of the black revolutionary artist. It means, most of all, staying close enough to them to be there whenever they need you.

But the work of the black artist is also to create and to preserve what was created before him. It is knowing the words of James Weldon Johnson's "Negro National Anthem" and even remembering the tune. It is being able to read "For My People" with tears in the eyes, comprehension in the soul. It is sending small tokens of affection to our old and ancient poets whom renown has ignored. One of the best acts of my entire life was to take a sack of oranges to Langston Hughes when he had the flu, about two weeks before he died.

We must cherish our old men. We must revere their wisdom, appreciate their insight, love the humanity of their words. They may not all have been heroes of the kind we think of today, but generally it takes but a single reading of their work to know that they were all men of sensitivity and soul.

Only a year or so ago did I read this poem, by Arna Bontemps, "The Black Man Talks of Reaping":

I have sown beside all waters in my day.
I planted deep within my heart the fear
That wind or fowl would take the grain away.
I planted safe against this stark, lean year.

I scattered seed enough to plant the land
In rows from Canada to Mexico.
But for my reaping only what the hand
Can hold at once is all that I can show.

Yet what I sowed and what the orchard yields
My brother's sons are gathering stalk and root,
Small wonder then my children glean in fields
They have not sown, and feed on bitter fruit.

It requires little imagination to see the author as a spiritual
colossus, arms flung wide, as in a drawing by Charles White,
to encompass all the "Adams and the Eves and their countless
generations," bearing the pain of the reaping but brooding on
the reapers with great love.

Where *was* this poem in all those poetry anthologies I read
with eager heart and hushed breath? It was not there, along
with all the others that were not there. But it must, and will,
be always in my heart. And if, in some gray rushing day, all
our black books are burned, it must be in my head and I must
be able to drag it out and recite it, though it be bitter to the
tongue and painful to the ears. For that is also the role of the
black revolutionary artist. He must be a walking filing cabinet
of poems and songs and stories, of people, of places, of deeds
and misdeeds.

In my new college of the young I am often asked, "What
is the place of hate in writing?" After all we have been
through in this country it is foolish and in any case useless to
say hate has no place. Obviously, it has. But we must
exercise our noblest impulses with our hate, not to let it
destroy us or destroy our *truly precious heritage*, which is
not, by the way, a heritage of bigotry or intolerance. I've
found, in my own writing, that a little hatred, keenly directed,
is a useful thing. Once spread about, however, it becomes a

web in which I would sit caught and paralyzed like the fly who stepped into the parlor. The artist must remember that some individual men, like Byron de la Beckwith or Sheriff Jim Clark, should be hated, and that some corporations like Dow and General Motors should be hated too. Also the Chase Manhattan Bank and the Governor of Mississippi. However, there are men who should be loved, or at least respected on their merits, and groups of men, like the American Friends, who should not be hated. The strength of the artist is his courage to look at every old thing with fresh eyes and his ability to re-create, as true to life as possible, that great middle ground of people between Medgar Evers' murderer, Byron de la Beckwith, and the fine old gentleman John Brown.

I am impressed by people who claim they can see every person and event in strict terms of black and white, but generally their work is not, in my long-contemplated and earnestly considered opinion, either black or white, but a dull, uniform gray. It is boring because it is easy and requires only that the reader be a lazy reader and a prejudiced one. Each story or poem has a formula, usually two-thirds "Hate whitey's guts" and one-third "I am black, beautiful, strong, and almost always right." Art is not flattery, necessarily, and the work of any artist must be more difficult than that. A man's life can rarely be summed up in one word; even if that word is black or white. And it is the duty of the artist to present the man *as he is*. One should recall that Bigger Thomas was many great and curious things, but he was neither good nor beautiful. He was real, and that is sufficient.

Sometimes, in my anger and frustration at the world we live in, I ask myself, What is real and what is not? And now it seems to me that what is real is what is happening. What is real is what did happen. What happened to me and happens to me is most real of all. I write then, out of that. I write about the old men that I knew (I love old men), and the great big beautiful women with arms like cushions (who would really rather look like Pat Nixon), and of the harried fathers and mothers and the timid, hopeful children. And today, in Mississippi, it seems I sometimes relive my Georgia childhood. I see the same faces, hear the same soft voices, take a nip, once in a while, of the same rich mellow corn, or wine. And when I write about the people there, in the strangest way it is as if I am not writing about them at all, but about myself. The artist then is the voice of the people, but she is also The People.

The Right To A Decent Life And Human Dignity
Coretta Scott King
1970

As I was preparing to leave my home in the east, the President of the United States was involved in a unique ceremony. On Wednesday he was publicly celebrating the reaching of the trillion dollars mark in the annual output of American goods and services. The trillion dollars is a lot of money—one thousand billion dollars—so much it is hard to understand. But what is easy to understand is that even with such fabulous wealth there is poverty in this country.

A trillion dollar economy takes care very handsomely of the people at the top. It takes care generously of the people near the top. It rewards people in the middle, but it starves and brutalizes people at the bottom. The weight is like a mountain crushing millions who are below it and especially those poor who are Black, Brown and Red.

We live in a day when great unions are institutionalized in the structure of our society. This means in ordinary terms that the long established unions no longer have to fight to survive. They are recognized and accepted and certainly they should be. They no longer lose strikes, they struggle only for a greater share of the proceeds of their work.

Yet your union, in this day, fights to live. Those who control the billion dollar economy have said Blacks and Chicanos do not have the right to a decent life or to human dignity. They must live on the crumbs from the tables groaning with food.

For more than thirty years farm workers were thought to be unorganizable and so powerless they could not demand and achieve security and dignity. But Cesar Chavez challenged the tyrants, organized the working poor and became a threat, so they have jailed him. But as my husband so often said, "You cannot keep truth in a jail cell." Truth and justice leap barriers, and in their own way, reach the conscience of the people. The men of power thought my husband was a powerless man with grandiose ideas. He had nothing but an idea that people at the bottom could be aroused to fight for dignity and equality.

The power structure became alarmed when his ideas were transformed into marching millions and the right to vote, the right to use facilities, the right to jobs, and the right to private dignity were won.

Our struggle, like yours—that is, the struggle of Black people—could not be won by us alone, we had to find allies among the Americans of good will, Black, Brown, and White, who are ashamed of poverty in a trillion dollar economy. That is why your boycotts have succeeded. While some Americans are willing to forget the poor and if necessary suppress them with violence and brutality, there are still many Americans who cannot live with the immorality of inequality.

They believe the heritage of this nation is decency and fair play. They would not eat grapes when grapes became a symbol of oppression and they will not eat lettuce, now that it has become tainted with injustice.

Social progress has always come when the people on the bottom, who in organized strength and from the foundation shook the whole structure. Social change does not come from voluntary good will and charity from the top. It comes from motion at the bottom.

Black people and Brown people are herded at the bottom and told to be quiet and to wait for slow change. But change has never come to us in waiting. Waiting has multiplied the profits of the rich, but it deadens and depresses those below.

We are tens of millions strong, and waiting not only offends our dignity, but leaves us in deprivation. We know our own history, waiting and patience have resulted in economic exploitation and racial abuse, and finally together, we have said there is an end to waiting.

We are not enemies of the nation, but we are treated as if we were conquered and enslaved. We have fed and clothed the nation by our sweat and toil but our share in its goods is the share of prisoners.

I know we will win our common fight because we are more united and have more mutual respect than ever in our history and because in mass ranks, we are moving forward.

I hope as we look for allies, we will give special attention to women. First of all most women in this country, like nonwhites, are not equal. They can understand our profound need for freedom and equality. They also have special power to make a boycott punishing for the exploiters. It is they who buy lettuce and when lettuce becomes the symbol of inequality and oppression, women will know that they, too, have a stake in our struggle.

In closing I want to express a personal note. I do not have to read books or stimulate my imagination to understand how grueling it is to work in a sun-baked field all day. I was born on the land in rural Alabama and worked in the cotton fields. Although my family owned the land, the system was organized to keep the earning from cotton too low to maintain an adequate subsistence. My father worked two jobs in advance, and he managed to educate his children and provide security. Often I think what a remarkable man he is and what a greater contribution he would have made to society if it had given him opportunities that it gave to others.

So I know that among you your children are undiscovered, undeveloped people of talent. Cesar Chavez is not an accident; he is a genius of his people and their union; the farm workers' union, is a hero union. When you have succeeded in making your lives more secure and richer, the whole nation will benefit. That is why your struggle has deeper dimensions than a strike for wages. You are demanding a place in the halls of man. You are saying there are no lowly people, there are only people who are forced down.

If this nation can produce a trillion dollars every year, it is a disgrace in the eyes of God that some people should be haunted by hunger and hounded by racism. The President of the United States should not gloat and take pride in a trillion dollar economy. He should be ashamed and mortified to acknowledge that abundance exists while the system producing it still cheats the poor. His days should be restless until the crime and violence of poverty is rooted out of the land rich beyond imagination. While the President stands before the flashing lights of the computer that says a trillion dollars, we stand before a dark jail that says oppression. America cannot be both and be America.

Introduction to Barbara Jordan's
"Democratic Convention Keynote Address"

Barbara Jordan's keynote address before the Democratic National Convention in 1976 represented a noteworthy historical milestone and demonstrated the speaker's rhetorical acumen as well. The address affirmed the mythic concept of America as a country of inclusion and claimed a similar character for the Democratic Party. In the speech, Jordan addresses basic beliefs of Americans, suggesting that these beliefs comport well with the conduct and traditions of the Democratic Party. Jordan enumerates the corpus of beliefs that comprise the democratic ideal and calls for a sense of "national community" reflective of a republic claiming non-preferential treatment for its citizenry. A *Washington Post* reviewer described the atmosphere surrounding this historic speech as follows: "She was there to bear witness to a dream they yearn to claim, and the congregation responded with an 'amen' chorus that would do credit to the Second Coming."

Barbara Charline Jordan was born in Houston, Texas, the youngest of three daughters. The skills of declamation she brought to the Keynote Address in 1976 have been attributed to several factors: good teachers, speaking opportunities early in her life, and talented parents who emphasized the importance of effective communication skills. Whatever external factors might have contributed to Jordan's professional success and acclaim, certainly her own innate ability and resiliency cannot be minimized. Characterized by determination and ambition, she systematically assessed her losses and formulated plans of action that would better ensure her future success. Even in failure, she was astute enough to analyze the techniques of the successful and evaluate her shortcomings objectively. This attitude prevailed whether she was considering her second-place finish in an Elks Oratorical contest, her appointment as a first affirmative constructive speaker on the Texas Southern University debating team because she was underprepared for refutation, or her losses in two races for the Texas State House of Representatives following her graduation from the Boston University Law School in 1959.

Shelby Hearon, Jordan's co-biographer of *Barbara Jordan: Self Portrait*, gives a brief but efficient image of the speaker as she stood before the Democratic National Convention: "Hunched over, reading through her new, lightweight aviator glasses, she gave the throng one more First Time" (Hearon and Jordan 1979, 230). Jordan addressed the "first time" issue obliquely, with no explicit reference to race, no condemnation of the legacy of discriminatory practices that made this occasion the first time—after one hundred and forty-four years—that an African American woman had been invited to deliver the keynote address. The audience was witnessing an unprecedented phenomenon and though her reference to race was an oblique one, the point could not be lost on an audience fully cognizant of the history of race relations in this country.

Democratic Convention Keynote Address
Barbara C. Jordan
1976

One hundred and forty-four years ago, members of the Democratic Party first met in convention to select a Presidential candidate. Since that time, Democrats have continued to convene once every four years and draft a party platform and nominate a Presidential candidate. And our meeting this week is a continuation of that tradition.

But there is something different about tonight. There is something special about tonight. What is different? What is special? I, Barbara Jordan, am a keynote speaker.

A lot of years passed since 1832, and during that time it would have been most unusual for any national political party to ask that a Barbara Jordan deliver a keynote address . . . but tonight here I am. And I feel that notwithstanding the past that my presence here is one additional bit of evidence that the American Dream need not forever be deferred.

Now that I have this grand distinction what in the world am I supposed to say?

I could easily spend this time praising the accomplishments of this party and attacking the Republicans but I don't choose to do that.

I could list the many problems which Americans have. I could list the problems which cause people to feel cynical, angry, frustrated; problems which include lack of integrity in government; the feeling that the individual no longer counts; the reality of material and spiritual poverty; the feeling that the grand American experiment is failing or has failed. I could recite these problems and then I could sit down and offer no solutions. But I don't choose to do that either.

The citizens of America expect more. They deserve and they want more than a recital of problems.

We are a people in a quandary about the present. We are a people in search of our future. We are a people in search of a national community.

We are a people trying not only to solve the problems of the present: unemployment, inflation . . . but we are attempting on a larger scale to fulfill the promise of America. We are attempting to fulfill our national purpose; to create and sustain a society in which all of us are equal.

Throughout our history, when people have looked for new ways to solve their problems, and to uphold the principles of this nation, many times they have turned to political parties. They have often turned to the Democratic Party.

What is it, what is it about the Democratic Party that makes it the instrument that people use when they search for ways to shape their future? Well I believe the answer to that question lies in our concept of governing. Our concept of governing is derived from our view of people. It is a concept deeply rooted in a set of beliefs firmly etched in the national conscience, of all of us.

Now what are these beliefs?

First, we believe in equality for all and privileges for none. This is a belief that each American regardless of background has equal standing in the public forum, all of us. Because we believe this idea so firmly, we are an inclusive rather than an exclusive party. Let everybody come.

I think it no accident that most of those emigrating to America in the 19th century identified with the Democratic Party. We are a heterogeneous party made up of Americans of diverse backgrounds.

We believe that the people are the source of all governmental power; that the authority of the people is to be extended, not restricted. This can be accomplished only by providing each citizen with every opportunity to participate in the management of the government. They must have that.

We believe that the government which represents the authority of all the people, not just one interest group, but all the people, has an obligation to actively underscore, actively seek to remove those obstacles which would block individual achievement obstacles emanating from race, sex, economic condition. The government must seek to remove them.

We are a party of innovation. We do not reject our traditions, but we are willing to adapt to changing circumstances, when change we must. We are willing to suffer the discomfort of change in order to achieve a better future.

We have a positive vision of the future founded on the belief that the gap between the promise and reality of America can one day be finally closed. We believe that.

This my friends, is the bedrock of our concept of governing. This is a part of the reason why Americans have turned to the Democratic Party. These are the foundations upon which a national community can be built.

Let's all understand that these guiding principles cannot be discarded for short-term political gains. They represent what this country is all about. They are indigenous to the American idea. And these are principles which are not negotiable.

In other times, I could stand here and give this kind of exposition on the beliefs of the Democratic Party and that would be enough. But today that is not enough. People want more. That is not sufficient reason for the majority of the people of this country to vote Democratic. We have made mistakes. In our haste to do all things for all people, we did not foresee the full consequences of our actions. And when the people raised their voices, we didn't hear. But our deafness was only a temporary condition, and not an irreversible condition.

Even as I stand here and admit that we have made mistakes I still believe that as the people of America sit in judgment on each party, they will recognize that our mistakes were mistakes of the heart. They'll recognize that.

And now we must look to the future. Let us heed the voice of the people and recognize their common sense. If we do not, we not only blaspheme our political heritage, we ignore the common ties that bind all Americans.

Many fear the future. Many are distrustful of their leaders, and believe that their voices are never heard. Many seek only to satisfy their private wants. To satisfy private interests.

But this is the great danger America faces. That we will cease to be one nation and become instead a collection of interest groups: city against suburb, region against region, individual against individual. Each seeking to satisfy private wants.

If that happens, who then will speak for America?

Who then will speak for the common good?

This is the question which must be answered in 1976.

Are we to be one people bound together by common spirit sharing in a common endeavor or will we become a divided nation?

For all of its uncertainty, we cannot flee the future. We must not become the new Puritans and reject our society. We must address and master the future together. It can be done if we restore the belief that we share a sense of national community, that we share a common national endeavor. It can be done.

There is no executive order; there is no law that can require the American people to form a national community. This we must do as individuals and if we do it as individuals, there is no President of the United States who can veto that decision.

As a first step, we must restore our belief in ourselves. We are a generous people so why can't we be generous with each other? We need to take to heart the words spoken by Thomas Jefferson:

"Let us restore to social intercourse that harmony and that affection without which liberty and even life are but dreary things."

A nation is formed by the willingness of each of us to share in the responsibility for upholding the common good.

A government is invigorated when each of us is willing to participate in shaping the future of this nation.

In this election year we must define the common good and begin again to shape a common good and begin again to shape a common future. Let each person do his or her part. If one citizen is unwilling to participate, all of us are going to suffer. For the American idea, though it is shared by all of us, is realized in each one of us.

And now, what are those of us who are elected public officials supposed to do? We call ourselves public servants but I'll tell you this: we as public servants must set an example for the rest of the nation. It is hypocritical for the public official to admonish and exhort the people to uphold the common good if we are derelict in upholding the common good. More is required of public officials than slogans and handshakes and press releases. More is required. We must hold ourselves strictly accountable. We must provide the people with a vision of the future.

If we promise as public officials, we must deliver. If we as public officials propose, we must produce. If we say to the American people it is time for you to be sacrificial; sacrifice. If the public official says that, we (public officials) must be the first to give. We must be. And again, if we make mistakes, we must be willing to admit them. We have to do that. What we have to do is strike a balance between the idea that government should do everything and the idea, the belief, that government ought to do nothing. Strike a balance.

Let there be no illusions about the difficulty of forming this kind of a national community. It's tough, difficult, not easy. But a spirit of harmony will survive in America only if each of us remembers that we share a common destiny. If each of us remembers when self-interest and bitterness seem to prevail, that we share a common destiny.

I have confidence that we can form this kind of national community.

I have confidence that the Democratic Party can lead the way. I have that confidence. We cannot improve on the system of government handed down to us by the founders of the Republic, there is no way to improve upon that. But what we can do is to find new ways to implement that system and realize our destiny.

Now, I began this speech by commenting to you on the uniqueness of a Barbara Jordan making the keynote address. Well I am going to close my speech by quoting a Republican President and I ask you that as you listen to these words of Abraham Lincoln, relate them to the concept of a national community in which every last one of us participates: "As I would not be a slave, so I would not be a master." This expresses my idea of democracy. Whatever differs from this, to the extent of the difference is no democracy.

Last Will And Testament
Mary McLeod Bethune
1955

Sometimes as I sit communing in my study I feel that death is not far off. I am aware that it will overtake me before the greatest of my dreams—full equality for the Negro in our time—is realized. Yet, I face that reality without tears or regrets. I am resigned to death as all humans must be at the proper time. Death neither alarms nor frightens one who has had a long career of fruitful toil. The knowledge that my work has been helpful to many fills me with joy and great satisfaction.

Since my retirement from an active role in educational work and from the affairs of the National Council of Negro Women, I have been living quietly and working at my desk at my home here in Florida. The years have directed a change of pace for me. I am now seventy-eight years old and my activities are no longer so strenuous as they once were. I feel that I must conserve my strength to finish the work at hand.

Already I have begun working on my autobiography which will record my life-journey in detail, together with the innumerable side trips which have carried me abroad, into every corner of our country, into homes both lowly and luxurious, and even into the White House to confer with Presidents. I have also deeded my home and its contents to the Mary McLeod Bethune Foundation, organized in March, 1953, for research, interracial activity and the sponsorship of wider educational opportunities.

Sometimes I ask myself if I have any other legacy to leave. Truly, my worldly possessions are few. Yet, my experiences have been rich. From them, I have distilled principles and policies in which I believe firmly, for they represent the meaning of my life's work. They are the product of much sweat and sorrow. Perhaps in them there is something of value. So, as my life draws to a close, I will pass them on to Negroes everywhere in the hope that an old woman's philosophy may give them inspiration. Here, then, is my legacy.

* *I leave you love.* Love builds. It is positive and helpful. It is more beneficial than hate. Injuries quickly forgotten quickly pass away. Personally and racially, our enemies must be forgiven. Our aim must be to create a world of fellowship and justice where no man's skin, color or religion, is held against him. "Love thy neighbor" is a precept which could transform the world if it were universally practiced. It connotes brotherhood and, to me, , brotherhood of man is the noblest concept in all human relations. Loving your neighbor means being interracial, interreligious and international.

* *I leave you hope.* The Negro's growth will be great in the years to come. Yesterday, our ancestors endured the degradation of slavery, yet they retained their dignity. Today, we direct our economic and political strength toward winning a more abundant and secure life. Tomorrow, a new Negro, unhindered by race taboos and shackles will benefit from more than 330 years of ceaseless striving and struggle. Theirs will a better world. This I believe with all my heart.

* *I leave you the challenge of developing confidence in one another.* As long as Negroes are hemmed into racial blocs by prejudice and pressure, it will be necessary for them to band together for economic betterment. Negro banks, insurance companies and other businesses are examples of successful, racial economic enterprises. These institutions were made possible by vision and mutual aid. Confidence was vital in getting them started and keeping them going. Negroes have got to demonstrate still more confidence in each other in business. This kind of confidence will aid the economic rise

of the race by bringing together the pennies and dollars of our people and ploughing them into useful channels. Economic separatism cannot be tolerated in this enlightened age, and it is not practicable. We must spread out as far and as fast as we can, but we must also help each other as we go. * *I leave you a thirst for education.* Knowledge is the prime need of the hour. More and more, Negroes are taking full advantage of hard-won opportunities for learning, and the educational level of the Negro population is at its highest point in history. We are making greater use of the privileges inherent in living in a democracy. If we continue in this trend, we will be able to rear increasing numbers of strong, purposeful men and women, equipped with vision, mental clarity, health and education.

* *I leave you a respect for the uses of power.* We live in a world which respects power above all things. Power, intelligently directed, can lead to more freedom. Unwisely directed, it can be a dreadful, destructive force. During my life-time I have seen the power of the Negro grow enormously. It has always been my first concern that this power should be placed on the side of human justice.

Now that the barriers are crumbling everywhere, the Negro in America must be ever vigilant lest his forces be marshalled behind wrong causes and undemocratic movements. He must not lend his support to any group that seeks to subvert democracy. That is why we must select leaders who are wise, courageous, and of great moral stature and ability. We have great leaders among us today: Ralph Bunche, Channing Tobias, Mordecai Johnson, Walter White, and Mary Church Terrell. [The latter two are now deceased.] We have had other great men and women in the past: Frederick Douglass, Booker T. Washington, Harriet Tubman, Sojourner Truth. We must produce more qualified people like them, who will work not for themselves, but for others.

* *I leave you faith.* Faith is the first factor in a life devoted to service. Without faith, nothing is possible. With it, nothing is impossible. Faith in God is the greatest power, but great, too, is faith in oneself. In fifty years the faith of the American Negro in himself has grown immensely and is still increasing. The measure of our progress as a race is in precise relation to the depth of the faith in our people held by our leaders. Frederick Douglass, genius though he was, was spurred by a deep conviction that his people would heed his counsel and follow him to freedom. Our greatest Negro figures have been imbued with faith. Our forefathers struggled for liberty in conditions far more onerous than those we now face, but they never lost the faith. Their perseverance paid rich dividends. We must never forget their suffering and their sacrifices, for they were the foundations of the progress of our people.

* *I leave you racial dignity.* I want Negroes to maintain their human dignity at all costs. We, as Negroes, must recognize that we are the custodians as well as the heirs of a great civilization. We have given something to the world as a race and for this we are proud and fully conscious of our place in the total picture of mankind's development. We must learn also to share and mix with all men. We must make an effort to be less race conscious and more conscious of individual and human values. I have never been sensitive about my complexion. My color has never destroyed my self respect nor has it ever caused me to conduct myself in such a manner as to merit the disrespect of any person. I have not let my color handicap me. Despite many crushing burdens and handicaps, I have risen from the cotton fields of South Carolina to found a college, administer it during its years of growth, become a public servant in the government of our country and leader of women. I would not exchange my color for all the wealth in the world, for had I been born white I

might not been able to do all that I have done or yet hope to do.

I leave you a desire to live harmoniously with your fellow men. The problem of color is world-wide. It is found in Africa and Asia, Europe and South American. I appeal to American Negroes—North, South, East and West—to recognize their common problems and unite to solve them.

I pray that we will learn to live harmoniously with the white race. So often our difficulties have made us hypersensitive and truculent. I want to see my people conduct themselves naturally in all relationships—fully conscious of their manly responsibilities and deeply aware of their heritage. I want them to learn to understand whites and influence them for good, for it is advisable and sensible for us to do. We are a minority of fifteen million living side by side with a white majority. We must learn to deal with these people positively and on an individual basis.

I leave you finally a responsibility to our young people. The world around us really belongs to youth for youth will take over its future management. Our children must never lose their zeal for building a better world. They must not be discouraged from aspiring toward greatness, for they are to be the leaders of tomorrow. Nor must they forget that the masses of our people are still underprivileged, ill-housed, impoverished and victimized by discrimination. We have a powerful potential in our youth, and we must have the courage to change old ideas and practices so that we may direct their power toward good ends.

Faith, courage, brotherhood, dignity, ambition, responsibility—these are needed today as never before. We must cultivate them and use them as tools for our task of completing the establishment of equality for the Negro. We must sharpen these tools in the struggle that faces us and find

new ways of using them. The Freedom Gates are half a-jar.
We must pry them fully open.

If I have a legacy to leave my people, it is my philosophy
of living and serving. As I face tomorrow, I am content, for
I think I have spent my life well. I pray now that my
philosophy may be helpful to those who share my vision of
a world Peace, Progress, Brotherhood and Love.

PART FOUR

PERSPECTIVES ON THE GENRE

The oratory of African American women essentially conforms to the primary theoretical expectations emanating from the traditional canon. Yet, like artistic expression in other types of prose across time, simplicity has replaced the ornate, with the net effect of fewer pronounced tropes and schemes and other attributes characteristic of Greek and Roman origins. All eloquence, however, is by no means lost in this simplification of expression in that the oratory continues to communicate in compelling fashion the best thoughts of the best thinkers of a given era.

Invention
Topics Or Lines Of Argument

The traditional rhetorical canon includes common topics, or lines of argument, this phase of operations classified under invention. The common topics include definition, comparison, relationship, circumstance, and testimony, each with subheadings. Definition includes division and genus; comparison includes similarity, difference, and degree. Relationship contains four sub-categories: cause and effect, antecedent and consequence, contraries, and contradictions. Circumstance encompasses the possible and impossible as well as past fact and future fact, and testimony covers authority, statistics, maxims, law, and precedents or examples. Corbett refers to these topics as "depositories of general arguments" that initiate or suggest lines of argument for the discourse. (Corbett 1971, 146).

Special topics fall into three categories, usually according to the type of oratory under consideration—deliberative, judicial, or ceremonial. The worthy and the good and the advantageous or expedient topics were generally invoked for deliberative discourse; justice and injustice, or right and wrong, for judicial discourse; and virtue and vice, or the noble and base, for ceremonial discourse.

Six speeches have been selected to illustrate the rhetorical application of the common and special topics. Speeches in this discussion include "The Unglamorous But Worthwhile Duties of the Black Revolutionary Artist" by Alice Walker (1970); "It Is Time For A Change" by Shirley Chisholm (1969); "A Plea for Industrial Opportunity" by Fanny Jackson Coppin (circa the 1890s); "The Burden of The Educated Colored Woman" by Lucy C. Laney (1899); "The Law and Moral Issues" by Patricia Roberts Harris (1963); and "Choose One of Five" by Edith Sampson (1965).

Comparison and definition are the primary lines of argument Walker uses to clarify the role of the black revolutionary artist. Coming to the full realization of the complexity of this task required some time. Her evolution is clarified by the common topic of comparison. Her matriculation at Sarah Lawrence initially suggested to her so many improvements over Spelman, her first undergraduate college. She considered the first school "opposed to change, to freedom, and to understanding that by the time most girls enter college they are already women and should be treated as women" (Par. 1). She found the freedom she sought at Sarah Lawrence. The freedom there enabled her to make significant artistic contributions, writing and publishing her first short story and book.

The next section is more subtle in its revelation of the shortcomings of the institution that led to her transformation in perception, to the belief that she had "found happiness and peace" in her own time; that is, until she discovered that so much of her own heritage had been omitted in the education she received at Sarah Lawrence.

Using a form of definition, she explains the "college of books" she entered as a corrective to her "miseducation." The definition includes rather extensive enumeration as she lists the essential works by African Americans that must be included in a comprehensive education. Without an understanding of W. E. B. DuBois and Richard Wright, for example, certain concepts and periods of history simply could not be understood. The enumeration not only advances her major thesis but offers substantial information to auditors interested in understanding realities descriptive of the essence and the texture of this nation and the world.

The speaker notes, with some satisfaction, the changes that had taken place at Sarah Lawrence since her matriculation there. Using the common topic of contrast or difference she notes: "When I was here there were six of us and none of us was entirely black. Much has clearly changed, here as in the rest of the country" (Par. 9). The college had, since Walker's attendance there, established a center for black studies. This contrast or difference noted here, she emphasizes, does not mean that there is no more work to be done in clarifying the true character of this country and recognizing the inclusiveness that defines America.

Definition as a line of argument is again invoked as Walker attempts to clarify her own identity. In a series of sentences, she explains: "I have not labeled myself yet. I would like to call myself revolutionary, for I am always changing, and growing, it is hoped for the good of more black people. I do call myself black when it seems necessary to call myself anything, especially since I believe one's word rather than one's appearance adequately labels one" (Par. 11). This definition is instructive to auditors in that it reveals the philosophical stance of the speaker, thereby giving the audience a backdrop against which to evaluate the primary assertions of the discourse. Her definition of the artist and the role of the artist in the community forms the substantive thrust of her discourse.

She uses enumeration to suggest the responsibilities devolving upon the black revolutionary artist. Her listing supports the generalization that follows: "*The real revolution is always concerned with the least glamorous stuff*" (Par. 15). The enumeration is corrective in that conventional wisdom could suggest that the work of the artist is one of detachment from the real problems of society and a life of fame and glory. She amends this perception in her explanation that "the work of the black revolutionary artist is concerned with raising a reading level from second grade to third. With simplifying history and writing it down (or reciting it) for the old folks. With helping illiterates fill out foodstamp forms—for they must eat, revolution or not." (Par. 15). The speaker continues her definition using illustrations and the common topic of difference to clarify the full implications of the life of an artist.

Hate, as an incentive or agent of immobilization, receives considerable attention in her discussion. Again, she uses contrast to emphasize the discrimination that should be exercised in the determination of accepting groups and individuals. She also explicates, through a form of definition and antecedent-consequent, the possible effects of hate. Her description accords to hate ambiguous possibilities. It is an emotion that has the potential of mitigating or paralyzing, and auditors should be aware of the dual possibilities, carefully eschewing the hate that paralyzes.

Walker also uses the common topic of definition to clarify what art is and what it is not in paragraph twenty-three. And the common topic of comparison that concludes the discourse makes a compelling statement. Comparing the people with whom she currently interacts in Mississippi with those she knew in her Georgia childhood, she makes a compelling observation: "I see the same faces, hear the same soft voices . . . And when I write about the people there, in the strangest way it is as if I am not writing about them at all, but about myself" (Par. 23). Here the speaker implies a profound notion concerning the invisible cord that binds all humanity together.

Shirley Chisholm employs several traditional lines of argument, or common topics, to develop her argument in "It Is Time For A Change." Comparison is the line of argument used to dramatize what the speaker perceives to be the folly of "spending nine billion dollars . . . on elaborate, unnecessary and impractical weapons when several thousand disadvantaged children in the nation's capital get nothing" (Par. 2). Words used to characterize each emphasis produce a strong emotional effect deriving primarily from the connotative potential of such words as *elaborate*, *unnecessary*, and *impractical* set in contrast against disadvantaged children. Invoked here as well is the special topic of the worthy and the unworthy as the speaker's comparative evaluations of the two emphases clearly reveal her perceived view that attention to disadvantaged children is a more worthy enterprise.

The speaker resorts to past fact to dramatize the prudent imperatives of the present. In an oblique reference to the misguided actions of former President Lyndon Johnson in the Vietnam War and the corresponding political price paid for that misdirection, she refers sarcastically to Melvin Laird's announced commitment to spend at least two more years in Vietnam. In her attack on Laird, she emphasizes that he seems not to have profited from the lessons of history in assessing the course of action appropriate for the Vietnam tragedy: "To hear him, one would have thought it was 1968; that the former Secretary of State was defending the former policies, that nothing had ever happened—a President had never decided not to run because he knew the nation would reject him, in despair over this tragic war we have blundered into" (Par. 11).

A considerable amount of enumeration occurs in paragraphs twelve and thirteen in a litany of consequences attending the willingness to spend two more years in Vietnam: hunger, death, suffering, high taxes, poverty, prejudice, neglect, "fantastic waste in the Defense Department and of penny pinching on social programs." The accrued effect of this enumeration is rhetorically significant. Enumeration, a form of definition, illuminates issues, focusing as it does on specific, concrete manifestations or attributes of the matter under consideration.

Another line of argument employed by the speaker is antecedent-consequent. In paragraph seventeen, Chisholm dramatizes the high cost of hypocrisy: "Unless we start to defeat the enemies of poverty and racism in our own country and make our talk of equality and opportunity ring true, we are exposed as hypocrites in the eyes of the world when we talk about making other people free." Antecedent-consequent is a sub-category of the common topic of relationship. A special topic also inheres in the discussion of possible consequences revealed by this common topic. The special topic of the advantageous and disadvantageous obtains here and, when construed in its positive form, translates into the advantage of living true to the country's espoused ideals and demonstrating by practices our worthiness to promote worldwide freedom.

Chisholm uses the common topic of difference to explain how different standards are applied to assess the efficacy of results obtained in defense programs and those in social programs. Referring to the severe criticism of the Job Corps, the speaker argues that "If it had been a military research and development project, they [accounting discrepancies] would have been covered up and explained away, and Congress would have been ready to pour more billions after those that had been wasted on it." This discrepancy underscores the misplaced values and shifting criteria characteristic of decision makers in this country.

Testimony is a common topic that includes statistics, and Chisholm uses statistics strategically in paragraph sixteen to reinforce her argument concerning the illogicality that inheres in misplaced values. She points to the investigation of Pride, a black Washington-based organization. The statistics are revealing: "They worked seven months and spent more than $100, 000. They uncovered a fraud. It was something less than $2100. Meanwhile, millions of dollars—billions of dollars, in fact—were being spent by the Department of Defense, and how many auditors and investigators were checking into their negotiated contracts? Five." The statistics confer significance on the disparity emphasized throughout the address. She resorts to the use of statistics again in the concluding paragraph, noting that "We are now spending eighty billion dollars a year on defense—that is two-thirds of every tax dollar." Statistics, if used with integrity, typically confer credibility on an argument.

Another speech demonstrating the effective use of common and special topics is Fanny Jackson Coppin's "A Plea for Industrial Opportunity" delivered toward the end of the nineteenth century. Considering the speaker's rhetorical objective to promote industrial opportunity, her use of past fact is particularly appropriate. Her appeal for expanded opportunities carries with it the possibility of promise, revealing both the means and the ability to handle competently privileges deriving from the opportunity: "That the colored people of this country have enough money to materially alter their financial condition was clearly demonstrated by the millions of dollars deposited in the Freedmen's Bank; that they have the good sense, and the unanimity to use this power, are now proved by this industrial exhibition and fair" (Par. 1). The speaker thus provides at the outset a refutation of the most probable opposition, the claim that African Americans are unprepared for the requested consideration. This strategy represents a clear demonstration of the common topic of the possible. The group on whose behalf the request is made possesses both the desire and the means to capitalize on opportunities extended in their behalf. This statement of fact, technically an introductory rebuttal of commonly held assumptions, provides the framework for more extensive rebuttals designed to force her auditors to reconsider stereotypical notions of the economic dependence and lack of industry among African Americans.

One major misconception Coppin seeks to correct is that African Americans must leave the South to experience economic advancement. Using a form of definition, the enumeration of alternatives, she suggests possible courses of action that could develop and solidify the economic power of African Americans in the South. These possibilities include consolidating their funds so as to be able to lend to the poorer classes until crops were harvested and the opening of co-operative stores. She clinches the "self-help" concept with a maxim, claiming "self-help" to be "the best help that any man can have, next to God's." The maxim itself is a powerful rhetorical tool in that its centrality in the mythic consciousness of Americans evokes a ready sympathetic resonance.

Coppin uses the common topic of comparison to differentiate between this fair and those events that require lavish announcements and verbosity. Although this low-key approach had permitted some to overlook the event, Coppin implicitly approves the chosen course of action by assigning negative descriptors—"noisy and demonstrative babblings, which are so often the vapid precursors of promises as empty as those who make them"—to describe competitors. She then invokes the common topic of enumeration to suggest ways in which the group addressed can carry out the directive seeming to derive from divine origin, "Speak to the people that they go forward (Par. 2). The strategies enjoined include public relations combined with a collaboration of means and efforts to secure employment comparable to the employment of the general population. The enumeration continues as she cites the number of occupations from which African Americans are excluded, the enumeration rendering more concrete and urgent her appeal for economic opportunity.

Ethical appeal is evident as Coppin recalls the legacy of slavery but quickly removes attribution of blame: "Slavery made us poor, and the gloomy, malicious shadow tends to keep us so. I beg to say, kind hearers, that this is not spoken in a spirit of recrimination. We have no quarrel with our fate, and we leave your Christianity to yourselves" (Par. 3). The speaker places the responsibility for ultimate success on the efforts of African Americans and favorable circumstances, a concession that does not comport well with reality but averts possible confrontation.

Coppin employs the special topics of the advantageous and the expedient to justify her emphasis on industrial education, a traditionally controversial topic in the African American community. Posing the negative "starving 'time' between the reception of a diploma [in medicine or law] and the time that a man's profession becomes a paying one," she discourages an exclusive emphasis on the professions and implies the practical benefits of the industrial occupations.

The speaker here makes use of the special topic of the expedient. Opportunities for African Americans to penetrate the prestigious professions in significant numbers are limited; the race will, therefore, be better served by selecting those occupations offering more immediate, concrete rewards. Her language is suggestive of the opposition faced by African Americans in their efforts to gain meaningful employment. She refers to the "closed doors of employment" and the "cold metallic voice within" to dramatize the plight of the race in the professional arena.

With muted sarcasm, she attacks the emphases attending efforts to elevate the status of the race. Alluding to efforts made on behalf of the minds and souls of African Americans, she reminds the benefactors: ". . . We haven't quite got rid of our bodies yet, and until we do, we must feed and clothe them, and this attitude of keeping us out of work forces us back upon charity" (Par. 7). This antecedent-consequent argument deviates from the prevailing structure for this kind of topic, but the essence and effect are the same. Her essential argument is that given the circumstances set in motion when members of the race are denied equal employment, the inevitable result is a group dependent upon charity.

Testimony is a rhetorical strategy that figures prominently in the last paragraph that, technically, could be classified as part of the body of the speech in that Coppin continues her argument. She quotes Henry C. Carey, whose work reveals the relationship between material prosperity and intellectual advancement. This cultural notion of physical well being as a necessary antecedent of creativity and productivity receives rather automatic assent from most people who recognize the interdependence of mental and physical health. Thus, the speaker's invocation of a commonly accepted premise has the potential of connecting with the social and psychological consciousness of a sensitive audience.

The common topic of the possible strengthens the speaker's argument. She argues that changing times have rendered the acceptance of African Americans in public places more palatable, asserting, "I am satisfied that the employment of a colored clerk or a colored salesman wouldn't even be a 'nine days wonder.'" But the following paradox illustrates the complexity of her appeal. She admits, "It is easy of accomplishment, and yet it is not" (Par. 8). She chooses, however, to end on a positive note and appeals to the enlightened among them to accept their obligation to extend the privilege of industrial opportunity to African Americans.

Lucy Laney uses several common and special topics in "The Burden of the Educated Colored Woman." In clarifying her use of the word *burden*, Laney employs the common topic of comparison by explaining, "What it is can be readily seen perhaps better than told for it constantly annoys to irritation; it bulges out as did the load of Bunyan's Christian—ignorance—with its inseparable companions, shame and crime and prejudice." (Par.1). The speaker thus communicates the urgency of her message, the language and allusion connoting the motivational pull of issues that tug at the conscience and command attention, reflection, and action. These are not issues that can be casually evaded because they evoke irritation and bulge out—defying complacency and neglect.

The speaker continues the topic of comparison as she invokes the memory and character of people like Phillis Wheatley, Sojourner Truth, and John Chavers. The point she makes here is that their potential should have been readily recognized by people or schoolmasters who might have generalized these abilities to other members of the race and thereby enhanced the productivity of talented minds. She compares these "dull teachers" with many modern pedagogues and school-keepers who fail to challenge and explore the possibilities of similarly capable pupils.

Cause and effect, a subdivision of relationship, is the topic that most accurately describes Laney's discussion of the African American's legacy of marriage. Charges of immorality, commonly leveled against African Americans, appear unwarranted if one reviews the legacy of marriage evolving from the institution of slavery. The callous disregard for stable marriages and fidelity demonstrated by slave-masters could not be logically expected to translate into traditional mainstream respect for the sanctity of marriage. The failure to bestow legal sanction on unions, the possible—even probable—separation of married couples, and the casual regard for the sanctity of the marriage vows demonstrated by slave owners who "consoled those thus parted with the fact that he could get another wife; she, another husband . . . " certainly offered little incentive to African Americans to confer upon the institution of marriage the appropriate respect for its indissolubility. Nontraditional behavior was thus spawned by the very circumstances surrounding the institution of marriage as it applied to people of color at the time.

This same line of argument extends to the prevalence of "untidy and filthy homes." Slave women were not taught to value homemaking since "homes were only places in which to sleep" and "house cleaning was sometimes enforced as a protection to property, but this was done at stated times and when ordered" (Par. 4). Incentives of ownership and pride had no place in the slave community and therefore careful housekeeping did not emerge as a practice of value to people who owned no homes. Although Laney clearly establishes the cause-effect relationship of history to the current conditions, she does not condone untidiness and calls upon the more favored, or the educated, to take corrective measures and seek to instill pride in the care of the home and hygiene among the lesser prepared.

In her discussion of the disproportionate number of incarcerated young black men, Laney uses several lines of argument. One is comparison. She discusses the differences obtaining in the conditions of black and white prisoners, noting, "It is true that white criminals by the help of attorneys, money and influence, oftener escape the prison, thus keeping smaller the number of prisoners recorded . . ." (Par. 5). And she implicitly invokes the argument of antecedent-consequent in describing the indiscriminate associations produced by prison life, where the younger and more innocent were placed in close, constant contact with hardened criminals. Clearly implied here is the probable consequences of increased corruption on the part of the young as they were exposed to the harsher elements of society.

Enumeration, a division of definition, is prominent in the speaker's discussion of prejudice. Her catalogue of illustrations includes: "In the South, in public conveyances, and at all points of race contact; in the North, in hotels, at the baptismal pool, in cemeteries; everywhere, in some shape or form, it is to be borne" (Par. 6). The cumulative effect of this enumeration is not only instructive, but potentially emotionally overwhelming. She cites ignorance and immorality as possible causes of this prejudice, but immediately asserts that the cure is more relevant than the cause. The antecedent-consequent line of argument is used in her appeal for better homes. She laments the fact that "the work of the schoolroom has been completely neutralized by the training of the home. Then we must have better homes, and better homes mean better mothers, better fathers, better born children." She also invokes the topic of testimony by quoting Emerson's eloquent claim "To the well-born child all the virtues are natural, not painfully acquired." (Par. 11).

Precedent, a form of testimony, is employed in the speaker's anecdote that demonstrates the power and capacity of women. The key term in the anecdote is the command: "Call the women. . . " The fact that women came and successfully pulled to the top of the building a heavy piece of timber the men had been unable to move evinces woman's potential power and strengthens Laney's argument that the current burdens of society can indeed be lifted by women.

Patricia Harris's explication of the relationship between law and morality includes rather comprehensive use of common topics. Following the introductory section, she uses stipulated definitions of the two major concepts in her discourse—law and morality. Noting the contentious nature of those inclined to consider these concepts, she stipulates the definitions applicable to her discussion. She defines law as "that body of rules and regulations established by official governmental units to control public and private behavior, the observance of which is secured by the threat of the imposition of penalties in the nature of fine, imprisonment, or withdrawal of a government granted benefit" (Par. 6) and morality as "that body of concepts of right behavior accepted by substantial segments of our society as standards for the evaluation of the conduct of individuals" (Par. 7). The definitions, thus stipulated, preclude the likelihood of misunderstanding and conflicting connotations usually accompanying theoretical discussions of these concepts. The example is the next evident rhetorical strategy used to develop her thesis. Her use of adultery as a case in point demonstrates the complementarity of law and morality, as the need to control behavior does indeed derive from moral imperatives codified by law.

Common topics of comparison and difference clarify the respective provinces of the two concepts. These topics are complemented by the implied irony that the clergy, as arbiters of morality, had forfeited their traditional role as interpreters of morality. This discrepancy between expectation and reality is central to her message, dramatizing the shifting parameters of moral considerations. She invokes past fact in a description that underscores her primary assertion. Noting the failure of the religious community to respond to the desecration of a Negro church and the loss of four lives, she leads up to a compelling observation: "But in that city, on the day of the desecration, one voice spoke to the city and to the world of the immorality of the event, and that voice was not the voice of a minister. It was the voice of a lawyer" (Par. 18). In referring to the bombing of a Birmingham church and the deaths of four young girls attending Sunday School, she implicitly, but dramatically, emphasizes the failure of that segment of the community most frequently expected to denounce immorality. The rhetorical application of the topic of difference is evident; the expected results did not occur under the circumstances they would most likely be expected to occur. The strategy highlights the eroding obligation to moral interpretation and responsibility demonstrated by the clergy.

The speaker also uses the common topic of difference to illustrate divergent perceptions of law "as the true embodiment of everything that's excellent," explaining that lawyers actually "subject it [the law] to a continuing critical scrutiny, seeking to ascertain if the law does in truth support the highest ethical and moral values of the society as it is expected to do or if, instead, it perverts them" (Par. 22). She continues with the common topic of difference to emphasize the liberty of community members to contemplate issues of morality with a broader perspective than can lawyers, bound as the latter are to the specific interests and imperatives of their clients. Paragraph twenty-seven is an artistic demonstration of difference used in an extended argument, as she examines the moral and legal dimensions of several current emphases. She argues that "whether or not we are permitted to pray in public schools is a legal issue, but whether or not we ought to pray in school is a question with which all of us are competent to deal." She supplements this example with the issues of the death penalty for rape or murder and the Fourteenth Amendment. The series of contrasts distinguishing between what the law permits and the inherent moral dimensions of these issues strongly emphasize the obligation of communities to establish "concepts of right behavior . . . for the evaluation of the conduct of individuals." Harris intimates that this ideal is at variance with current practice, and this observation becomes a compelling point in the speaker's exegesis of law and morality.

Continuing with the common topic of difference, she contrasts de Tocqueville's perception of Americans in 1836 to the prevailing attitudes of Americans at the time of her speech. Alexis de Tocqueville's view of the flux evident in American society, as views of perfection shift, is contrasted with a near complacency or fear of change described by the speaker as "a general wish not to rock the boat; not to change the imperfections of today's world, because the world of tomorrow, if we change things, may be worse" (Par. 29). We note here a subtle indictment of the comfort of stability as opposed to the less orderly dynamics of flux, the appealing—though frequently unsettling—tendency of Americans to question and reevaluate national issues in response to shifting ideals.

The predominant line of argument, or common topic, is that of comparison—similarities and differences. The speaker utilizes this topic to emphasize the complementarity of the law and morality by pointing out dimensions in each concept that differ from the other, and by noting the discrepancy between expectations and reality in the interpretation and enforcement of morality and law. This line of argument carries the primary thrust of her message, continuing even into the conclusion where she contrasts de Tocqueville's idealized view of Americans with reality. Comparison is an effective line of argument for the explication of concepts as commonly connected as are law and morality; it also provides for the necessary differentiations that clarify contrary dimensions of the two concepts.

Antecedent-consequent is the rhetorical scheme that essentially articulates logical outcomes of given situations. Harris employs this scheme obliquely in paragraph four. In many instances, this scheme is used to warn so as to avert a possible disaster. Here, however, it is applied with more positive intent—the expression of an ideal and the prerequisites for the attainment of the ideal. The speaker argues, "And if it is the purpose of law to so order society that it may achieve the goal it has set for itself, the adoption of that part of the moral code deemed to constitute the imperative for the living of the good life would seem essential." The nation's attainment of its goals requires the articulation and adoption of a moral code that comprehensively reflects the society's interpretation of the good life.

Harris's conclusion that "the most significant initiators of national dialogue are these custodians of the law and not the would-be custodians of morality" seems to be less of an idolization of the legal profession than an implied reprimand of the religious community and the community in general for their failure to identify and raise the moral arguments that characterize the national conscience. The legal profession, then, by default, takes on the task of consciousness raising traditionally expected from other segments of the population, particularly the clergy.

In "Choose One Of Five," Edith Sampson so skillfully weaves the lines of argument into the address that she meets the ultimate criterion of art: "the highest art is to conceal art." The enumeration in the first section catalogues the numerous issues that should engage the mental energies of educated people. And although the speaker dismisses these issues as the emphasis of her presentation for this occasion, the enumeration—a form of definition—outlines a plethora of modern dilemmas that must ultimately require the considered reflection of the audience. The audience cannot forget the monumental social issues placed before them: international, national, and local. Selecting another emphasis for the presentation at hand cannot remove the haunting of these detractors of the abundant life and purposeful living. Consideration of choice one through five is couched in antecedent-consequent context. Auditors are warned that having chosen a particular option, certain eventualities or circumstances naturally follow. Closing their minds to the continuing task of learning and exposure has its consequences. They will have to insulate themselves from situations and people that provoke thought and ambiguity. And though the speaker prefaces these consequences with "You will have to," the ultimate outcome is obviously unsatisfactory. Invoked here also is the special topic of the worthy and the advantageous. Auditors can readily comprehend the emptiness and lack of involvement this course of action represents and realize immediately that their preparation deserves more purposeful direction.

The common topic of comparison illustrates the difference between choice one and choice two. Although choice two will also prove unsatisfactory ultimately, it does expand the options and activities possible for those subscribing to this choice. The special topic of the disadvantageous emphasizes the consequences of conformity. The inner self will become frustrated and the ensuing anguish she describes dramatizes the disadvantage of yielding to conformity.

Sampson continues the antecedent-consequent line of argument undergirded by comparison as she explores the third choice. The disadvantage is obvious here as well. Subscribers to this option escape the duty of challenge, but they also sacrifice the excitement of challenge in their affiliation with elite groups that limit experimentation and expansion. The dead-end consequences of this choice are dramatized in the statements: "One thing you can't have if you go the third-choice way—at least not today—and that's a conviction that human beings and the history they have made is important. Nothing is important really—nothing that is, except your one staked-out small field of specialization."

The scope broadens in the explication of choice four. Enumeration renders this choice a bit more complex. By affiliating themselves with the far right or the far left, they can embrace philosophical factions, but the ultimate consequences are similar. Individuality and freedom of choice are similarly sacrificed, removing the challenge and provocation of making choices since these extreme positions have their own built-in philosophies and biases. The topic of comparison emerges near the end of this discussion as the speaker notes: "In sharp contrast to choice-three people, choice-four people are convinced that everything is important because everything links somehow to the cause."

The speaker's explication of choice five reverses somewhat the veiled sarcasm evident in the preceding discussions. The eventualities are more sobering, divested as they are of the surface sarcasm characterizing the previous choice. Strong words such as *strenuous* and *demanding* characterize this part of the presentation. The enumerated challenges are indeed demanding and the rewards stripped of glory and comfort. In two short paragraphs, Sampson outlines the realities of choice five: "If only choice five involved only one thing or the other—thought or action—it would be ever so much easier. It doesn't though. It involves both . . . And if that weren't bad enough, this choice usually brings with it a certain amount of inner ache, because this way is a lonely way." Ironically the only choice that ambitious, responsible people would find truly worthy is shrouded in difficulties and complications.

Throughout Sampson's discourse, the primary lines of argument are antecedent-consequent, enumeration, and comparison. In the conclusion, the speaker begins with choice four and enumerates the disadvantages of each choice, concluding that choice five "makes life exciting . . . challenging, at least intermittently rewarding. But comfortable? No." Sampson's presentation is provocative; eschewing the didactic tone, she simply describes the consequences of choices, the descriptions themselves making the advantageous choice obvious.

Arrangement

Arrangement in rhetorical discourse consists of five parts: introduction, statement of fact, confirmation, refutation, and conclusion. Barbara Jordan's speech delivered before the National Democratic Convention in 1976 illustrates effective arrangement and will serve as the representative example of this dimension of the canon.

In the introduction, Jordan sets the 1976 Democratic National Convention in historical perspective, alluding to the origin and traditions of the party. Using the general topic of comparison—the difference component—she dramatizes the uniqueness of this convention. Her speech begins: "One hundred and forty-four years ago, members of the Democratic party first met in convention to select a Presidential candidate. Since that time Democrats have continued to convene once every four years and draft a party platform and nominate a presidential candidate. And our work this week is a continuation of that tradition. But there is something different about tonight. What is different? I, Barbara Jordan, am a Keynote speaker" (Par.1-2).

Her reference to time is particularly strategic; the Party has met every four years for almost one and half century and has this year, for the first time, lived up to its implicit promise of inclusiveness. Considered in isolation, this observation could be viewed as negative, but the speaker softens the reality by conferring the optimistic interpretation that the inclusiveness demonstrated at this moment stands as "evidence that the American Dream need not forever be deferred" (Par. 3). The historical moment is also critical since the nation had not at this time rendered due penitence for the unfavorable social climate of the previous decade. The corrective potential of the Party's strategy becomes apparent and is consistent with the democratic concept of governing Jordan emphasizes in the body of her speech.

The introduction as a whole reveals features of a strategy termed Introduction Preparatory, according to the taxonomy of introductions set forth in Richard Whately's *Elements of Rhetoric*. Introduction preparatory proposes "to explain an unusual mode of developing our subject; or to forestall some misconception of our purposes" (Corbett 1971, 306). After appropriately acknowledging the distinctive honor that is hers, Jordan poses the rhetorical question: "Now that I have this grand distinction what in the world am I supposed to say?" She then goes on to list the issues she could address on this occasion:" I could list the many problems which Americans have. I could list the problems which include lack of integrity in government; the feeling that the individual no longer counts; the reality of material and spiritual poverty; the feeling that the grand American experiment is failing or has failed" (Par. 6). Following this enumeration, she announces that she will not settle for such a listing because the people want and deserve more.

The rhetorical strategies employed in the introduction are multifaceted. Although the speaker ultimately rejects the option of emphasizing the issues enumerated, she, nonetheless, gains the rhetorical advantage of bringing these issues to the attention of the American public. And the problems are precisely those that the Democratic Party, in recent history, has professed to counteract. Another dimension of her introduction comports well with the *ethos* in the classical system, the ingratiation of oneself with the audience. She has introduced concerns that evoke sympathetic resonance in most Americans, yet she rejects these as somehow unworthy of this audience, thus evincing the highest regard for her audience. The direction of her discourse is also intimated: her address will be "more than a recital of problems."

Thus the tone of her discourse was set—the rejection of the negative for the positive. The centrality of the fulfilled dream in all its mythic import defines the positive nature of her presentation. Her decision not to dwell on America's problems complements the metaphoric emphasis employed in the beginning paragraphs of the address. She chooses uplifting considerations in which was couched the essence of numerous positive mythic elements central to the American consciousness to motivate her auditors to strive for the common good.

The confirmation, or main body of argument, in Jordan's address is divided into four major sections: the traditional needs to which the Party appeals in paragraphs eight through eleven; the set of beliefs or concept of governing that justifies the Party's appeal in paragraphs twelve through twenty; mistakes of the past that render imperative a reexamination of the concept of governing in paragraphs twenty-one and twenty-two, and an agenda for the future efforts of the Party in paragraphs twenty-three through forty-one.

The concluding paragraphs address the restoration of public trust and, in consequence, the unity crucial to the success of the Democratic Party. The essence of this section of the discourse is adequately summarized in the statement that "we cannot improve on the system of government handed down to us by founders of the Republic; there is no way to improve upon that. But what we can do is to find new ways to implement that system and realize our destiny" (Par. 41). She then quotes Abraham Lincoln, "As I would not be a slave, so I would not be a master" (Par. 42).

Style

Style is the third component of the complete rhetorical canon, the five dimensions including invention (topics or lines of argument), arrangement, style, memory, and delivery. Selected stylistic features used in this analysis include limited attention to diction and sentence structure as well as paragraph development and more extensive treatment of schemes and tropes.

Sentences And Paragraphs

Sentence analysis often provides additional insight into a speaker's style and method of development. The several sentence features often noted by rhetoricians and linguists include length, sentence openers, functional types—declarative, interrogative, imperative, and exclamatory; and grammatical types—simple, compound, complex, and compound-complex. Mary McLeod Bethune's "A Century of Progress of Negro

Women" has been selected to illustrate the role of sentence study in rhetorical analysis.

Sentence length in the discourse ranges from eight to ninety-eight words. The significance of sentence length in rhetorical criticism applies primarily in the consideration of extremely short or long sentences. The theoretical expectation of the short sentence is that it provides emphasis or effect. Bethune's speech contains four sentences with fewer than ten words. Three of these sentences are simply informational and exert limited rhetorical effect. The last sentence in the discourse, "She [the Negro woman] has made and is making history" is after the Aristotelian model of brief concluding sentences.

Long sentences are of interest to rhetorical critics because of their potential for cognitive overload since auditors do not have the advantage of immediate review. The longest sentence in the text appears in paragraph eighteen and reads "the educational institutions she has established and directed have met the needs of young people; her cultural development has concentrated itself into artistic presentation accepted and acclaimed by meritorious critics; she is successful as a poet and a novelist; she is shrewd in business and capable in politics; she recognizes the importance of uplifting her people through social, civic, and religious activities; starting at a time when as a "mammy" she nursed the infants of the other race and taught him her meagre store of truth, she has been a contributing factor of note to interracial relations." Six instances of psychological closure occur in this sentence, the actual effect being the same as that of six sentences. Only the technicality of end punctuation classifies this long passage as a single sentence. With the intermittent closure, the sentence is readily accessible and imposes no significant cognitive overload.

The declarative sentence is the dominant mode of presentation throughout the discourse. Although emotional appeals and implied argument permeate the speech, Bethune's obvious rhetorical objective is to convey information that illustrates the progress of Negro women of the past century. The declarative sentence is an appropriate rhetorical vehicle for this purpose. She poses no rhetorical questions and avoids the use of hortatives or imperatives.

Simple sentences are the grammatical sentence type used most frequently. Bethune's diverse methods of amplification, however, do not necessarily conform to Richard M. Weaver's claim of the simple sentences's "unclouded perspective," yet her disciplined thinking patterns produce no convoluted passages. The absence of competing elements informed Weaver's commendation of the simple sentence for clarity. Weaver also attributes to the compound sentence the effect of finality and authority and to the complex sentence logical ordering and ranking. Weaver's primary argument is that grammatical sentence types do more than provide sentence variety; they communicate atmosphere as previously described. The complex sentence follows the simple sentence in frequency of occurrence in this address.The compound and compound-complex structures receive little representation in the discourse.

The dominant sentence opener in the speech is the subject-first construction. Prepositional phrase openers follow next in frequency of occurrence. Other openers include single-word adverbs and adverb clauses, expletives, conjunctions, and a few verbals. Overall, the speaker's use and distribution of sentence openers is sufficiently varied to avoid monotony and succeed in enhancing the rhythm of the prose.

Paragraph analysis is often imposed by the editor of the speech text. The relevance of paragraph analysis in rhetorical studies is the information it yields about a given speaker's perception of the nature and amount of proof necessary to support assertions. In many instances, a given idea receives continuing consideration in the speech text despite the formal paragraph marker. No speech is presented as a model of paragraph development inasmuch as the amount of evidence presented in the majority of speeches demonstrate appropriate, and varying, assessments of the complete rhetorical situation.

Schemes And Tropes

Schemes and tropes in the traditional canon include deviations from the ordinary in either thought or expression. Corbett lists both under figures of speech, with schemes representing a transference of word order and tropes a transference of thought. Schemes include such figures as parallelism and repetition, polysyndeton, polyptoton, alliteration, antithesis, anaphora, epistrophe, anastrophe. These schemes are clarified both in the text of this section and in the Glossary. Tropes include metaphor, irony, erotema (the rhetorical question), synechdoche, metonymy, puns, etc. Classical rhetoricians as well as modern speakers and writers resort to these schemes for deliberate effect.

Parallelism and repetition are prominent rhetorical schemes and have the potential of evoking predictable reactions from a listening audience. These devices can serve as organizing principles, and they also reduce the cognitive burden because the repetition or parallel form provides for continuity in thought and allows the listener appropriate time to receive the substantive part of the message. Speeches demonstrating use of these schemes include "The Progress of Colored Women" delivered by Mary Church Terrell in 1904; "The Ethics of The Negro Question" by Anna J. Cooper delivered before the Society of Friends at Asbury Park in 1892; "A Challenge To

Artists" by Lorraine Hansberry in 1963; and "Liberty for Slaves" delivered in 1857 by Frances E. W. Harper.

Mary Church Terrell makes effective use of parallelism and repetition in "The Progress of Colored Women." Discussing the attributes of women of African descent, she notes "*So great* has been their thirst for knowledge and *so Herculean* their efforts . . . " In addition to contributing to the flow of the oratory, the repetition allows auditors to reflect on key words that characterize the ambition and industry of African American women. The repetition of the word *so* also provides a coherent framework for the listeners' organization of the idea articulated.

Another example of repetition is the section justifying the continuing determination of women of color to the issue of human rights and dignity. In condemnation of the convict-lease system, the speaker explains, "*So long as* hundreds of their brothers and sisters . . . are thrown into cells . . . *and so long as* children are born to the women in these camps . . ., colored women who are working for the emancipation and elevation of their race know where their duty lies" (Par. 8). The repetition of *so long as* exerts a cumulative effect that communicates an amalgam of factors that indeed render understandable the determination of the women to eradicate the evils enumerated. The parallel series in the closing paragraph achieves several rhetorical objectives. "*Lifting* as they climb, onward and upward they go *struggling* and *striving* and *hoping* . . ." conveys the vitality characterizing the work of African American women in various capacities. Each verbal lends its own testimony to the depth and scope of the sacrifices made daily by women of color and confers a tone of optimism suggesting these efforts would not come to naught. The obvious auditory advantage achieved in the rhythm of the series strengthens the articulation of continuity characterizing the struggle. And "seeking no favors because of their color . . ." complements the preceding series, clarifying the dignity and self-determination informing their motivation.

Anna J. Cooper in "The Ethics of The Negro Question" employs both parallel repetition and anaphora, a particular type of repetition that occurs at the beginning of successive structures. In the first paragraph of her speech, the mere repetition of *her* produces several rhetorical effects. In the sentence beginning with "America can boast *her* expanse of territory, *her* gilded domes, *her* paving stones of silver dollars . . .," the repetition of the pronominal adjective does contribute to the rhythm of the sentences, but it also organizes the series and allows auditors time to focus on the concrete attributes enumerated.

The past participle construction forms yet another example of parallelism. The passage, "*uprooted* from the sunny land of his forefathers by the white man's cupidity and selfishness, ruthlessly *torn* from all the ties of clan and tribe, *dragged* against his will over thousands of miles of unknown waters to a strange land among strange peoples . . . " provides continuity of presentation, the parallel elements serving the additional rhetorical function of accrued emotional intensity as each participle reinforces the actions attending the African American's forced presence in this country. This notion of forced presence confers significance on the speaker's claim of ethical responsibility devolving upon America's power structure.

Following the speaker's assertion that even charity does not study his [the Negro's] needs as an individual person but the good that love has planned for him must be labeled and basketed "*special* for the Negro" (Par. 17), an anaphoric series follows: *special* kinds of education, *special* forms of industry, *special* churches and *special* places of amusement, *special* sections of our cities during life and "*special*" burying grounds in death." The form complements the substance of this passage, the repetition of *special* underscoring the alienation inherent in the unique apparatus set in place to deal with people of color.

Speaking of the peculiar plight and special responsibility of artists, Lorraine Hansberry uses repetition to clarify the realities. *"Having discovered that* the world is incoherent, they . . . also come to the conclusion that it is also unreal. . . . *Having determined that* life is . . . an absurdity, they have not yet decided that the task of the thoughtful is to try and help impose purposefulness on that absurdity." These verbal beginnings unify two significant components of the speaker's self awareness, thereby serving an organizational purpose as well as contributing to the flow and rhythm of the prose.

Other schemes of repetition include the infinitive phrase series in paragraph ten, a passage that enumerates the realities impinging upon the writers of Hansberry's generation: "We were ceaselessly told, after all, *to be* everything which mutilates youth: *to be* silent, *to be* ignorant, *to be* without sanctioned opinions, and *to be* compliant, and above all else, obedient. . ."

Repetition of the introductory preposition in paragraph eight also demonstrates the rhetorical possibilities of this strategy. In Hansberry's statement: "Among my contemporaries and colleagues in the arts the search for the roots *of* war, the exploitation *of* man, *of* poverty, and *of* despair itself," the repetition of the work *of* lends strength to the series and provides more time for auditors to consider the substantive concepts enumerated. The scheme has the effect of slowing down the discourse to an extent without becoming cumbersome or intrusive.

Another speaker, Frances E. W. Harper, reflecting upon the motivations for slavery in "Liberty for Slaves," used parallel repetition to communicate how different states and regions contributed to the institution of slavery. "*Ask Maryland*, with her tens of thousand of slaves, if she is not prepared for freedom and hear her answer: 'I help supply the coffee gangs of the South.'" "*Ask Virginia*, with her hundreds of slaves, if she is not weary with her merchandise of blood and anxious to shake the gory traffic from her hands, and hear her reply: '*though* fertility has covered my soil, *though* a genial sky bends over my hills and vales, *though* I hold in my hand a wealth of water-power . . . one of my chief staples has been the sons and daughters I send to the human market and shambles . . . '*Ask the farther South*, and all the cotton-growing states chime in, 'We have need of fresh supplies to fill the ranks of those whose lives have gone out in unrequited toil on our distant plantations' (Par. 2).

Several other rhetorical schemes make up the traditional rhetorical canon. Among them are polyptoton, the use of variants from the same root; antithesis, contrasting ideas presented in juxtaposition, usually with syntactic balance; and ellipsis, the omission of words that can be reasonably inferred from the context; epistrophe, the use of the same word at the end of successive clauses; anastrophe, a reversal of sentence order. An illustration of several of these schemes follows.

Maria Stewart, "In African Rights And Liberty" uses schemes effectively to force the free sons of Africa to contend for the freedom of everyone. Fear is a mythic element that Stewart casts in rhetorically strategic prominence. Using the scheme polyptoton, the use of variants from a common root, Stewart chides African American males: "Or has it been the *fear* of offending whites . . ." If it has O ye *fearful* ones, throw off your *fearfulness*" (Par. 2). She also makes effective use of at least two devices to obtain emphasis. One represents repetition that focuses on the projection of a key image and an inversion of word order, a psychologically common way of gaining attention by deviating from the expected. "If you are *men*, convince them that you possess the spirit of *men*; and as your day, so shall your strength be" combines epistrophe, the use of the same word at the end of successive clauses, and anastrophe, which reverses sentence components of what could be paraphrased to read, "Your strength shall be sufficient to the task."

The antithesis in paragraph nine has the potential of motivating African Americans to close the gaps between their own limited achievement and the more commendable ones of their white counterparts. The contrast dramatized in "Our minds are vacant and starving for knowledge; theirs are filled to overflowing" is sufficient to agitate the ambitious or those possessed of race pride. Here the mythic element used to characterize the status of African Americans foreshadows the social satire of the 1960s designed to shame the race into closing the gap between their actual accomplishments and their potential. This technique is complemented by another antithetical series in paragraph five: "We have pursued the shadow; they have obtained the substance; we have performed the labor; they have received the profits; we have planted the vines; they have eaten the fruits of them." If the speaker could evoke outrage on the part of African Americans when they considered the reality that the beneficial results of their labor had gone to the oppressors, she would have achieved her rhetorical objective to "fire the breast of every free man of color in these United States," an objective presented at the beginning and end of her discourse.

She relents somewhat in the next few paragraphs employing the scheme parenthesis to acknowledge the limited options of African American males by saying that "Had those men amongst us, who have had an opportunity, turned their attention as assiduously to mental and moral improvement as they have to gambling and dancing, I might have quietly remained at home, and they stood contending in my place"

(Par. 6). The clause "who have had an opportunity" calls attention to limited opportunities for men of the race.

Tropes figured prominently in the traditional canon. Erotema, the rhetorical question, is classified as a trope. "What If I Am A Woman?" by Maria Stewart demonstrates functional uses of the rhetorical question. Most of the rhetorical questions in this speech are contained in pivotal paragraphs. Paragraph two, for example, contains four consecutive rhetorical questions: "What if I am a woman? Is not the God of ancient times the God of modern days? Did he not raise up Deborah to be a mother and a judge in Israel? Did not Queen Esther save the lives of the Jews? And Mary Magdalene first declare the resurrection of Christ from the dead?"

Each question is obviously an affirmation of the speaker's major point, focusing on historical evidence that women played important roles in pivotal times. The testimony also conveys the possibility of the continuing centrality of women in significant events. Another pair of questions appears in paragraph seven: "Why cannot a religious spirit animate us now? Why cannot we become divines and scholars?" These questions, as do those in paragraph two, elicit affirmative responses and underscore Stewart's major premises.

Another speaker who uses the rhetorical question effectively is Constance Baker Motley in her "Keynote Address" before the Southern Christian Leadership Conference. Motley uses the rhetorical question strategically both as a rebuttal of competing information and as a provocation to action. In paragraph fourteen, she refers to a rotation system in the election process of the Manhattan borough that had brought a series of African Americans to important offices. Citing the historical pattern of ethnic emphasis traditionally attached to these elections, she inquires: "Where were all these critics when Negroes were excluded from candidacy or public office because of their race?" (Par. 14). Through the rhetorical question, she offers an effective rebuttal to those who argue against the consideration of race in these elections. In paragraph twenty, she uses the rhetorical question more as a call to action. The two rhetorical questions introducing the paragraph are: "But how many Negroes will go to school with whites come September 1965? How many Negro teachers who will teach white children are now teaching Negro children?" Both questions are designed to agitate, to stir the consciousness of African Americans to take advantage of unprecedented opportunities and also to guard against exploitation. She follows the questions with a series of possibilities. But it is the rhetorical questions that provide the framework for the presentation of possibilities.

In "Breaking The Bars To Brotherhood," Mary McLeod Bethune couches her appeal for vision in a series of rhetorical questions. She establishes her argument in an antecedent-consequent chain of reasoning in paragraph six, "Unless the people have vision, they perish." The rhetorical questions that follow elicit considerations with the potential of focusing the vision. In enjoining this vision, she poses several possible responses to dramatize what the vision entails. When she raises the two-part question about what they see now and what they are willing to venture, she follows with other rhetorical questions that clarify what she means by vision: "Do we see our large opportunity for the race to produce? Do we see an intellectual interpretation of our religious thought unhampered by superstitious belief or limited by too great a satisfaction? Do we see the brotherhood of the peoples of the world working out an abundant life in their activities, of duty, of art, of business, of everyday living?" (Par. 6). The questions are expansive in their potential in that they suggest the important components of vision with the lone caveat in the second question. Here she addresses the influence of their religious thought, perceived variously as the sustaining force of the race and also as an opiate militating against assertive action. She presents three questions, two of them evocative of positive affirmation, and the other, though suggestive of the possibility for limited success, actually   offering an alternative escape.

Irony and metaphor are tropes with significant rhetorical potential in all kinds of literature, and African American orators have used them to considerable advantage. Mary Church Terrell, in "What It Means To Be Colored In The Capital Of the United States," uses irony to dramatize a disturbing reality. Her reference to the failure of churches and sanctuaries to grant admission to people of color is particularly poignant. The sanctuary of God would obviously be expected to offer all the warmth and comfort required by the human heart. The fact that African Americans were denied access to theaters or restaurants or that they were forced to ride in the Jim Crow sections of street cars can certainly be sources of discomfort and shame. But the ultimate irony is that people of color are unwelcome even in the sanctuary of God, a serious indictment of any locale endorsing such blatant discrimination.

Another case of compelling irony appears in paragraph two in the speaker's commentary, "As a colored woman I cannot visit the tomb of the Father of this country, which owes its very existence to the love of freedom in the human heart and which stands for equal opportunity to all without being forced to sit in the Jim Crow section of an electric car which starts from the very heart of the city—midway between the Capitol and the White House." Three public monuments are mentioned in this passage, each emblematic of the essence of the American ideal, yet the embarrassing reality is the denial of access to the most highly symbolic monuments of this country.

Another ironic situation dramatized in the address is the reality that perquisites Americans traditionally claim help citizens gain access mean little, if anything, to the mobility or elevation of African Americans. "It matters not what my intellectual attainments may be or how great is the need of the services of a competent person," she explains, "if I try to enter many of the numerous vocations in which my white sisters are allowed to engage, the door is shut in my face." This reality is antithetical to the promise of America, the assumptions governing life in a democratic republic, and the incentives that encourage effort. Attributes and achievements purported to provide access are rendered irrelevant when the seekers are people of color.

Terrell uses the metaphor of the chasm to conclude the speech and complement the ironic thread that unifies the address. She describes the "chasm between the principles upon which this Government was founded . . . and those which are daily practiced under the protection of the flag yawns so wide and deep." The concluding statement adequately captures the ironic construct of the discourse that attests to, through a multiplicity of rhetorical strategies, the emotional upheaval and humiliation deriving from being colored in the capital of the United States.

"Why Slavery Is Still Rampant" by Sarah Parker Remond also employs irony in her discussion of the role played by the church in slavery. Her reproach is compelling: "You send missionaries to the heathen; I tell you of professing Christians practising what is worse than any heathenism on record" (Par. 5). The emotional intensity of the passage is enhanced in her continuing revelation that includes the irony of slavers plying on the seas "which were previously guarded by your ships." And the following paragraph dramatizes the unexpected consequences of a church member's sale of slaves. The expected reprimand from fellow Christians was not forthcoming, this situation couched in the words "But Mr. Butler has in no wise lost caste among his friends." In actuality his influence seemed strengthened by his participation in the slave trade.

Ironic as well is the observation that the respect normally accorded achievement does not apply to free people of color in the North. Remond notes that "whatever wealth or eminence in intellect and refinement they may attain to, they are treated as outcasts . . ." This reality contradicts expectations governing similar situations for the general population. The logical expectation is that social and economic respect accrues in relation to effort and achievement. These virtues, however, do not receive just compensation in the case of African Americans, a condition essentially parallel to that of receiving none of the monetary benefits deriving from their labor.

Remond's appeal to the British to "raise the moral public opinion until its voice reaches the American shores" is a subtle personification demonstrating the power of public outrage. Similar in impact to such allusions as "the shot heard round the world," the speaker implies that sufficient indignation on the part of the people of England would resound across the seas, giving both literal and figurative significance to attestations of moral integrity. The figurative appeal continues in the sentence, "Aid us thus until the shackles of the American slave melt like dew before the morning sun" (Par. 8).

A speech illustrating the power of metaphor in public address is Sojourner Truth's "When Woman Gets Her Rights Man Will Be Right." Metaphors of "troubled waters" and "track" contribute to the development of the speaker's message. The latter reference appears in the passage, "I know that it is hard for men to give up entirely. They must run in the same old track." Here Truth identifies a perennial enemy of equal rights for women and underscores the role of tradition in perpetuating the subjugation of women. Prior to this statement, she likens the attitude of men to that of slaveholders, accusing them of having held the reins so long that they are reluctant to give up: "You have been having our rights so long, that you think, like a slaveholder, that you own us. I know that it is hard for one who has held the reins for so long to give up; it cuts like a knife. It will feel all better when it closes up again."

The metaphor of troubled water in Truth's speech is symbolic of the agitation and unrest accompanying efforts to gain equal rights for women. Throughout the speech, the speaker has kept the image of agitation before the audience. In sentences such as "There is a great stir . . . , So I am keeping the thing going while things are stirring . . . I want to keep the thing stirring, now that the ice is broken . . . " She then leads to the articulation of the image, "And now when the waters is troubled, and now is the time to step in the pool." The concept here invokes other rhetorical strategies as well, particularly the special topic of the expedient embodied in the wisdom of taking advantage of existing opportunities. Her closing words, in fact, underscore her determination to continue the agitation and take advantage of the unrest out of which most social change evolves. In two closing sentences, Truth proclaims: "I am going round to lecture on human rights. I will shake every place I go to."

"We Need To Be United" by Coretta Scott King also demonstrates effective use of the metaphor and irony. The metaphor of the sleeping giant in paragraph five suggests the significance of the gains Martin Luther King, Jr. was making for the working people of America at the time of his assassination. King had championed the cause of the working people, understanding better than most the latent power of this segment of the population. The figure of the road or journey, prominent in world literature, has held special significance for African Americans. King uses this metaphor in paragraph nine to emphasize the unity she so strongly endorses throughout the speech. In the statement, "Some trade-unionists are hostile to the freedom movement, and some blacks are spreading the illusion that a separatist road exists in the journey to emancipation," she obliquely attacks the nationalist movement endorsed by some African Americans, a movement that hostile attitudes on the part of unionists can indeed promote. Evident here is the mutual destruction that can be spawned by extreme attitudes.

Dialectical Tension Through Cultural Referents

In *Modern Rhetorical Criticism* (1991) Roderick P. Hart emphasizes the potential of cultural and mythic considerations in rhetorical analysis. The potential effectiveness of a discourse derives in part from the cultural and mythic referents the speaker invokes to gain sympathetic resonance from the audience. The interplay of positive and negative cultural elements creates dialectical tension and dramatizes both the pragmatic and transcendent qualities of public address. Juxtaposition or contrast of the negative and positive has the dual effect of according to evil sufficient potency to encourage its eradication. On the other hand, the positive cultural elements keep before the audience the possibility of transcendence—the hope or the expectation that the affected group does indeed possess the wherewithal to avert ultimate failure.

Several speeches in this collection effectively dramatize this dialectical tension. Among them are Shirley Chisholm's

"For The Equal Rights Amendment," delivered before the United States House of Representatives on 10 August 1970; Angela Davis's "Let Us All Rise Together: Radical Perspectives on Empowerment For Afro-American Women," delivered at Spelman College on 25 June 1987; Georgia Washington's 1902 address, "The Condition of The Women in The Rural Districts of Alabama: What Is Being Done To Remedy The Condition," delivered before the Hampton Conference; Sadie T.M. Alexander's "Founders Day Address," presented at Spelman College in 1963; Margaret Walker-Alexander's "Religion, Poetry, And History: Foundations For A New Educational System" delivered before the National Urban League Conference in New Orleans on 29 July 1968; and Audre Lorde's "Learning From the 60s," delivered at Harvard University in 1982.

Shirley Chisholm invokes the mythic American dream of equality and hope, implying all the optimism that this attitude connotes. The negative elements of prejudice and discrimination are used to demonstrate challenges to this dream. The pervasiveness of the evils of prejudice and discrimination is a key point in her presentation for the Equal Rights Amendment.

The possible is argued as she attempts to disarm the detractors who shed doubt on the possibilities of this amendment to eradicate the problems it purports to eradicate. Alluding to past fact—the fact that such an argument could well have been used against civil rights legislation—she implies that the same just results could well obtain in this instance. The possibility of an enlightened and encouraged citizenry falls into the category of the transcendent.

She enumerates some elements that undermine the possibilities of women, holding the ideal of due process as the goal to which we should aspire. The culprit of exclusion, the negative force emphasized in one segment of the speech, she categorizes as an agent antithetical to constitutional promise. She places the passage of the bill in the realm of the possible, thereby negating the negative claims of confusion and excess litigation made by opponents of the bill. References to the success of civil rights litigation that once elicited the same caveats lend credibility to her optimism.

Positive cultural elements enumerated in the discourse include equal opportunity and better material progress for women. Overall gain for both sexes is another distinct possibility; a future free from the relics of the past is a hopeful and an optimistic element. The chance to correct the Founding Fathers' exclusion of daughters from the covenant of promise offers America the chance to be all that its possibilities imply.

The speaker's entire delineation of practical solutions sets in motion a transcendent line of thought in that it communicates the vision of a better, more complete life for all Americans. Taken separately, these suggestions could be classified as pragmatic. But the achievement itself would be emblematic of the possibilities of America—an abstract and empowering vision.

Manifestations of the emphasis on opportunity are numerous and diverse. Recognition of the negative qualities that retard progress—discrimination, prejudice, exclusion, and exploitation—render future progress more accessible. Chisholm rules out restrictive forces by offering practical remedies for successful implementation of the amendment. She asserts that the negative forces can indeed be eliminated, thereby providing a more inclusive society that will ultimately redound to the benefit of all.

The concept of empowerment is in itself a powerful cultural referent with positive connotations. Angela Davis, in "Let Us All Rise Together," thus establishes as an ideal a concept with the potential of obtaining intellectual assent and emotional commitment from her audience. Closely connected to this ideal are unity and perseverance, both similarly positive. Davis's use of empowerment as a desired goal for women has the potential of persuading the audience to accept her proposals and call to action. Such a noble goal seems intrinsically worthy of consideration, even commitment. Difficulties suffered by the race, and women in particular, render empowerment a highly desirable goal, and such an ideal conveys optimism. People have greater incentive to act when hope is projected, and visions of this ideal no doubt elicited strong emotional commitment from her audience.

To make this ideal more appealing, the speaker invokes some negative cultural referents. The discord then existing between white women and Afro-American women seems antithetical to the concept of empowerment if auditors perceive unity to be a prerequisite for ultimate success. This referent encompasses insensitivity and exclusion, both of which serve as deterrents to the ultimate realization of the ideal established early in the speech, indeed even in the title.

These negative referents serve an important rhetorical function in evoking discontent, even outrage. Davis's use of the negatives is no doubt designed to dramatize the diminution of success that lack of unity engenders. Responsibility is a cultural value receiving considerable emphasis in Davis's address. In paragraphs thirteen and fourteen, she urges the active participation of black women scholars and professionals, indicating that "[We] cannot afford to ignore the straits of our sisters who are acquainted with the immediacy of oppression in a way many of us are not." This declaration reaffirms the theme of her address, "Lifting as we climb." Davis's use of this cultural referent is rhetorically powerful in that it reminds those who are more fortunate of their responsibility to the lesser fortunate. This appeal is both emotional and moral, capable of evoking strong intellectual assent from auditors.

Precedence is another highly valued cultural referent. Though precedence is formally categorized as a common topic or line of argument, it exerts force as a cultural value. People receive inspiration and motivation when they recognize that a given goal is not only desirable, but possible. Thus, the speaker's invocation of achievement wrought by noble women of color throughout history communicates the possibility of replication. In fact, precedence suggests obligation since no generation can claim progress if it fails to build upon the foundation established by its forbears.

Georgia Washington's address at Hampton demonstrates effective use of negative cultural referents. Deprivation is a negative referent invoked by the speaker to depict the situations undergirding her concern. She recounts a cyclical legacy of deprivation, a strategy with the rhetorical potential of evoking sympathetic resonance from the audience. Washington describes a dozen or more families living in facilities once occupied by only a master and mistress to dramatize the cramped and obviously unsatisfactory conditions in which these people lived. Negative referents are forceful agents in rhetorical appeals since they speak to innate principles of decency and justice, evoking shame on the part of perpetrators and eliciting sympathy and eventual assistance from sensitive auditors. The establishment of need is also effectively achieved through the presentation of unsatisfactory or inhumane conditions.

Washington's description of the unrelenting toil of the typical family in these conditions carries strong emotional appeal. A sense of the just and the good assumes lifestyles that permit time for the renewal of the spirit and the maintenance of attractive surroundings. The articulation of exceptions to this expectation is a powerful rhetorical tool, one that invokes the special topics of the just and the good. Any disciplined sensitivity will respond to the denial of these basic rights to human beings, and the speaker's invocation of serious violations of these privileges carries significant rhetorical potential. Home as a place of repair and pleasure is a valued cultural ideal, and deviations from this ideal produce an emotional intensity to which most audiences will respond.

Lack of self-determination is another negative element the speaker employs to arouse the indignation of her audience. Hampton graduates and friends, in all probability, value freedom highly and feel committed to its promotion in all segments of the society. Washington's reference to the mothers before the war who "belonged to the master body and soul" is rendered more poignant by the realization that their offspring enjoy scarcely more freedom than did their mothers. Conditions, according to her description, differ little from those before the war: "These people handle very little money; whenever they work by the day or month a written order is given by their employer to some store in the village, and they get their food and their clothing too on this" (Par.7). News of this continuing dependency has the potential of arousing the Hampton audience to action. Again, the speaker's use of a negative cultural referent serves a significant rhetorical function; it has the potential of evoking indignation, or, at the very least, sufficient empathy for their suffering sisters to assist in efforts for relief.

The speaker's invocation of the work ethic consistently espoused by Tuskegee and Hampton Universities is a rhetorically compelling strategy. Her audience at Hampton is obviously committed to this value, and she enhances her ethical appeal because she has retained that value and seeks to instill it in those she teaches. Despite the fact that arduous labor has yielded few benefits for this disadvantaged group, the continuing belief in the ultimate reward for diligent labor remains a critical part of their value system. So the speaker's appeal for help in perpetuating the work ethic undoubtedly confirms Hampton's philosophy of the rewards of diligence and industry. Survival and transcendence are two cultural referents frequently invoked by the speaker as she chronicles the current plight of women in the rural districts and anticipates a time when their quality of life will improve. The negative referents serve well rhetorical purposes of agitation, but prospects for survival and transcendence were also necessary as incentives for continued improvement. The negative referents, in essence, must necessarily lead to, or at least imply, the possibility of progress. When Washington speaks of the organizations committed to the improvement of existing conditions and of the need for encouragement from Hampton and Tuskegee, she supplies the element that communicates to her auditors prospects for change and progress.

Important to the cultural pride of a group is a noteworthy legacy of effort or growth. Sadie Alexander's "Founders' Day Address" provides ample motivation for continuing effort by recounting the efforts of preceding groups that led to significant social gains for the race. This positive cultural referent has strong rhetorical potential in that it imbues auditors with a sense of heightened possibilities of their own ability to pursue similar actions, the testimony of the past providing as it does the possibility of success. Thus, the appeal to past success is a potent mythic element, one capable of demonstrating possibilities and, in consequence, increased motivation.

Negative images invoked by the speaker are the holocaust and concentration camps. These images demonstrate the impact of negative mythic referents in conveying the potency of evil. Auditors are thus reminded of the atrocities of which humankind is capable unless vigilance prevails. The possibility of evil is a particularly forceful rhetorical strategy since the natural inclination is to take precautions to avert similar future atrocities. Images of the indiscriminate destruction of Jewish people and the inhumane confinement of Japanese Americans evoke fear and natural psychological resistance in any sensitive audience, and the speaker thereby achieves a level of emotional intensity with the potential of arousing within the audience a commitment to action.

The superiority of democracy over competing systems of government is another powerful cultural referent used by Alexander. Linking Communism and other forms of government with annihilation underscores the advantages of democracy. This reference is strategic in that the speaker implicitly argues the importance of maintaining the essence of democracy, an essence now tainted with discrimination. The argument has a two-fold impact in that it motivates African Americans to strive for democracy in its purest sense, but it also suggests to those who violate the spirit of democracy the risk of eroding credibility and ultimate defeat.

The image of closed doors carries strong mythical implications since the parameters of the image are so inclusive. Exhaustive enumeration is not required, for this image in itself represents every thwarted opportunity against which the race struggles. In a given audience, such a reference may evoke a multitude of memories and particulars that stagger the imagination because the image speaks to individuals as well as to the group. The speaker can therefore state one example or a few examples and achieve a multi-level response as each auditor associates the spoken example with innumerable obstacles in his or her own experiences.

The expansion of expectations is another motivational cultural referent suggesting the the race need not confine itself to "low horizons, limited aspirations and motivation

. . . " (Par. 12). Such vision enables members of the race to speculate on greater achievements than it has yet known. Thus the possibilities of success form a cultural referent that militates against low expectations and acceptance of the status quo. Visions of expanded freedom and advancement are potent motivational tools capable of eliciting effort and commitment from an audience initially demoralized.

In her demonstration of the domain of students' concerns, Alexander enumerates several blights upon the current society. Her discussion of student participation includes a statement specifying the scope of their involvement, "Where there has been hunger, imperialism, dictatorship, exploitation, college students have in many countries often demonstrated against what they believe to be unjust" (Par. 5). The social evils against which student had fought were both inclusive and expansive, encompassing issues of community and world-wide significance. The range of issues addressed by students suggests their concerted action against negative forces. The invocation of the negative mythic elements does not denote pessimism; rather, the cultural referent implied here is the ability to persevere despite overwhelming odds.

Margaret Walker Alexander also uses cultural referents effectively in "Religion, Poetry, and History." In establishing the need for a new education, Walker refers to disturbing realities: ideological and military conflict, economic problems, chaos in the inner cities, and confusing drama on college campuses. The speaker invokes these negative cultural referents because they render concrete the import of her major appeal—the need for a new education. The rhetorical advantage of the negative elements is that they foster discontent, even outrage. And these emotions are provocative to auditors who have contemplated the full implications of the conditions she describes. Negative elements, therefore, function as motivational agents in the discourse since potency must be conferred upon evil for the audience to comprehend fully the necessity of eradicating these forces.

The speaker's reference to the young is a compelling rhetorical strategy. The national and cultural ethic has traditionally attributed to young people the power of the future. She begins with a discussion of their discontent but moves quickly to possibilities. The value the culture attaches to children certainly requires attention to environmental conditions negatively affecting their well being. Describing the characteristics of youth, Walker explains: "Like the youth of every generation they want to know and they demand to be heard. Like youth in every age they are the vanguard of our revolutionary age" (Par. 3). The promise of youth automatically connotes a brighter future, a future requiring that the current mature generation ensure against societal forces threatening the potential promise preserved for future generations.

Walker also explicates the antecedents and manifestations of bigotry and discrimination. Her criticism of the social distortions perpetuated by various agents in the society is provocative and descriptive of the transformation required in education to counteract the effects of stereotypes suggesting inherent superiority or inferiority based on race alone. Again, negative cultural referents with negative connotations reinforce the urgency of the speaker's message and provide the motivation for listeners to commit their energies to the task of eradicating stereotypes that militate against understanding and mutual respect between races.

A particularly provocative set of cultural referents are those referring to our basic institutions—the home, the school, and the church. For an American audience, these referents evoke common feelings because of the value the culture places on the influence of its basic institutions. If the speaker can instruct or motivate the audience to reflect on the centrality of these basic institutions in the American culture and delineate possible threats to their continued functions, her rhetorical intentions are being fulfilled.

Christianity as a promoter of good and an incentive to charitable living is a significant referent since so much of the national psyche derives from religious foundations. This issue can be manipulated rhetorically since the speaker can achieve her objectives either by emphasizing its absence or suggesting its possibilities when its precepts are appropriately implemented or practiced.

A stable sense of history and cultural continuity also carries strong rhetorical potential in that it speaks to the near universal appeal of an enduring legacy. If a speaker can appeal to the centrality of legacy and cultural continuity, she can depend upon substantial sympathetic resonance from the audience. Traditionally African Americans have linked their legacy of difficulty and suffering to their prospects for success so as to indicate the nature of the struggle.

Three other speeches particularly rich in cultural and mythic referents are Edith Sampson's "Choose One Of Five," Frances E. W. Harper's "The Great Problem To Be Solved" and, in intriguing contrast, Angela Davis's "I Am A Black Revolutionary Woman."

In her formulation of five choices of action available to her audience, Edith Sampson invokes a time-tested mythic element, the power and possibilities of the inner self. The challenge that she places before her auditors, she informs them, will be self-scoring, but there will be proctors—among them "the hardest taskmaster of all, your inner self." This appeal is linked to both religious and ethical myths of the society since the will, determination, and pride of the individual are deemed critical to an individual's prospects for success. And the American consciousness is attuned to those intangibles that emanate from the inner being to sustain the motivation and drive generally valued as antecedents of success.

The negative referents receive an oblique presentation and display their own destructive attributes. Sampson's reference to college graduates who have "wrapped themselves in an apathy so thick that they're in a position to say in all truth, 'no opinion' to any Gallup or Roper pollster who might question them on any subject" is a negative referent that carries the theoretical potential of achieving the opposite effect, the determination not to be numbered among the mindless group with no convictions or philosophical base.

Sampson confers negative connotations on conformity and extremist positions, both concepts antithetical to the character of Americans, particularly those who aspire to make a difference in future events. The accompanying attributes receive sufficient description to render them unacceptable to the audience, and the speaker—through strategic manipulation of positive and negative cultural and mythic elements—attains her rhetorical objective.

The difficulties that she attaches to choice five, the challenging choice, are provocative in that they encompass the resolution and diligence that vibrant living requires. She admits the restlessness and the loneliness that will be the lot of those courageous enough to select choice five, but these are challenging concepts to the ambitious. Acknowledging the reality that "choice-five people have to live constantly with an acceptance of the fact that there are no simple answers in this world because there are no simple questions" is a concept with strong cultural underpinnings.

"Exciting". . . "challenging". . . and "rewarding" are words that evoke positive emotional responses in listeners. These descriptors are used to emphasize the wisdom inherent in choice five. Throughout the explication the speaker uses negative features sarcastically, yet the aim of her discourse is inspiration, challenging auditors to a full exploration of possibilities. When she speaks of "the anguish of those moments in your middle age when you lie sleepless at 2 A.M. or 3 and wonder whatever happened to all your bright ambitions of college days—that anguish and those moments don't count too much," listeners are well aware that this anguish can be averted; that is, if they live up to their potential and promise, they need never experience the anguish Sampson describes.

The interplay of negative and positive cultural referents work together to confer an optimistic tone to the address. The students and graduates can, of course, opt for the less challenging options presented in choices one through four, but they can also envision the rewards of choice five—with all its loneliness, restlessness, uncertainty, and sacrifice. The mythic connotations of perseverance against challenging odds and the sacrifice required for success and achievement speak to the psyche of Americans who traditionally value the success story.

In "The Great Problem To Be Solved," Frances E. W. Harper emphasizes the hypocrisy of claiming to have reverence for God while simultaneously exhibiting only contempt and hate for fellow human beings. She argues that if any one factor should inform the esteem in which we hold one another it should be the knowledge "that we all come from the living God and that he is the common Father," the discoveries of ethnologists notwithstanding. The work of Thomas Huxley and Charles Darwin will not negate this important principle, she maintains. This section of her address closes with the sobering translation of a Biblical principle, "The nation that has no reverence for man is also lacking reverence for God and needs to be instructed."

Progress is a positive cultural referent invoked by Harper in her skillful manipulation of chronology that dramatizes the continuing progress of the race, but the progress is presented through the filter of degradation and inhumane treatment. "One hundred years ago Africa was the privileged hunting ground of Europe and America . . . Less than fifty years ago mob violence belched out its wrath . . . Less than twenty-five years ago slavery clasped hands with King Cotton and said slavery fights and cotton conquers for American slavery" (Par. 1).

The economic motivations of slavery seem more acceptable to some than the harsher censure of moral apathy. But this economic reality receives no justification from Harper. In fact, in another excellent speech, "Liberty For Slaves" delivered in 1857, Harper vehemently denounced the greed that permitted the sacrifice of twenty thousand lives on plantations. She recalled the horror of "a hundred thousand new born babies . . . annually added to the victims of slavery" and suggested that greed won out over moral courage. Describing the horrors of slavery, she notes, "Such a sight should send a thrill of horror through the nerves of civilization and impel the heart of humanity to lofty deeds. So it might, if men had not found out a fearful alchemy by which this blood can be transformed into gold. Instead of listening to the cry of agony, they listen to the ring of dollars and stoop down to pick up the coin" (Sterling 1984, 162).

Harper requests the indulgence of the audience, acknowledging that "It may not seem to be a gracious thing to mingle complaint in a season of general rejoicing. It may appear like the ancient Egyptians seating a corpse at their festal board to avenge the Americans for their shortcomings when so much has been accomplished" (Par. 1). Conditions described in the following statement clearly demonstrate the need for the intrusion of complaints. Recognizing again the victories and triumphs won by freedom and justice, she injects a sobering observation that she did not know of "another civilized nation under heaven where there are half so many people who have been brutally and shamefully murdered, with or without impunity, as in this Republic within the past ten years." (Par. 2).

In this address before the Pennsylvania Abolition Society, Frances Watkins Harper balances effectively the contrary forces that prevent the country from living up to its possibilities and resources, both spiritual and material, that bode well for the nation's future. For a country with our tradition of accomplishments, failing to pursue its potential for excellence is morally untenable. She appeals to the conscience of the nation and then balances the moral appeal with a more practical one, the advantages to be gained by a productive citizenry. Her rebuke for the atrocities so unbecoming to a nation with the expressed ideals of America is balanced with an account of some concrete accomplishments that justify hope. Harper's final call to action reflects a clear understanding of the numerous obstacles that accrue with any protracted undertaking. Though hostilities and misfortune may plague their efforts, she urges an understanding of the nature of failure and success: "Apparent failure may hold in its rough shell the germs of a success that will blossom in time, and bear fruit throughout eternity. What seemed to be a failure around the cross of Calvary and in the garden has been the grandest recorded success" (Par. 4). Thus, despite the discouraging nature of current racial problems, possibilities for transcendence, as established by precedent, remain within the realms of reality.

Mary Church Terrell uses positive and negative mythic indicators strategically in "Frederick Douglass," a reasonable expectation in ceremonial discourse. She invokes past fact to demonstrate the possibilities of race achievement, a strategy that dramatically illustrates the powerful effects of strength, courage, and commitment. The illustrious history of Douglass was no doubt widely circulated in relation to the general race picture, and she uses this impressive past to dramatize his specific contributions to the women's suffrage movement.

In compelling rhetorical fashion, the speaker rationalizes what could normally be construed as negative social attitudes. Yet her boast of feeling "several inches taller than her sisters in the more favored race" is reminiscent of extraordinary circumstances that permitted heroes and heroines to call attention to their privileged status without invoking social scorn. Since women of color so seldom have anything to boast about, her restrained boast in this instance is thereby justified and also dramatizes the traditional disadvantages of African American women.

Recalling a more romantic past that, although to a large extent seems incongruous at the time of her presentation, is nonetheless an effective invocation of nostalgia—a continuing practice of a society inclined to recall the past with more glory than it warrants. By placing Frederick Douglass in the courtly tradition, she thereby underscores more emphatically the nature and extent of the positive qualities synonymous with his reputation.

Dialectical tension produced rhetorically by polarities is rendered concrete by the situation Douglass himself faced when forced to confront the wrenching choice between race and gender. Terrell appropriately acknowledged this intense dilemma by conceding that "if at any time Mr. Douglass seemed to waver in his allegiance to the cause of political enfranchisement of women, it was he realized as no white person no matter how broad and sympathetic he may be, has been ever able to feel or can possibly feel today just what it means to belong to my despised, handicapped and persecuted race."

These negative cultural referents do not evoke pity, scorn, or bitterness. Rather, they underscore the astounding strength implied in the ability of African Americans to endure and survive these tremendous odds. In a somewhat inverted pattern, she uses negative terms to demonstrate positive results: the determination and forbearance that must have characterized people of color who constantly faced these deprivations and prevailed. The triumph is not articulated as concretely as it might have been, the contemplation of the hardships endured carrying sufficient rhetorical potency to dramatize the triumph.

Terrell's judicious use of linguistic features also complements her central argument.Referring earlier to Douglass as "incomparable," she astutely reinforces this notion through a comparison.Conceding the strength of Elizabeth Cady Stanton, Terrell nonetheless depicts Douglass's more impressive strength in an apt contrast:" If Elizabeth Cady Stanton manifested sublime courage and audacious contempt for the ridicule and denunciation she knew would be heaped upon her as a woman, how much more were these qualities displayed by Frederick Douglass, the ex-slave." The comparison serves to emphasize the positive cultural referent invoked by Douglass's characteristic perseverance. In this address Terrell not only illustrates the plight of African American women plagued by disadvantages of race and gender; she articulates as well an eloquent and fitting tribute to one of the race's most distinguished advocates of freedom.

Audre Lorde invokes a series of cultural referents in her address explaining her evolving respect for Malcolm X. In "Learning From the 60s," Lorde notes the vision and evolving flexibility of the Muslim leader. Both of these values have the potential of evoking sympathetic resonance in an audience by suggesting a balance between principle and the wisdom of acknowledging flaws in one's own agenda and merit in another's. The balance indicated is consistent with cultural values and commends the integrity of the person whose legacy is being celebrated on this occasion. This stance enables the speaker to introduce information that is corrective in that the leader's attitude toward women was ultimately altered in a positive way. The ability to admit wrong is a highly respected cultural value, and the speaker thereby elicits good will by tapping into a system of beliefs valued by the society.

The speaker dramatizes effectively the nature of unity. Across time, Biblical injunctions, myths, and cliches have proliferated around this concept. Although the speaker's analysis of this concept may differ from some commonly-held perceptions, the reality is that the word itself is sufficient to gain ethical appeal for the speaker and to influence the audience's acceptance of other tenets of the speaker's argument. And the speaker informs as well as exhorts by defining unity in a different way, imbuing it with more expansive dimensions.

Lorde refers to the "promise and excitement" of the 60s, a characterization indicative of the vitality of the period. She notes as well the "isolation and frustration" of the era. Again here a sense of balance is achieved and auditors are thus enabled to consider the dual nature of transition. The pivotal principle here is that of balance, a concept that generally comports well with the national consciousness. To admit that isolation and frustration accompany promise and excitement is not a negative referent in the American psyche; rather it is indicative of the proverbial "ups and downs" or "valleys and peaks" deeply entrenched in the national consciousness.

Another cultural referent the speaker uses to advantage is determination. This attribute is almost synonymous with America and certainly with the African American experience. Consequently, when Lorde speaks of determination and its effects, she could logically expect receptivity from her audience. Implications presented in conjunction with an accepted value take on the positive attributes of that value, essentially assuring the speaker of tacit approval from the audience.

Some sections of the text point to the evils that had plagued African Americans and the country across time: burning cities, the Vietnam War, unjust imprisonments, and beatings. Lorde's enumeration of these negative features of the society appear in paragraph twelve in an intense series. Implicit in this catalogue of evil is the necessity of determination and transcendence, yet evil has to be accorded its full potential so that auditors can appreciate the struggles, the tolerance, and the pain of those affected by these negative societal forces. The waste of energy and spirit spawned by these conditions cannot be erased by transcendence; reviewers can commend the transcendence, but the reality of the pain and humiliation incurred is a part of history that must be relived each time these realities are considered.

Imperialism, presented as a negative force, confirms the reality that people of color are expendable. Lorde illustrates this reality by referring to nations occupied mainly by people of color that had been overrun by America. The concept condemned here is the unjust use of power, and she cites as an example the irony of the claim that the small republic of Grenada could be considered a threat against the power of the United States. The violation of human rights is another negative referent that evokes outrage and thereby the need to protect individual and group rights since they can be so easily eroded.

The devastating effects of lack of compassion also receive attention in the address. Lorde refers to reduced aid for the terminally ill, the elderly, and dependent children. She speaks as well of callous suggestions to use elderly citizens in atomic plants because of their limited remaining time. These examples demonstrate the necessity of a transformation of values and a reordering of priorities. The concreteness, the callousness, and the lack of compassion exhibited in the actions and attitudes enumerated certainly have the potential of mobilizing action. Thus the speaker here dramatizes the potency of negative referents in arousing the emotions of auditors to the extent that anything short of concentrated action is unconscionable.

Despite the emphasis of negative referents in Lorde's speech, the possibility of transcendence is evident. In fact the objective is to remind auditors of the errors of the past so that the future can be free from such impediments.

Conclusions

Perhaps the most promising avenue of future research in the oratory of African American women resides in the evaluation of cultural referents that orators select to evoke sympathetic resonance from their audiences. Obviously, public address will continue to demonstrate the basic imperatives of organization, with appropriate attention to arrangement and orderly development of ideas and concepts. And figurative language will no doubt continue to adorn these ideas and concepts. The primary distinguishing feature, however, will in all probability derive from the manipulation of prevailing values rather than from the manipulation of language.

An analysis of the oratory across the ages reveals an amalgam of emphases and ideologies, with no linear pattern readily discernible according to chronology. Both restraint and militancy obtain in every era. Thus, rhetorical generalizations, based on historical periods, with the possible exception of an evolving simplicity in prose style, may yield little by way of illumination of the cultural legacy represented in the oratory. This reality may be peculiar to African American oratory because of the reversals so prevalent in the history of the race. The cultural emphases in the public address are particularly revelatory in that the ideals and aspirations of the race manifest themselves in a formal codification peculiar to the genre.

In "Ndebele," one of the poems in Alice Walker's *Her Blue Body Everything We Know* (1991), she refers to the tenacity of African women and women of African descent, claiming "Ours the privilege/of not/even comprehending/what it means/to give up." This characterization certainly deserves examination so as to assess the extent of its peculiarity. Productive approaches to studies of this nature could include such considerations as to whether this tendency toward optimism, even in situations where optimism is not indicated or empirically warranted, is more prevalent in the oratory of African American women than in the oratory of men of the race or in the oratory of women of other races. The selections represented in this collection reveal few instances of hopelessness, manifesting limited or restrained bitterness and generally some view of transcendence despite the unsettling realities of prevailing situations.

Whether or not this inclination is directly and consistently related to gender or race is indeed a necessary assessment in attempts to ascertain the place of the public address of African American women in the traditional rhetorical canon. The extent to which the tone of the oratory derives from acculturation is a worthy, and necessary, avenue of exploration. Steps in such an exploration imply a consideration of the rhetorical devices contributing to the tone: images, figuration, and cultural referents. An indispensable component of this evaluation would be systematic comparative analyses so as to avoid inaccurate or forced generalizations about the genre under consideration.

Despite the remaining questions and challenges that inhere in attempts to clarify the character of the genre, this study certainly attests to the centrality of women in national and international affairs across time. Certain realities and limitations can be conceded without denigrating the obvious and significant insights gained from a study of the oratory of African American women. We need not, for example, reject categorically the claim that women were less likely than men to keep written records of their speeches, nor the fact that for a time public speaking by women was considered inappropriate. Yet preliminary indications that the oratory does indeed afford its own imprimatur while at the same time evincing considerable conformity to the protocol of the traditional canon affirm the scholarly significance of the genre.

Although the emphasis of this work has not been strictly historical, the recursive nature of the struggle *is* a significant historical phenomenon. Women of African descent have had to fight more than once for the ballot and many times witnessed the erosion of gains attained through excessive hardships, learning firsthand that gains for the race, or for the gender, could not automatically be assumed as permanent attainments. Thus, the struggle of women, even when studied thematically, is revelatory of historical and sociological realities that are indeed peculiar to African American women.

Viewed in cosmic perspective, however, the struggle of women of color must ultimately be considered in relation to the total society in which the struggle occurred. This symbiosis does not necessarily require identical parallels in the struggles of men of the race or the general struggles of women of all races. It does, however, require sufficient categorization to determine the relationship of this struggle to that of the general society, this categorization necessarily reflective of both its distinguishing attributes and corresponding characteristics.

"Not even comprehending what it means to give up" indeed seems to be a consistent echo in the public address of African American women across time. Even as they declaimed the dehumanizing effects of slavery, the subjugation of women, and the reversals endured in the struggle, the preponderance of the oratory retains the possibility, indeed even the hope, of transcendence. Although this hope has not been traditionally accompanied by evidence that suggested fruition, it communicates more than wishful thinking, more than an evasion of reality. Rather it seems to communicate a spirit of determination that resists pessimism or defeat.

As scholars continue to explore the nature and dimensions of this genre, careful analysis of the use of positive and negative cultural and mythic referents is imperative. The means whereby the orators maintained the possibilities for transcendence require examination in relation to profit and loss, reality and illusion. Systematic evaluation of this genre, representing as it does the codified, public articulation of the fears and aspirations of both a striving race and a striving gender, holds the potential for illuminating the nature and dynamics of the struggle.

GLOSSARY OF KEY WORDS AND TECHNICAL TERMS

Definitions and examples are taken in whole or in part from Edward P. J. Corbett's Glossaries and examples in *Classical Rhetoric For The Modern Student*, 2nd ed. unless otherwise noted. (*)

Alliteration—repetition of initial sounds (she sells sea shells by the sea shore.)*

Anastrophe—inversion of the normal syntactic order of words (To the market she went.)*

Anidiplosis—repetition of the last word of one clause at the beginning of the following clause—"The crime was common, common be the pain."—Alexander Pope, "Eliisa to Abelard" (475).

Antecedent-consequent—a line of argument, or common topic: a subclass of relationship—"If the current course of action persists, risks to the integrity of our institution will accrue."*

Antithesis—the juxtaposition of contrasting ideas, often of parallel structure—"Our knowledge separates as well as it unites; our orders disintegrate as well as bind; our art brings us together and sets us apart."—J. Robert Oppenheimer, *The Open Mind* (1955)" (464).

Aristotle—Greek philosopher and student of Plato. Author of *Rhetoric*, a classic work still widely used by rhetoricians and students of rhetoric.*

433

Arrangement—the five parts of a discourse labeled in traditional classical rhetoric: exordium (introduction), narratio (statement of fact), confirmatio (proof), refutatio (refutation or rebuttal), peroratio (conclusion).

Cause-effect—a common topic, or line of argument, and a subtopic of the common topic of relationship—Jonathan Swift's argument that selling two year old infants would result in poorer tenants having something of value to offer.

Ceremonial discourse—the oratory of display (referred to variously as panegyrical, epideictic, demonstrative, and declamatory).

Circumstance—a common topic, or line of argument, that includes possible and impossible and past fact and future fact.

Cognitive burden—the amount of short-term memory required to comprehend and retain the semantic and syntactic units of a sentence.

Common topics—general strategies of development based upon the tendency of the human mind: definition, comparison, relationship, circumstance, testimony.

Comparison—a line of argument or common topic including similarity, difference, and degree.

Definition—a line of argument or common topic including genus and division.

Deliberative discourse—discourse in which the speaker seeks to persuade someone to do something or to accept a given point of view; usually concerned with the future.

Delivery—the fifth part of rhetoric, concerned primarily with voice and gestures.

Epanelepsis—a scheme characterized by repetition at the end of a clause of the word that occurred at the beginning of the clause "Blood hath bought blood, and blows have answer's blows:—"(Shakespeare, *King John*, II, i, 329-30) 474.

Epideictic discourse—see ceremonial discourse.

Epistrophe—repetition of the same word or group of words at the ends of successive clauses "I'll have my bond! Speak not against my bond!"—(*The Merchant Of Venice*, III, iii, 3-4) 473.

Erotema—see rhetorical question.

Ethos (Ethical appeal)—the appeal of personality or character.

Expletive—a word or phrase added to a sentence in order to ease syntax or rhythm, as the word *there* and *it* in the following sentences: There are many reasons given. It is nice to see you.

Forensic discourse—see judicial discourse.

Functional sentence types—the classification of sentences according to their functions in the sentence: statements, questions, commands, exclamation (declarative, interrogative, imperative, exclamatory).

Future fact—a common topic, or line of argument concerned with whether or not something could or would happen.

Grammatical sentence types—sentences classified according to number and kinds of clauses: simple, compound, complex, and compound-complex.

Hortatives—sentences actively engaging the audience in calls to action: "Let us not cease striving. Let us work together."

Hyperbole—the use of exaggerated terms for the purpose of emphasis or heightened effect. "His eloquence would split rocks." (486).

Invention—a system or method for finding arguments; topics or lines of argument suggesting material from which to obtain proof.

Irony—use of a word in such a way as to convey a meaning opposite to the literal meaning of the word—"For Brutus is an *honorable* man/So are they all, *honorable* men." (489).

Judicial discourse—legal oratory or any oratory in which a person offers condemnation or defense as proof (also known as forensic discourse).

Litotes—deliberate use of understatement—"I am a citizen of no mean city."—St. Paul (487).

Logos (logical appeal)—appeal to reason.

Memory—the fourth part of rhetoric, the complete catalogue including invention, arrangement, style, memory, and delivery.

Metaphor—implied comparison between two things of unlike nature . . . "On the final examination, several students went down in flames." (479).

Metonymy—substitution of some attributive, or suggestive word for what is actually meant [crown for royalty, wealth for rich people, bottle for wine, pen for writers] (481).

Oxymoron—the yoking of two terms which are ordinarily contradictory—[sweet pain, conspicuous by his absence, thunderous silence, make haste slowly] (491).

Paradox—an apparently contradictory statement that nevertheless contains a measure of truth . . . "Art is a form of lying in order to tell the truth."—Pablo Picasso (492).

Parenthesis—insertion of some verbal unit in a position that interrupts the normal syntactical flow of the sentence. "There is even, and it is the achievement of this book, a curious sense of happiness running through its paragraphs."—Norman Mailer (467).

Past fact—a common topic, or line of argument concerned with whether something has or has not happened.

Pathos (emotional appeal)—appeal to the emotions.

Personification—investing abstractions for inanimate objects with human qualities or abilities..."O, eloquent, just, and mighty Death!..." (486).

Polyptoton—repetition of words from the same root . . . "Not as a call to *battle*, though *embattled* we are." John F. Kennedy (478).

Polysyndeton—deliberative use of many conjunctions . . . "For thine is the kingdom and the power and the glory."*

Psychological closure—the point of equilibrium achieved when the listener/reader has sufficient information to satisfy the curiosity raised at the initiation of a given statement.

Quintilian—(Marcus Fabus Quintilianus) Roman rhetorician of the first century A.D.*

Relationship—a common topic, or line of argument, that includes cause and effect, antecedent and consequence, contraries, and contradictions.

Rhetoric—the faculty of discovering all the available means of persuasion in any given situation [Aristotle] (3).

Rhetorical question—(erotema) a question elicited for the purpose of asserting or denying something obliquely . . . "How can the uneducated have faith in a system which says that it will take advantage of them in very possible way?"—Edward Kennedy (488).

Schemes—a deviation from the ordinary pattern or arrangement of words; a transference of order. Schemes include strategies such as repetition, parallelism, and omission.

Simile—explicit comparison between two things of unlike nature..."He had a posture like a question mark." (479).

Special topics—particular lines of argument used when discussing some particular subject: the worth or the good and the advantageous or expedient or useful for deliberative discourse; justice and injustice for deliberative discourse; virtue and vice or the noble and base for ceremonial discourse.

Synecdoche—figure of speech in which the part stands for the whole . . . [vessel for ship, bread for food, hands for helpers, silver for money] (480).

Syntagmatic analysis—a schematic presentation that labels sentences according to their relationship to the main assertion and to each other. Major generalizations are usually designated as level one, and sentences of support are ranked according to their level of specificity.

Style—the third part of rhetoric associated with word choice and eloquence; the other parts of the traditional canon include invention, arrangement, memory, and delivery.

Testimony—a common topic, or line or argument, that includes authority, statistics, maxims, law, precedents (examples).

Topics—methods of development or lines of arguments, suggesting strategies for clarifying an idea. Common topics are definition, comparison, relationship, circumstance, and testimony; special topics are the worthy or the good and the advantageous or expedient or useful.

Tropes—a deviation from the ordinary meaning of a word; a transference of meaning. Standard figures of speech are classified as tropes; simile, metaphor, irony, synecdoche, etc. are commonly used tropes.

SELECTED BIBLIOGRAPHY

Anderson, Judith. *Outspoken Women: Speeches by American Women Reformers 1635-1935.* Dubuque, Iowa: Kendall Hunt, 1984.

Barksdale, Richard and Keneth Kinnamon. *Black Writers Of America.* New York: Macmillan, 1972.

Baym, Nina, et al., eds. "Zora Neale Hurston." In *The Norton Anthology of American Literature.* 3rd ed. Vol. 2. New York: W. W. Norton, 1989,: 1424-26.

Bethune, Mary McLeod. Papers. Amistad Research Center, New Orleans, Louisiana, Tulane University.

Black, Edwin L. *Rhetorical Criticism: A Study In Method.* Madison: University of Wisconsin Press, 1978.

Boulware, Marcus M. *The Oratory Of Negro Leaders 1900-1968.* Westport, Connecticut: Negro Universities Press, 1969.

Brigance, William N. *A History Of American Public Address.* 2 vols. New York: MacGraw Hill, 1943.

Brock, Bernard L., and Robert L. Scott, eds. *Methods of Rhetorical Criticism: A Twentieth Century Perspective.* 2nd rev. ed. Detroit: Wayne State University Press, 1980.

Brown, Delindus R., and Wanda F. Anderson. "A Survey of the Black Woman and the Persuasion Process: The

Study of Strategies of Identification and Resistance," *Journal of Black Studies* 9 (Dec. 1978): 233-248.

Bryant, Ira B. Barbara Charline Jordan: *From The Ghetto To The Capital.* Houston: D. Armstrong Co., Inc., 1977.

Carter, Steven. "Lorraine Hansberry" In *Dictionary Of Literary Biography.* Vol. 38. Detroit, Michigan: Gale Research, 1985.

Cathcart, Robert. *Post Communication: Rhetorical Analyses and Evaluation.* 2nd ed. Indianapolis: Bobbs-Merrill, 1981.

Chisholm, Shirley. *The Good Fight.* New York: Harper and Row, 1973.

Chisholm, Shirley. *Unbought And Unbossed.* Boston: Houghton Mifflin, 1970.

Cooper, Anna Julia. *A Voice From The South By a Black Woman of The South.* Xenia, Ohio: Adline Printing House, 1982.

Cooper, Anna Julia. Papers. Moorland-Spingarn Research Center, Washington, D. C., Howard University.

Corbett, Edward P. J. *Classical Rhetoric For The Modern Student.* 2nd ed. New York: Oxford University Press, 1971.

Davis, Angela. *Women, Culture and Politics.* New York: Vintage, 1990.

Duffy, Bernard K. and Halford R. Ryan. *American Orators Of The Twentieth Century*. Westport, Connecticut: Greenwood, 1987.

Dunbar, Alice Moore, ed. *Masterpieces Of Negro Eloquence*. New York: The Bookery Publishing Company, 1914. Rpt. Johnson Reprint Corporation, 1970.

Foner, Philip S., ed. *The Voice Of Black America: Major Speeches By Negroes In The United States 1797-1971*. New York: Simon and Schuster, 1972.

Franklin, John Hope. *From Slavery To Freedom*. 5th ed. New York: Alfred A. Knopf, 1980.

Giddings, Paula. *In Search Of Sisterhood: Delta Sigma Theta And The Challenge Of The Black Sorority Movement*. New York: The Feminist Press, 1988.

Giddings, Paula. *When And Where I Enter: The Impact Of Black Women On Race And Sex In America*. New York: Bantam, 1984.

Glenn, Robert W. *Black Rhetoric: A Guide To Afro-American Communication*. Metuchen, N. J.: Scarecrow Press, 1986.

Golden, James L. and Richard D. Rieke, eds. *The Rhetoric Of Black Americans*. Columbus, Ohio: Charles E. Merrill, 1971.

Graham, John, ed. *Great American Speeches Of The Twentieth Century*. New York: Appleton-Century Crofts, 1970.

Hansberry, Lorraine. *To Be Young, Gifted And Black*. Adapted by Robert Nemiroff. New York: New American Library, 1969.

Hart, Roderick P. *Modern Rhetorical Criticism*. Glenview, Illinois: Scott, Foresman/Little Brown Higher Education, 1990.

Hill, Roy L., ed. *Rhetoric Of Racial Revolt*. Denver: Golden Bell Press, 1964.

Jordan, Barbara and Shelby Hearon. *Barbara Jordan: A Self Portrait*. New York: Doubleday, 1979.

Jordan, Vernon. "Eulogy For Patricia Roberts Harris." *Howard Law Journal* 29.3 (1986): 419-421.

Lerner, Gerda, ed. *Black Women In White America*. New York: Vintage Books, Random House, 1975.

Lomax, Charles W. *The Agitator In American Society*. Englewood Cliffs, N. J.: Prentice Hall, 1978.

Lorde, Audre. *Sister Outsider: Essays and Speeches*. New York: Crossing Press (Feminist Series), 1984.

Mullen, Robert W. *Rhetorical Strategies Of Black Americans*. Washington, D. C.: University Press of America, 1980.

Neverdon-Morton, Cynthia. *Afro-American Women Of The South: And The Advancement Of the Race 1895-1925*. Knoxville: The University of Tennessee Press, 1989.

O'Neill, Daniel J., ed. *Speeches By Black Americans.* Belmont, California: Dickenson Publishing Co., 1971.

Peare, Catherine Owens. *Mary McLeod Bethune.* New York: The Vanguard Press, Inc., 1951.

Quarles, Benjamin. *Black Abolitionists.* New York: Oxford University Press, 1969.

Walker, Alice. *Her Blue Body Everything We Know.* New York: Harcourt Brace Jovanovich, 1991.

Williams, Jamye Coleman and McDonald Williams, eds. *The Negro Speaks: The Rhetoric Of Contemporary Black Leaders.* New York: Noble and Noble, 1970.

Windt, Theodore. *Presidential Rhetoric 1961 To The Present.* 3rd ed. Dubuque, Iowa: Kendall Hunt, 1983.

Woodson, Carter Godwin. *The Negro In Our History.* Washington, D. C.: Associated Publishers, 1924.

Wrage, Ernest J. and Barnet Baskerville, eds. *Contemporary Forum: American Speeches On Twentieth Century Issues.* Seattle: University of Washington Press, 1962.